Culture, Growth and Economic Policy

Panagiotis E. Petrakis

Culture, Growth and Economic Policy

Springer

Panagiotis E. Petrakis
Department of Economics
University of Athens
Athens
Greece

ISBN 978-3-642-41439-8 ISBN 978-3-642-41440-4 (eBook)
DOI 10.1007/978-3-642-41440-4
Springer Heidelberg New York Dordrecht London

Library of Congress Control Number: 2014932054

Printed on acid-free paper

Springer is part of Springer Science+Business Media (www.springer.com)

To Eleni and Isabella

Contents

Introduction

1

When looking at the economic history of the world, it becomes apparent that development economic thinking has evolved with only a handful of examples regarding the emergence of developmental transformations (i.e., mainly economies in Southeast Asia). Therefore, it is not surprising that no significant theoretical construction has emerged to accurately interpret economic growth, and as a consequence, policies regarding universal growth and development economics have not been proposed. In such an environment, there is a constant search for solutions to various development issues and new formations.

In their book *The Economics of Growth*, Aghion and Howitt (2009) concluded that their exploration into growth had been one into uncharted territory. That is, they identified a key issue that should concern growth economists but has remained largely ignored: culture. Thus, the present book refers to the role of cultural background[1] in the process of growth, development and the application of economic policy.

Cultural background and culture (including civilization) are concepts rooted in cultural anthropology. The cultural background of a society is what memory is to an individual (Kluckhohn 1954). It includes values, ideas and other symbolic systems that shape behavior and are passed from generation to generation (Kroeber and Kluckhohn 1952). A similar view considers that anything that was functional at some point in the history of a group deserves to be transferred to following generations (Triandis 2009). Furthermore, this can be defined as a group's shared ideas, behavior theories or mental parameters (Allaire and Firsirotu 1984; Hofstede 1994). As far as the economy is concerned, North (1990) approached cultural background as a source of informal restraints that direct our everyday transactions and its significance can be ascertained by looking at typical norms. When one looks

[1] Throughout this book, the concepts of "culture" and "cultural background" are used interchangeably. However, the writer prefers the latter, given that it is generally believed that the former is much broader (i.e., it encompasses amongst other things elements of education and material facts regarding cultural life), whereas the focus of this book is on behaviors, habits and values.

P.E. Petrakis, *Culture, Growth and Economic Policy*,
DOI 10.1007/978-3-642-41440-4_1, © Springer-Verlag Berlin Heidelberg 2014

at the norms of different societies, different cultural backgrounds are found. Generally, in defining cultural background, we will include those customary beliefs, preferences and values that influence individual economic behavior (Acemoglu 2009) and that ethnic, religious and social groups transmit from generation to generation (Guiso et al. 2006).

The origin (endogenous or exogenous) of cultural values and the way they are shaped within a society determines the development of policies that concern cultural background. It is surprising then that the interrelationship between cultural values and economic growth remains unclear (Triandis 2009) when the relationship is so clear (Harrison and Huntington 2000; Harrison and Kagan 2006). The "disclosure" of the aforementioned interrelation is one of the issues pursued in this book. Nevertheless, it is not sufficient to merely determine that cultural background is related to economic growth. We also need to clarify the extent to which cultural background is subject to change, whether or not by way of human intervention. In other words, the issue of whether cultural background is interrelated to the process of economic growth is indeed important, but what is of greater importance is whether cultural background changes, and if so how and to what extent. This is the only way to ultimately understand whether we can influence (and to what extent) the process of economic growth.

From Rostow's stages of development to the Washington Consensus and institutional reorganization, from the formation of Solow's productive coefficients to the Neoclassical synthesis and the Post-Keynesian view of the macroeconomic management of mature economies, economic thinking has taken (whether directly or indirectly) various elements from the human sciences of psychology, social psychology and anthropogeography. This is not unexpected given that the individual and society are at the center of economic thinking as a social science. To the extent that concepts (e.g., the role of institutional background) are introduced then the inclusion of cultural values is absolutely understood. But even when notions such as the expectations -which constitute a primarily analytical tool of the economic theoretical synthesis (neoclassical and Keynesian thinking)—are introduced, in reality the entrance gateway pumps elements of a cultural and an anthropological nature to economic thinking and the economic analysis of human behavior.

Therefore, while we intuitively consider that the presence of similar elements in economic thinking and economic policy is very natural, we should admit that until today, except from the Neoclassical and the Keynesian management of expectations for the confrontation of uncertainty, the way in which the cultural and anthropological elements are introduced, remains at least piecemeal and is surrounded by skepticism. It should be noted that the Neoclassical and the Keynesian management of expectations did not solve the problem of the introduction of cultural elements to economic thinking, but they in fact banished them and replaced them with an absentmindedly management of the past. Therefore, we understand that we are probably sailing through unknown waters. This particularly concerns economic thinking and policy and more specifically macroeconomic thinking and policy and, of course, growth and development thinking.

An important reason why this occurs is the fact that as far as the relationship between culture and economic output is concerned, the theoretical thinking is not easily offered for empirical confirmation. By extension, it is not easy to form integrated theoretical structures allowing for empirical control. Therefore, the relevant research results are troubling. Of course, the capacity for empirical verification has increased over the last years (data are produced, techniques are improved etc.), either at a microeconomic or a macroeconomic level, which fact allows the in-depth study of the subject-matter.

In essence, although economic thinking has felt the need to define its relationship with, for instance, politics and technology, this has not yet occurred with cultural values and cultural background. One reason for this delay is the fact that economics is based on general interpretative rules, while the concept of cultural values is highly temperamental as it promotes the relativity of values in separate societies. In addition, other factors have hindered the theoretical development of this topic. Although A. Smith and J.S. Mill "opened the door" to cultural constraints in the 1800s, the influence of the Marxist relationship (which required controlled constructions via productive relationships) and that of the neoclassical synthesis (which required the prevalence of markets in economic result) slowed the study of the issue.

The global recession of 2008 showed that the human factor and cultural values played and continue to play a significant role. For example, the animal spirit (Akerlof and Shiller 2009) had a strong presence in the emergence of the crisis (e.g., an underestimation of the accumulation of risk by excessive banking and national debt) and regarding how nations chose to exit the crisis (e.g., societies' denials and renaming of any problems, the avoidance confrontation and the development of nationalistic beliefs). Consequently, we consider that the great recession resulted in an obvious need for economic thinking to include a cultural dimension.

Is it true that we need not consider the effect of cultural background when planning developmental policy because cultural values have only a slight influence on such policy? Or are there "toxic" cultures (Landes 1999) that act to overturn or limit developmental prospects? If they do indeed exist then ignoring this issue is likely to lead us in the wrong direction.

Thus, this book aims to analyze the basic relationships among cultural background, growth, development and economic policy. It also raises a number of fundamental questions, including:

- Is the relationship between cultural background and economic behavior (at a microeconomic level) established? We may intuitively understand the significance of cultural background to economic behavior, but is this relationship scientifically confirmed?
- Is the relationship among cultural background, growth and development (at a macroeconomic level) scientifically confirmed? Do the observed associations also hide causes and effects?
- Do specific levels of cultural background shape (under certain conditions) developmental stagnation, thus causing "cultural growth traps"?

- What is the relationship between cultural background and the ability to activate economic policy? In other words, is cultural background deactivating (under certain conditions) economic policy to a lesser or greater extent?
- Is there an ideal cultural background in terms of economic growth and development? If so, how can it be adopted by a society?

While including the elements leading to the creation of a cultural background (because it is important to realize its structures and time endurances), this book does not attempt to interpret the different expressions of cultural background that were or are dominant in various geographical regions, national or social groups. On the contrary, it studies their economic consequences in growth and development.

Regarding the logic behind the analysis of this book, it becomes clear that these chapters intend to provide some answers to the questions surrounding the relationship between cultural background and growth *and* to explore the impact of the relationship on economic policy in relation to growth and development.

This book comprises three parts: The first analyzes the relationship between cultural background and economic system. The second analyzes cultural background on the basis of its basic components, and the requirements for change are also investigated. The final part encompasses an empirical examination of the creation of the relationship between economy and cultural background at micro and macro levels. The relationship between cultural background and growth and development from an economic policy perspective is also raised.

I wish to warmly thank the following people who contributed to the completion of this book: a special thank you to Mr. D. Valsamis, whose cooperation was invaluable and to Mr. P. Kostis, Mrs. K. Kafka and Mrs. N. Daniilopoulou who untiringly contributed to the entire project; to Mrs. V. Kontodaimon for her invaluable help with the first chapter; to Mrs. S. Zacharogianni for the electronic manuscript preparation and to Mrs. K. Anomitri who offered me administrative assistance throughout the project. The final responsibility for the presentation of this book lies with the author.

My scientific work would not have been completed without the help of my colleagues at the University of Athens, and in particular, E. Gkiouli, who contributed significantly to the development of this scientific project.

References

Acemoglu D (2009) Introduction to modern economic growth. Princeton University Press, Princeton, NJ

Aghion P, Howitt P (2009) The economics of growth. MIT, Cambridge

Akerlof G, Shiller R (2009) Animal spirits: how human psychology drives the economy, and why it matters for global capitalism. Princeton University Press, Princeton, NJ

Allaire Y, Firsirotu ME (1984) Theories of organizational culture. Organ Stud 5:193–226

Guiso L, Sapienza P, Zingales L (2006) Does culture affect economic outcomes? J Econ Perspect 20(2):23–48

Harrison LE, Kagan J (2006) Developing cultures: essays in culture change. Routledge, New York, NY

Harrison LE, Huntington SP (2000) Culture matters: how values shape human progress. Basic Books, New York, NY

Hofstede G (1994) Cultures and organizations. Software of the mind. Harper Collins, London

Kluckhohn C (1954) Culture and behavior. Free Press, New York, NY

Kroeber AL, Kluckhohn C (1952) Culture: a critical review of concepts and definitions. Peabody Museum of American Archaeology and Ethnology, Harvard University, Cambridge, MA, c1952

Landes D (1999) The wealth and poverty of nations: why some are so rich and some so poor. WW Norton, London

North D (1990) Institutions, institutional change and economic performance. Cambridge University Press, Cambridge

Triandis HC (2009) Ecological determinants of cultural variation. In: Wyer RS, Chiu C, Hong YY (eds) Understanding culture: theory, research and application. Psychology press, New York, NY, pp 189–210

Part I

The Foundations

The first part of this book aims to highlight the way in which cultural background interacts with economic system. Although it is easy to intuitively accept such a relationship, it is nonetheless quite difficult to establish it in a manner withstanding a methodologically organized approach.

The first part comprises six chapters. Chapter 2 refers to the way in which the primary procedure for satisfying human needs is undeniably linked to the development of cultural background. Chapter 3 attempts to analyze how cultural background is shaped. Chapter 4 presents the role of cultural background in economic thought. Not all theoretical constructions are equally hospitable to the introduction of cultural background. Nevertheless, the manner in which the cultural background is introduced shapes the analytical ability to understand its role in economic evolution, growth and development. Chapter 5 studies the way in which cultural background and the economic system are interrelated. Chapter 6 presents the relationships between cultural background and incentives, growth and distribution. Finally, the relationship between cultural background and rationality is analyzed in Chap. 7.

Human Needs and Cultural Background 2

The purpose of this chapter is to show how cultural background is firmly interconnected with the way in which societies attempt to satisfy their basic human needs. A brief outline of the relationship governing human needs, cultural background and a society's economic development is presented below.

The concept of human needs is presented in the first Sect. 2.1. The following Sect. 2.2, discusses the relationship between needs and economic growth. The third Sect. 2.3 shows the relationship among needs, economic growth (development) and cultural background. Finally, the fourth Sect. 2.4 raises the issue of the relationship between the individual and society.

2.1 Human Needs

The concept of human needs has been a focus of philosophy and psychology, as well as political, economic and social sciences (Rosenfeld et al. 1992). Thus, there is extensive literature on this particular field.

The first documented investigation into the area of human needs was carried out in the field of psychology. Maslow (1943) was one of the first scholars to study human needs as a separate thematic field. He attempted to determine whether there are particular factors that push humans to behave in accordance with particular rules. Following his research, Maslow developed "A Theory of Human Motivation", citing five motivations that constitute "basic human needs". These need categories are interrelated and follow a hierarchy—only when the lower category of need has been appropriately satisfied will the next level of need emerge. These needs dominate the conscious life of the individual and serve as the basis for the organization of their behavior until they reach the next category. The five categories are as follows (from the lowest to the highest):

(a) Physiological needs: At the first level, humans universally seek to satisfy their basic biological needs, which are directly connected to their survival, for example food, shelter and clothes.

P.E. Petrakis, *Culture, Growth and Economic Policy*,
DOI 10.1007/978-3-642-41440-4_2, © Springer-Verlag Berlin Heidelberg 2014

(b) The need for safety: The satisfaction of the needs for safety and security is at the second level, where humans act to acquire a satisfactory feeling of safety and security against natural dangers. Issues concerning the satisfaction of their natural needs are also found here, as is the need for security in financial issues such as permanent employment and adequate savings.
(c) The need for love: At the third level, and provided that the two previous categories have been satisfied to an adequate degree, humans start to strongly feel the lack of friendship, love and family. As a result, they will seek to satisfy their need to establish personal relationships of any kind, for example with friends, partners or family.
(d) The need for esteem: At the fourth level and as an extension of the previous category is the satisfaction of the need for affiliation. Individuals aim at being esteemed and appreciated by other individuals through their successful affiliation in various social groups.
(e) The need for self-actualization: Even if all the previous needs have been adequately satisfied, an individual may still experience dissatisfaction or anxiety. Such feelings constitute the need for self-actualization and this will only be satisfied when an individual is able to engage in activities that make them feel fulfilled, in which they are probably more efficient.

People worldwide have an innate predisposition to seek the satisfaction of the aforementioned needs, with their ultimate goal being self-actualization. Maslow stated that all humans worldwide share the same needs (Maslow 1943).

Following Maslow (1943) and Alderfer (1968) also suggested the universality of needs. However, he simplified Maslow's (1943) five ranked stages of needs into three: a) the need to exist, which includes physiological and safety needs, b) the need for relatedness, which includes love and esteem and c) the need for growth, which refers to self-actualization. His theory is known in the literature as "Existence, Relatedness and Growth" (E.R.G.). Alderfer (1968) sees his three categories as having more continuity and less of a hierarchical structure. Thus, an individual may experience some of the stages at the same time without organizing changes in the hierarchy.

When comparing various theories on needs, it is clear that human needs can be categorized; however, they differ on two points: whether the categories of needs apply to all people worldwide and whether these needs follow a hierarchy in being satisfied.

The economist Max-Neef (1991) dealt with human needs from an economic perspective. More particularly, his research concerned the modeling of human development as a society's productive source. According to his theory, human needs can indeed be categorized. In fact, they constitute a system where needs interact and inter-correlate, and with no particular hierarchy. The sole exception is physiological needs, which must be sufficiently satisfied for an individual to survive. In addition, Neef stated that human needs are the same for all people worldwide (i.e., universal human needs). What *is* different among civilizations is the way in which an individual acts to satisfy them (satisfiers). Therefore, Max-Neef (1991) created a matrix known as the "Matrix of Needs and Satisfiers" to categorize needs and the means for the satisfaction of needs (satisfiers). In this model, the categories of needs are the same for all societies. However, each society can satisfy the needs using different methods (Max-Neef 1991) to determine how citizens choose to satisfy their needs.

Finally, human needs are objective in nature and, hence, may be considered universal in light of the doctrine that states needs constitute necessary requirements and elements for the molding of an individual's character. However, what do change and are subjective among humans are individuals' wishes and wants, which are in fact choices, likes and ambitions (Fernandez-Huerga 2008). Needs are aims with a universal form, whereas wishes and wants are aims that cannot be universal as they emerge from the subjective perception of each individual (Doyal and Gough 1984, 1991). The wishes and wants in fact constitute ways of satisfying needs, which are the same for all people worldwide, and wishes and wants, just like all the other means of satisfying needs, can be integrated into the need categories (Lutz and Lux 1979; Max-Neef 1991).

2.2 Needs and Economic Evolution

Streeten et al. (1981) conducted one of the first extended surveys regarding the relationship that links human needs to the economic growth of developing countries. The authors conducted a series of analyses in different samples from South America, Europe and Asia and reached two basic conclusions: high economic growth rates are neither necessary nor sufficient to improve the satisfaction of basic needs and a good performance in satisfying basic needs boosts, or at the very least does not delay, economic growth. More specifically, that study showed that the process of the satisfaction of needs in the form of mass investments in human capital can initially decrease growth to the extent that resources are transferred from investment to consumption. Later on, the process gradually becomes more productive and leads to the boost of economic growth in the future.

All economies follow a course of economic growth that comprises five categories with a hierarchical structure and every society falls in one of these categories based on its economic status (Rostow 1960). The categories are as follows (from lower to upper):

(a) Traditional society: This category includes those societies based largely on agricultural production. In these societies there is a maximum limit on the feasible production level of product per capita. This limit derives from the fact that the society cannot espouse and use the possibilities offered by modern science and technology in an organized and methodological way. Furthermore, such societies cannot effectively exploit productive resources for their economic benefit, and they have underdeveloped political systems. Hence, individuals within a traditional society seek to satisfy their physiological needs for food, shelter and clothing and nothing more.

(b) Preconditions for "Takeoff": Societies in a transitional stage of growth are placed in this category. The ideology of such a society is that economic growth is not only feasible but also necessary to gain national pride, private profit, general prosperity and a better life for following generations. At this level, one notices development in the education sector, which is extended to meet the needs for modern economic activity, the growth of entrepreneurship in public and private sector and the development of the banking system and institutional background. Such development means that the capital generated can be effectively managed and enables further growth in investments and trade. Nevertheless, the development pace at this stage is rather slow, given that it still employs low-productivity methods resembling those used in the traditional society.

(c) "Takeoff": This stage includes societies that have managed to move beyond the low-productivity methods of the traditional society and are now fully modernized. Hence, the ideology and practices of the previous stage are now supported by the appropriate "equipment", creating the prerequisites for rapid and constant economic growth. This stage shows significant development in the industrial sector and in mass production, accompanied by the modernization of the agricultural sector as farmers are starting to implement new methods and technologies both in their agricultural production and way of life. In this stage, it is expected that in one to two decades, the social and political organization of the society will be significantly transformed resulting in steady growth for society.

(d) Drive to maturity: This stage lasts for approximately 40 years, during which the society experiences growth in all sectors (Rostow 1960). At the same time, society starts to internationalize its activity and establishes its position in the international economy. Once a society achieves these milestones it is considered to have reached maturity. When a society has achieved total development in an industrial category, it is then able to focus on production in a new sector. An example is the switch from iron, coal and heavy railway to mechanical tools, chemicals and electrical equipment. Germany, Great Britain, France and the United States went through this phase at the end of the nineteenth century.

(e) Age of mass consumption: The predominant period of this stage is when the citizens of the society experience modern comfort, during which they focus on the constant consumption of consumer goods and can barely recall the issues they faced during previous stages. This is the stage where a society focuses on achieving its own balance among three states: military and security issues, prosperity and equality issues and the further development of the upper classes. As Rostow (1960) stated, every society attempts to define its uniqueness and the factors that shape it on political, economic, geographical and cultural levels.

Based on the approach by Rostow (1960) and Porter et al. (2002) conducted a modern study and defined three categories of economic growth within a society. The first and lowest category is one where society is led by productive resources (factor-driven stage). In this stage, society produces low-value products using existing knowledge, without creating any new knowledge or innovation. Furthermore, society clearly produces for self-consumption to meet its own needs because there is no export sector. This stage is similar to the first stage of the traditional society developed by Rostow (1960).

Table 2.1 Human needs and economic growth

Human needs	
Maslow (1943)	Alderfer (1968)
Physiological needs	Existence
Safety needs	Relatedness
The need for love	Growth
The need for esteem	
The need for self-actualization	
Economic growth	
Rostow (1960)	Porter (2002)
Traditional society	Factor-driven
Preconditions for "Takeoff"	
Takeoff	Efficiency-driven
Drive to maturity	Innovation-driven
Age of mass consumption	

The second category is where society is led by effectiveness (Porter et al. 2002). This category includes Rostow's (1960) other four categories, and represents the gradual attempts of a society to develop and become modernized, to make its debut in the international market and to acquire a national identity.

Finally, Porter et al. (2002) introduced a third category, which follows the previous two. This is the category where society has exhausted every resource (factor driven) and form of its efficient utilization (efficiency driven) and the only route for further growth is via knowledge and innovation (innovation driven). This stage can be considered parallel to the emergence and development of the notion of entrepreneurship, which is still examined and studied by many modern sciences.

By comparing the theories of Rostow (1960) and Porter et al. (2002) on economic growth with those of Maslow (1943) and Alderfer (1968) on human needs (Table 2.1), it is possible to state that there are clear similarities between the satisfaction of needs deriving from individual growth and changes in the stages of economic growth, and both can experience dual-direction causation. Lower (higher) levels of individual growth are parallel to lower (higher) levels of economic growth. Hence, the satisfaction of the need for food is parallel to the first stages of growth in primary production, whereas the stages of the economic actualization of the personality are connected with the growth stages of efficiency, entrepreneurship, creativity and innovation.

Economic growth leads to changes in the institutions related to economic activity. The anachronistic bureaucratic structures of the early industrialization were ineffective in the technologically modern societies with highly specialized labor force. This can also explain the efforts made over the last decades to cut the red tape, according to Inglehart (1997). Lastly, the external shocks in the economy can lead to changes in institutions and culture. The most distinctive example is war. The Second World War had a significant influence on the labor market for a great period of time (Fernandez and Fogli 2004). The lack of male population in the labor market due to the war led to the increase in working women, thus redefining their role in the society. As an external shock, hyperinflation in 1920 had a negative impact on the middle class of that time, since many savings were lost. This resulted in intense uncertainty, and had an impact on the way money markets and insurance funds were organized.

2.3 Needs, Economic Growth and Cultural Background

From the perspective of cultural background, the different phases of needs and economic growth also require individual constitutions of different qualities as well as various types of social organization. The meeting of primal needs requires people who are aggressive and good hunters or nomadic nations that can travel to find food. Innovation-driven economies require societies that have faith in the future because often their returns from investments are not realized for some time. In contrast, factor-driven economies can co-exist with high uncertainty avoidance, which is not consistent with higher growth levels. As a consequence, the development of the satisfaction of human needs and economic change in development and growth coexist in a constant process of cultural background.

The cognitive process of each individual is not fully conscious, particular or deliberate, and is instead limited and gradually developing throughout their lifetime (Hodgson 1988, 1997). The cultural and institutional background of each society provides each individual with information that has been created over the centuries and that mirrors the knowledge of the past (Hodgson 1988; Knight 1997; Streit et al. 1997). Such information directly affects the way in which the individual chooses and interprets their data and, hence, their cognitive background (Neisser 1967; Spradley 1972; Bourne et al. 1986). The fact that all individuals have access to this "ready-made" information also explains the existence of predictability (to a degree) in human behavior, to the extent that the cognitive level of each individual comprises information that is common and known to the other individuals within that society (Earl 1983; Heiner 1983; Hodgson 1988; Dequech 2004).

The internal psychological world is different and unique for each individual. The cognitive process, as mentioned above, is not a totally conscious, particular or deliberate procedure, meaning that it leaves room for diversity among individuals, and is formed in accordance with the different habits and experiences of each individual. In accordance with their internal world, each individual interprets data differently and extracts information that mirrors their personal imagination and creativity (Hodgson 1988; Loasby 2001). Hence, at any given time an individual forms a cognitive background that reflects their personal psychosynthesis and their cultural and institutional environment. Based on such background, an individual acts to understand and instantiate their needs and wishes. This is where the reasoning ability of each individual is defined, i.e., the ability to use information from their cognitive background to make decisions as to how to satisfy their needs and wishes.

The mentality of each individual is different regarding their ability to understand in great detail all the information included in their cognitive background (many

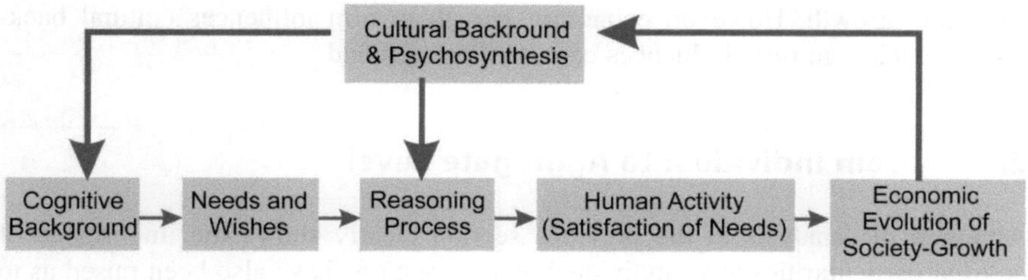

Fig. 2.1 Cultural background and economic growth

have very complex cognitive backgrounds) and to assess and process that information to make decisions and to then act. This problem is strengthened by the fact that there is a fundamental uncertainty as to how they will develop in the future, which then limits an individual's cognitive and assessment ability because it limits the information used in decisions and subsequent actions (Dequech 2000, 2006; Davidson 1996).

Because of these problems and through the reasoning process, an individual seeks and implements simple mechanisms that will help them identify the best methods to satisfy needs. At this stage, the role of the external environment and the internal psychological world of each individual is to reduce these problems and increase the reasoning ability of the individual.

As mentioned above, a society's cultural and institutional background offers each individual a storage room of data and information that the individual can use at any time to structure their cognitive background. The same information, however, can also be used by the individual as an axis on which they can structure their reasoning processes (Douglas 1987). In this way, the cultural and institutional background offers a series of habits and rules that the individual can use as a standard to check whether they have identified the best solution or to identify which existing solution is the best according to the standards set by their cultural and institutional background (Hodgson 1988, 1997). Thus, the reasoning behavior that determines the cultural background can be considered the potential behavior of an individual.

The internal psychological world of each individual plays a very important role at this stage of the reasoning process and action. Personal creativity and the personal emotional world differentiate the reasoning behavior of each individual regarding their needs and how to satisfy them. Through each action, an individual gains some experience, which is then added to their internal psychological environment. Such an environment, together with cultural background, repeatedly drives human activity (Fig. 2.1).

In fact, cultural background and an individual's psychosynthesis shape the reasoning process. However, it has already been influenced by their needs and wishes, which are obviously influenced by their cognitive background. The reasoning process is in the background of human activity aiming to satisfy human needs. Thus, human activity leads to society's economic development and economic growth. However, economic growth in turn influences cultural background, which, in turn, influences cognitive background.

2.4 From Individual to Aggregate Level

Although the analysis in the previous section clearly shows the importance of cultural particularities at an individual level, questions have also been raised as to how individual traits are expressed as social behaviors. For example, if we take the existence of general social traits for granted, the question arises regarding how such general traits shape individual behaviors. In other words, what is in fact posed is a question concerning the relationship between the individual and the group. There are some views (The Chicago School; Becker 1976, 2000) that support the scenario that social behaviors are an outcome of collective individual behavior. In contrast, others claim that social phenomena define individual behaviors (Polanyi 1975 [1944]). The latter is widely accepted in psychology, given that it offers an easy starting point for the interpretation of personal behaviors. For example, in a general collectivism environment, people are more likely to develop individual isolation fears (Markman et al. 2009).

These two views may be coalesced by a more mature approach, i.e., by accepting that the composition of individual behaviors leads to the adoption of social standards *and* that cultural background shapes individual behaviors; the New Institutional Economics is considered to represent a prime example (Beugelsdijk and Maseland 2011), comprising a good mix of institutions and behaviors. In such an approach, institutions and culture are not the outcomes of careful planning, but exist in a model of inter-correlations by using the result of their composition and the conflict of opposing forces as the right of their existence.

The issue of the relationship between individualism and aggregate has a further parameter related to time or (more generally) to the specific reference period of the analysis.

If we are at a reference period strongly characterized by distressing events (e.g., Hurricane Katrina), local communities will display special experiential behaviors that are gradually transformed to behavioral traits passed from generation to generation. In contrast, a period of prosperity highlights the significance of greater stability and creativity, which results in a decrease in the significance of other cultural differences among members of the population.

An interesting dimension in the analysis of the relationship between individualism and aggregates concerns the extent of the implementation of its conclusions. There is the general perception that economics as a science seeks general norms and laws with universal implementation. It is very difficult to tolerate the introduction of views that lead to the special handling of various geographical or population segments. In contrast, the analyses that include cultural elements and references to cultural background by nature refer to separate population organizations. However, the tension between the two opposing forces has a problematic background. General rules may exist without necessarily being based on space or time segmentation.

Therefore, what does matter is whether the presence of cultural traits influences behaviors and economic output.

References

Alderfer CP (1968) An empirical test of a new theory of human needs. Organ Behav Hum Perform 4:142–175
Becker GS (1976) The economic approach to human behaviour. University of Chicago Press, Chicago
Becker GS (2000) A comment on the conference on cost-benefit analysis. J Leg Stud 29(2):1149–52
Beugelsdijk S, Maseland R (2011) Culture in economics: history, methodological reflections and contemporary applications. Cambridge University Press, Cambridge
Bourne LE, Dominowski RL, Loftus EF, Healy AF (1986) Cognitive processes. Prentice Hall, Englewood Cliffs
Davidson P (1996) Reality and economic theory. J Post Keynesian Econ 18(4):479–508
Dequech D (2000) Fundamental uncertainty and ambiguity. E Econ J 26(1):41–60
Dequech D (2004) Uncertainty: individuals, institutions and technology. Camb J Econ 28(3):365–78
Dequech D (2006) The new institutional economics and the theory of behavior under uncertainty. J Econ Behav Org 72(1):70–78
Douglas M (1987) How institutions think. Routledge & Kegan Paul, London
Doyal L, Gough I (1984) A theory of human needs. Crit Soc Policy 10:6–38
Doyal L, Gough I (1991) A theory of human need. Palgrave Macmillan, New York
Earl PE (1983) The economic imagination: towards a behavioral analysis of choice. Wheatsheaf, Brighton
Fernandez R, Fogli A (2004) Culture: an empirical investigation of beliefs, work, and fertility. NBER working paper 11268
Fernandez-Huerga E (2008) The economic behavior of human beings: the institutionalist/post-keynesian model. J Econ Issues 42(3)
Heiner RA (1983) The origin of predictable behavior. Am Econ Rev 73(4):560–595
Hodgson GM (1988) Economics and institutions. A manifesto for a modern institutional economics. Polity Press, Cambridge
Hodgson GM (1997) The ubiquity of habits and rules. Camb J Econ 21(6):663–684
Inglehart R (1997) Modernization and postmodernization: cultural, economic and political change in 43 societies. Princeton University Press, Princeton
Knight J (1997) Social institutions and human cognition: Thinking about old questions in new ways. J Inst Theor Econ 153(4):693–699
Loasby BJ (2001) Cognition, imagination and institutions in demand creation. J Evol Econ 11 (1):7–21
Lutz MA, Lux K (1979) The challenge of humanistic economics. The Benjamin/Cummings Publishing Company, Menlo Park
Markman BA, Grimm RL, Kyungil K (2009) Culture as a vehicle for studying individual differences. In: Wyer RS, Chiu C, Hong YY (eds) Understanding culture: theory, research and application. Psychology Press, New York, pp 93–108
Maslow AH (1943) A theory of human motivation. Psychol Rev 50(4):370–396
Max-Neef M (1991) Human scale development – conception, application and further reflections. The Apex Press, New York and London
Neisser U (1967) Cognitive psychology. Appleton-Century-Crofts, New York
Polanyi K 1975 [1944] The great transformation. Rinehart, New York
Porter M, Sachs J, McArthur J (2002) Executive summary: Competitiveness and stages of economic development. In: Porter M, Sachs J, Cornelius PK, McArthur J, Schwab K (eds) The Global Competitiveness Report 2001–2002. Oxford University Press, New York, pp 16–25

Rosenfeld P, Culbertson AL, Magnusson P (1992) Human needs, a literature review and cognitive life span model. Navy Personnel and Development Center. Program Element 0603707N, Work Unit R1770
Rostow WW (1960) The process of economic growth, 2nd edn. Oxford University Press, London
Spradley JP (1972) Culture and cognition: rules, maps and plans. Chandler Publishing, San Francisco
Streeten P, Burki SJ, Hicks N, Stewart F (1981) First things first – meeting basic human needs in developing countries. Oxford University Press, International Bank for Reconstruction and Development/The World Bank
Streit M, Mummert U, Kiwit D (1997) Views and comments on cognition, rationality, and institutions. Editorial preface. J Inst Theor Econ 153(4):688–692

The Construction of Cultural Background 3

This chapter describes how cultural background is shaped. It is necessary to outline early in this book how cultural background is organized so that we can clearly study its interactions with development and growth. Thus, in the following sections of this chapter we establish how the characteristics and strength of cultural background are shaped over time.

In more detail, Sect. 3.1 presents the relationship between cultural background and cognitive ability. Section 3.2 makes reference to the procedures under which cultural background influences personal cognitive ability. Section 3.3 clarifies the elements of its organization, and Sect. 3.4 presents endogenous perceptions of the mechanisms and functioning of cultural background. Section 3.5 presents external influences of cultural background and Sect. 3.6 comments on the existence of multicultural equilibria.

3.1 History, Stereotypes and Information Processing

History as a concept includes facts and information. Facts refer to the actual delimitations and organizations of the external world. A change in a country's borders or political system constitutes facts. In contrast, information concerns the elements transmitted from a source to a receiver and refers to new knowledge. To the extent that information production occurs, the notion of information is very important to individuals within a society. One facet of information is its production and another is its processing. Individuals, therefore, as active gatherers rather than passive receivers, have the ability to control the nature and volume of information by either accepting or rejecting it via a process of assumption control.

When an assumption control process concerns the creation and function of cultural stereotypes, it is likely that the gathering of information ends up enhancing or maintaining stereotypes because of deficient information. The traffic of new information can therefore influence the shaping of stereotypes and "shared" knowledge through the creation of concepts and consequential information-gathering strategies. The key stages in shaping "new" concepts are concise understanding,

P.E. Petrakis, *Culture, Growth and Economic Policy*,
DOI 10.1007/978-3-642-41440-4_3,

the formation of entire thoughts and finally the expression of subjective judgments and decisions that ultimately shape behavior. A new knowledge-gathering strategy may be either diagnostic or confirmative. The diagnostic process aims at controlling knowledge assumptions regarding cultural background or formed stereotypes, whereas the confirmation process tends to accept such elements of cultural background as they are.

The gathering of new knowledge is followed by the processing of information, which takes place in three stages (Wyer and Srull 1989; Wyer et al. 2009). This process is influenced by a number of factors, namely the type of information, the intended goals and purposes for the information, as well as its time reference. The three stages are as follows:

(a) Inflow: This concerns the process where information is registered, organized and demonstrated in the memory under different purpose and goal conditions.
(b) Invocation: This concerns the process where the perception formed and then used to recall past information and syndromes.
(c) Decision (judgment): This concerns the way in which figurations are recalled and used to make various decisions.

These stages enable an individual to make social decisions, and both cultural background and the information gathering process are of significant importance in this process.

3.2 Cultural Background and Cognition

Cultural background can affect personal cognition and, hence, the psychological process of information processing and cognition via three methods (Markman et al. 2009).

(a) Communication and language: All cultural backgrounds include concepts that are systematically repeated. These are transferred to community members and contribute to the development of causal constructions. Furthermore, languages also differ from one another in terms of their emphasis. Thus, the way of thinking is also influenced.
(b) Manner in which strategies to resolve problems are shaped: Cultural background acts to enable every generation to benefit from the knowledge accumulated by previous generations. Hence, younger generations process new stimuli from a more favorable perspective compared with previous ones. Such stimuli are not just concepts but also thinking and problem solving processes. The ongoing process to improve problem-solving ability creates new resolution methods and occurs mainly through the educational system.
(c) Motivation and the existence of incentives: It is accepted that every cultural background can be distinguished by different priorities regarding the same particular concept, e.g., sovereignty of socialization over privacy. This particular priority is mainly based on the fear of isolation. Such a fear may interpret the influence of cultural differences in processing information.

3.3 Components of Cultural Background

A key reason to analyze the concept of cultural background is to identify the structures and compositions of internalized behaviors, characteristics and behavioral standards, as well as the relationships amongst them. Cultural background is also connected with a national entity (Hofstede 1980, 2001), within which particular characteristics of geographical boundaries can be defined, and in turn describe dominant cultural values. Therefore, cultural background is deemed to be a stable concept that does not change and is not diffused through human communication (Oyserman and Sorensen 2009). This, however, is a view that is subject to much debate.

Hong (2009) considered cultural background as the sum of "interconnected knowledge networks", which are jointly owned by private individuals and consist of three factors:

(a) Taught thinking processes;
(b) Constructions of beliefs, behaviors and values; and
(c) Underlying theories on the relationships between various sides of the natural and the social world.

Using the term "cultural syndromes" (Triandis 2009), Oyserman and Sorensen (2009) defined cultural background as the sum of hidden, conflicted interconnected characteristics and, depending on the circumstances, periodically rise to the surface or fall into oblivion. Hence, cultural background includes a way of thinking and produces meanings, i.e., cognitive situations or reconstructions. An example of cultural syndrome is individualism and collectivism, in which Triandis and Trafimow (2001) identified a number of factors that may "invite" one or the other. Similar factors include whether the individual belongs to a group, the size of the group, and whether rules of accession into the group were followed.

In contrast, Schwartz (2009) considered cultural background to be an extrinsic variable in relation to the individual. Despite not being intrinsically installed in the human mind, cultural background does influence individual behavior through oral communication, regulations and expectations. Nonetheless, it is difficult for an extra-individual construction to become accepted because the production of culture is an intrinsic (endogenous) process of the human species. The significance of extraneous influences (e.g., climate and geography) in shaping cultural background is clear, and this will be studied later in the book in the analysis of interpretative mechanisms for the production and operation of cultural background.

3.4 Endogenous Cognizance Regarding the Birth of Cultural Background

Listing the interpretation mechanisms for the production and operation of cultural background will contribute to understanding how cultural background influences an individual's cognition and comprehension of the way they behave.

Cultural background is defined as "shared knowledge", which includes anyone who participates in possessing and distributing knowledge. Although this definition is descriptive, it does not explain which components of "shared knowledge" are activated and how individuals choose to use such mechanisms. Mechanisms are influenced by natural and human constructions, through which some aspects of such knowledge are selected (Hong 2009). Furthermore, the diachronic use of shared knowledge for communication purposes is available in the individual's mind, which creates mental situations from which meanings are drawn and behavior is shaped. Such knowledge becomes shared when it enters the shared field of communication amongst generations and, thus, cultural background is formed.

The basic features of shared cultural knowledge, whether of intrinsic or extrinsic origin, are as follows:

(a) It has a dynamic character, meaning that it changes through time and space. Even though such dynamism is applied to different population groups at different speeds, the end result is the shaping of a loosely interconnected system of values for a given country or national entity.
(b) It has a declarative and procedural character. The declarative character of shared knowledge mainly concerns facts, notions, values, beliefs and solid views of ourselves, fellow human beings and society. Procedural shared knowledge includes "know-how", that is, behavioral practices and recurrent processes. Declarative and procedural knowledge give rise to the development of diachronic incentive processes.
(c) Shared knowledge has a perpetual character and ultimately becomes a shared reality for the group.
(d) Shared knowledge can be enjoyed by everybody but may not be distributed to everyone in the same manner. In other words, it has an unequal distribution. It is distributed in accordance with the requirements set by the theory of social impact (Latane 1996). "Neighboring" individuals are more likely to have the same system of shared knowledge. Furthermore, certain individuals may be able to influence the distribution of shared knowledge depending on how much power their position vests in them.
(e) Individuals have an active role in accumulating, maintaining and activating shared knowledge. This is because shared knowledge is closely linked to life experiences. Hence, it is used to define the identity of individuals themselves.

This approach establishes the basic process that shapes cultural background—the process of its activation. Activation in terms of shared knowledge includes availability, accessibility and applicability.

Availability refers to the situation in which particular knowledge is presented to an individual's cognition system. One example is supernatural superstitions, where some people "invest" and others do not. It should be noted that accessibility of shared knowledge is considered a given fact, as there are knowledge sums that may be temporarily available.

Applicability refers to an individual's ability to apply shared knowledge to all situations. In other words, an individual must be able to choose from an extensive store of shared knowledge, and that reference that is directly connected to the problem at hand.

The aforementioned organization leads to the activation of cultural process. It should be noted though that individuals are not passive receivers of their cultural environment. On the contrary, they use cultural background as a tool to understand their experiences (Hong 2009). For this reason, any matching of geographical boundaries and uniqueness in cultural background characteristics is not scientifically acceptable, as this would reduce the likelihood of the appearance of the same syndromes at the same periods of time in different societies. For example, all societies socialize their members both for individualism and collectivism. The only difference amongst societies lies in the extent that individualism or collectivism is used in various circumstances.

The following comments can be made regarding the syndromes mentioned above:

(a) A society's "portfolio of syndromes" and the specific weight of each syndrome within each portfolio is of particular importance.
(b) The extent to which a society cultivates the various syndromes in its population during the process of socialization is significant. For example, there are societies (monasteries) that impose the wearing of uniforms upon their members. Obviously, this is not a treatment favoring individualism. However, such societies also promote a personal relationship between the individual and God. Therefore, in this case, the uniqueness of the relationship is stressed as individualism as a value.
(c) Finally, the significance of the process of adducing syndromes is stressed. For example, the reporting of disasters, epidemics and plagues by the mass media clearly encourages the invocation for uncertainty syndromes. Such exposure can have a significant influence on "adducing" processes and in turn dynamically shape the cultural map of a society.

Cultural syndromes constitute a link between the distant factors that created such syndromes and today's cultural conditions. Nevertheless, different distant factors shaping cultural syndromes (history, language traditions, philosophical and religious beliefs such as Protestantism and Confucianism) can create similar cultural syndromes. Thus, while societies may not share common origins, cultural syndromes may have exceptional similarities. Collectivism, for instance, is characteristic of East Asia because of Confucianism but is also representative of Northern Europe, where Confucianism has had no significant impact.

The interconnection of the distant past with modern cultural consequences is realized through immediate external and internal realities. Immediate external realities are social structures that reflect invoked cultural syndromes. Hence, the syndrome of uncertainty is reflected in an unstable tax system and a shadow economy (without rules). Hence, we can claim that societies do not differ because they include different dominant cultural syndromes, but because they share comparable institutional structures. In contrast, immediate internal realities are subjective psycho-structural circumstances. An example would be bankruptcy, which constitutes a social circumstance and has the same outcome in many countries (loss of the owner's property or shares); however, the significance attributed to bankruptcy differs from country to country. There are societies that link bankruptcy

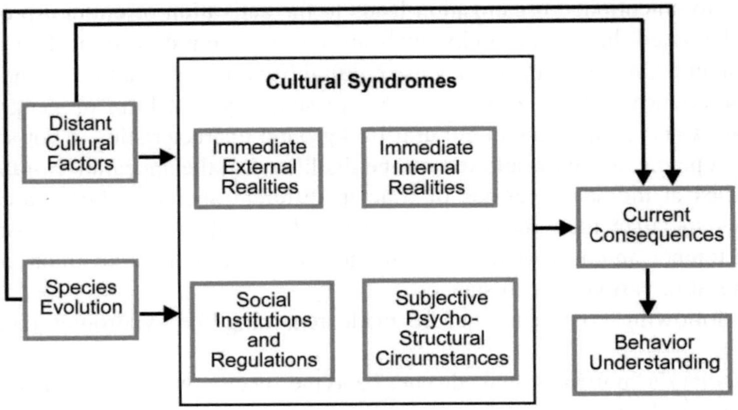

Fig. 3.1 The formation of cultural syndromes. *Source*: Petrakis and Kostis (2013)

to "dishonesty" and elbow out the "unsuccessful" businessman, whereas there are also societies that consider bankruptcy as an economic failure and give the businessman a second chance.

Hence, when cultural syndromes are used, cultural background can offer different notions according to everyday situations, and cultural syndromes may create different current real situations.

According to Fig. 3.1, to understand the way in which shared knowledge functions, we need to first understand two of its features, i.e., its declarative and procedural character. Declarative-type knowledge includes notions, values, beliefs that are formed in the individual's memory within the context of interconnected knowledge networks. In this way, when one notion of knowledge is activated, other related notions are also activated, thus activating an integrated knowledge system (Collins and Loftus 1975). Furthermore, the method used to access knowledge depends on the goals and (limited) ability of the individual to search their memory in detail for the all the relevant knowledge. Therefore, it is necessarily based on a small volume of knowledge, which is accessible according to the last time it was available and the frequency of its use. Procedural-type knowledge includes "know how", i.e., recurrent procedures characterized by automatic invocation. Hence, if x applies, then rule y is implemented (Anderson 1982): x is a mixture of innately produced and externally deriving stimuli and y is a sequence of behaviors that are triggered when the circumstances included in x materialize. The stimuli included in x are of particular importance. The entire "structure" of what is described as x may include thoughts, notions and signals. Furthermore, it may also include elements that have not been accurately and consciously defined. In addition, the way in which y is activated is of particular importance because it may include both self-conscious and unconscionable circumstances. If they are self-conscious, the way in which behavior is triggered may be identical every time. However, if they are unconscionable, then the activation of behavior may result in more than one action.

3.5 External Factors that Influence the Shaping of Cultural Background

Thucydides, and later Herodotus, identified a relationship between soil fertility and military conflicts in ancient Greece, thus highlighting the influence of external environments on a society's cultural background. Triandis (2009) noted that Athenians were not warmongers as they had no fertile soil to protect and were thus able develop a culture of dialogue and persuasion, i.e., democracy. From this perspective, the wider concept of external influences is understood.

The basic sources of external influences that shape cultural background are as follows (Triandis 2009):

(a) The availability of resources: The greater the resources (such as land and oil) of a society, the easier life is for its citizens. Therefore, it is more likely that people in such societies feel trust, optimism, secure and detest conspiracy theories.
(b) Mobility of resources: When available resources can be easily moved (e.g., farmers can easily move their flocks), "honor" psychologies develop as a means of protection against insults (theft) against mobile wealth by third parties.
(c) Cultural isolation: When a society is isolated in various ways (e.g., geographical), it tends to develop more homogeneous reactions and cultural backgrounds. Thus, tighter cultural regulations are more likely. In contrast, heterogeneity may lead to lax implementation.
(d) Interdependence activities: When cooperation with others is necessary for certain reasons (e.g., to construct vast projects), it is highly likely that "socialization", collectivism and cooperation behaviors will emerge. If not, then individualism behaviors will develop.
(e) Dangerous activities: A society in which individuals earn a living from dangerous activities is very likely to introduce rewards to compensate those who undertake risks and to confer power and respect upon them (e.g., knights in Europe during the Dark Ages). Many societies that accept the unequal allocation of power, influence and wealth encouraged individuals to undertake dangerous missions at some point in history (e.g., warriors in ancient Greece).
(f) Population density: As population density increases, it is likely that societal rules and norms become stricter. However, when a population becomes extremely dense, then it is possible that the society will turn to collectivism.
(g) Simple and complex societies: Simple societies (hunters and gatherers) have minimum resources at their disposal and generally such goods can be stored relatively easily. In contrast, rural societies have more complex hierarchies and organizations. In such a society, an individual may hold both a high social position (community leader) and a low hierarchical position (employee at the local factory).
(h) Immigration: Immigration leads to individualism, given that it includes the basic feature of separating from the group and surviving under private terms.

(i) Lack of ability to foresee natural events: The frequency natural disasters impacts on a society's cultural background. Therefore, in communities where disasters are frequently repeated, individuals do not develop scheduled activities. Furthermore, combined with limited resources, this situation enlarges the dimensions of uncertainty. If resources are plentiful, then a society may instead engage in over-scheduling for protection purposes (e.g., Japan and earthquakes).
(j) Geographic terrain: If an area has certain geographical traits that impact on the societies that live in that region, e.g., isolated communities, then certain particular isolation characteristics will develop.
(k) Climate: Studies have shown that climate influences both social psychology and cultural background. McClelland (1961) suggested an indirect relationship between climate conditions and cultural background. Furthermore, Tavassoli (2009) stressed a link between climate and the development of human behavior. The first study found that in countries with low temperatures and few sunshine hours, individualism prevails over collectivism because individuals are more isolated because of climate conditions. Furthermore, according to Triandis (1995), individuals are more disciplined and abide by society norms and rules (e.g., Northern European countries). In contrast, in warm climates (Hofstede 1980, 2001) where the sun shines most days of the year, collectivism is more likely to develop.

Climate is also directly connected with the shaping of cultural background via the influence of individual behavior. Individual psychology is affected through "homeostasis", i.e., the process where the human body adapts to the external environment through blood circulation (Tavassoli 2009). As a mechanism of "adaptation to temperature changes", homeostasis is the result of a control system that functions through basic human mechanisms—hormones, neurotransmitters, dopamine, serotonin and norepinephrine—connected to the hypothalamus in the human brain. This system concerns emotions and incentives. Dopamine is associated with reward expectations and activation incentives. In contrast, serotonin and norepinephrine are involved in the incentive development process. For example, sunshine enhances the human production of dopamine, whereas heat leads to the synthesis of norepinephrine. Therefore, the extent and duration of exposure to sunlight and, as a result, high temperatures create natural and psychological attitudes that regulate certain behaviors.

During the process of psychological homeostasis, human attitude adapts to the motivating stimuli it receives from the external environment because the individual wishes to maintain motivation processes that offer them the maximum possible pleasure. Therefore, when motivation stimuli from the environment are weak, individuals tend to increase the intensity with which homeostasis creates motivation requirements. The opposite happens when stimuli are powerful. Hence, when an individual finds himself/herself in an external environment where powerful motivation stimuli are created through natural functions (warm environment), homeostasis will lead them to repressive motivation conditions so that they can maintain an appropriate level of motivation. Hence, they are led to non-active attitudes. The opposite happens when external stimuli are weak. To follow is an example of risk assumption. Low levels of dopamine (little sunshine) are associated with "melancholic" moods that lead to a search for reward situations to lift mood levels. Hence, the requirements for bigger rewards are met at the expense of certainty, i.e., in the search for risk and profit. In contrast, individuals in a good mood (satisfactory sunshine and temperature) are more likely to avoid risk because they tend to maintain a healthy psychological state. When they are about to take risks, such individuals have less to gain and more to lose on an emotional level.

3.6 The Case of Multi-cultural Equilibria

The term multi-cultural equilibria (Beugelsdijk and Maseland 2011) implies that societies with a given economic level of effectiveness may have different cultural portfolios.

Here, we consider that culture does matter but produces different results. This ensures that there are no unambiguous correlations between cultural traits and specific economic results. As far as growth is concerned, a given cultural trait may have an enhancing presence in one economy yet act as a barrier in another.

Of course, the definition of economic effectiveness is relative and this makes ratiocination difficult. Hence, it is important to determine whether economic effectiveness is defined in terms of GDP per capita, productivity, happiness or rate of growth. Such relativity regarding effectiveness also makes the debate on the role of cultural background in economic results extremely difficult. If, however, we confine ourselves to the rate of growth as the criterion for effectiveness, then the starting level for these measurements is important—even so, more is required. Thus, the geographical reference and historical approach of the socioeconomic formation are also important. Finally, the content of cultural traits, as approached by separate societies, is of particular importance. Collectivism in Southern Europe is not the same as collectivism in Northern Europe.

The problem raised by the term multi-cultural equilibria concerns the procedure for proving their existence. If their existence is corroborated, then new requirements for research in this field are formed, given that more information on the exact nature of such equilibrium points is required. The debate among Hofstede (1980, 1991), Hofstede et al. (2010) and House et al. (2004) (Globe Project) regarding the cultural dimension of uncertainty avoidance is quite distinctive (a negative association in their results reaching −0.64) but is actually nothing more than the acknowledgement of the fact that multi-cultural equilibria do exist.

References

Anderson JR (1982) Acquisition of cognitive skill. Psychol Rev 89:369–406

Beugelsdijk S, Maseland R (2011) Culture in economics: history, methodological reflections and contemporary applications. Cambridge University Press, Cambridge

Collins AM, Loftus EF (1975) A spreading – activation theory of semantic processing. Psychol Rev 82:407–428

Hofstede G (1980) Culture's consequences: international differences in work-related values. Sage Publications, Beverly Hills, CA

Hofstede G (1991) Cultures and organisations. Harper Collins Business, London

Hofstede G (2001) Culture's consequences: comparing values, behaviors, institutions and organizations across nations. Sage Publications, London

Hofstede G, Hofstede GJ, Minkov M (2010) Cultures and organizations: software of the mind. McGraw-Hill, New York, NY

House RJ, Hanges PM, Javidan M et al (2004) Culture, leadership and organizations: the GLOBE study of 62 societies. Sage, Thousand Oaks, CA

Hong Y (2009) A dynamic constructivist approach to culture: moving from describing culture to explaining culture. In: Wyer RS, Chiu C, Hong YY (eds) Understanding culture: theory, research and application. Psychology Press, New York, NY

Latane B (1996) Dynamic social impact: the creation of culture by communication. J Commun 46:13–25

Markman BA, Grimm RL, Kyungil K (2009) Culture as a vehicle for studying individual differences. In: Wyer RS, Chiu C, Hong YY (eds) Understanding culture: theory, research and application. Psychology Press, New York, NY, pp 93–108

McClelland DC (1961) The achieving society. Van Nostrand, Princeton, NJ

Oyserman D, Sorensen N (2009) Understanding cultural syndrome effects on what and how we think: a situated cognition model. In: Wyer RS, Chiu C, Hong YY (eds) Understanding culture: theory, research and application. Psychology Press, New York, NY, pp 25–52

Petrakis P, Kostis P (2013) Economic growth and cultural change. J Socio-Econ. doi:10.1016/j.socec.2013.02.011

Schwartz SH (2009) Culture matters: national value cultures, sources and consequences. In: Wyer RS, Chiu C, Hong YY (eds) Understanding culture: theory, research and application. Psychology Press, New York, NY, pp 127–150

Tavassoli TN (2009) Climate, psychological homeostasis and individual behaviours across cultures. In: Wyer RS, Chiu C, Hong YY (eds) Understanding culture: theory, research and application. Psychology Press, New York, NY, pp 211–222

Triandis HC (1995) Individualism and collectivism. Westview Press, Boulder, CO

Triandis HC (2009) Ecological determinants of cultural variation. In: Wyer RS, Chiu C, Hong YY (ed) Understanding culture: theory, research and application. Psychology Press, pp 189–210

Triandis HC, Trafimow D (2001) Cross-national prevalence of collectivism. In: Sedikides C, Brewer MB (eds) Individual self, relational self, collective self. Taylor & Francis, Philadelphia, PA, pp 259–276

Wyer RS, Srull TK (1989) Memory and cognition in its social context. Erlbaum, Hillsdale, NJ

Wyer RS, Chiu C, Hong YY (2009) Understanding culture: theory, research and application. Psychology Press, New York, NY

Culture in Economic Thinking

4

Although the interconnection between "culture" ("cultural background")[1] and economic science is widely acknowledged among researchers, this relationship may seem odd to non-experts. In this chapter we first examine culture as part of economic theory. We then investigate developments that have led to the differentiation of culture and economy and to their interconnection again.

This chapter is structured as follows. Section 4.1 investigates cultural background as part of economic theory and Sect. 4.2 describes the divergence of the two concepts. Sections 4.3 and 4.4 focus on the re-emergence of cultural background in growth economics and economic thinking, respectively. Culture in the neoclassical model is presented in Sects. 4.5 and 4.6 refers to the relationship between cultural background and the post-Keynesian/institutional model. Finally, Sect. 4.7 focuses on the theory of rational expectations.

4.1 "Culture" in Economic Theory

The study of the relationship between culture and economic science constitutes a study of two different aspects of economic system (De Jong 2009) because since the late nineteenth century there have been at least two dominant economic paths. On the one hand, we have "marginal analysis" to make personal decisions and to maximize benefits; on the other hand, there is traditional economic science, which studies economies based on aspects of society, and incorporates production, consumption and the distribution of goods and services. In the first approach, culture does not play a significant role, but in the second one it constitutes a key element and a source of interest.

[1] For the purposes of the present book, it is not necessary to conduct a detailed examination of the concepts of "culture" and "cultural background" to identify the conceptual divergence of the two, if any. Hence, they are deemed synonymous. The use of the term "cultural background" is preferred, except in the present chapter where historical reference makes it necessary to use the concept of "culture".

P.E. Petrakis, *Culture, Growth and Economic Policy*,
DOI 10.1007/978-3-642-41440-4_4, © Springer-Verlag Berlin Heidelberg 2014

The term "culture", as we define it today, was first used by Cicero in his work *Tusculanae Disputationes* (circa 45 BC) to metaphorically express the cultivation of the philosophical soul. During the Middle Ages, this dimension disappeared as the focus turned to religious worship rather than the amelioration of human life. The Renaissance again revived the metaphoric use of culture. Until the early seventeenth century, culture reflected the moral and intellectual development of people at a personal level. During the seventeenth and eighteenth centuries, the term was expanded to express the development of not only humans at an individual level but also that of society as a whole. At the same time, attempts were made to include a set of social rules and standards. Therefore, culture, history and economic theory attempted to investigate and understand the differences between societies at a development level.

Adam Smith, the father of economic science, saw a relationship between culture and economy, and more particularly with economic history. For Smith and many of his contemporaries, the development of societies in terms of culture was universal; it was the degree of development that differed. This view is not surprising because even before his seminal work *An Inquiry into the Nature and Causes of the Wealth of Nations* (1776), Smith was already well known for his earlier piece *The Theory of Moral Sentiments* (1759), in which he outlined his views on ethics. In his earlier work, Smith expressed his view that an individual naturally shows solidarity towards his fellow human beings, and that an individual's ethics do not allow him to exploit others. Furthermore, the role of individualism is pinpointed, and acts as a lever for the moral development of society. In other words, the father of economic science by no means ignores the moral and cultural aspect of society.

Smith's book *An Inquiry into the Nature and Causes of the Wealth of Nations* moves in the same direction, although focusing on economic system. The "invisible hand" constitutes a mechanism that effectively guides the productive power of a society to act on the basis of its own wishes and its own personal benefit, with no state-imposed limitations. In turn, individual interest also tends to bring about social interest. In this work, Smith foresees a social order that includes motives, morality and social institutions.

The dawning of the Enlightenment period saw the divergence of the various views on the concept of culture and new elements were added. An important approach is that of the "essentialization" of culture, as mentioned by Beugelsdijk and Maseland (2011). According to this approach, culture and the identity of a group of people or a society are inherent.

The aforementioned interpretation of cultural background started to emerge in the late eighteenth century and peaked in the nineteenth century when nations began to make their political debuts. The division started with the Romantics, with their separation of culture (Kultur) and civilization (Zivilization). The conceptual differences that occurred during this period led to the incorporation of two important elements in the concept of culture: (1) culture was seen as a particular feature of each society, which distinguished it from primitive forms of social organization by achieving social prosperity and significant achievements in the fields of politics, arts and technology, and (2) it was also a means for growth, unique for every society.

This development path influenced thinking within economic science and was integrated in the ideas of Historical School scholars such as Wilhelm Roscher, Bruno Hildebrand, Karl Knies and Gustav Schmoller. This school of thought examined economics as a sum of principles, based on political, cultural and historical science. Its ideas had a particularly significant impact on discussions regarding the role of culture in economics. The "essentialized" views of the Historical School were structured around the matching of society and nation, which is understood as a closed and homogenous group of individuals and was not subject to doubt. Hence, every analysis of culture should place national entity as a point of reference.

In addition to the influence of culture within an entire school of thought (the Historical School), the divergence between culture and civilization also inspired criticism by representatives of political economy, including Karl Marx. Marx attempted to examine culture as a sum of social values from the perspective of political economy. In his work *Das Kapital* (1867), he described the operation of the capitalist system and the way in which the productive process is structured. Marx considered the exploitation of labor by capital to rely on a series of beliefs, perceptions and sociopolitical institutions that played a determinative role in the consolidation of the capitalist system. In other words, he deemed culture as one of the means used for the consolidation of capitalism.

Therefore, regarding the content of culture and its role in economics during the nineteenth century, two dominant trends emerged. On the one hand we have the Historical School, where culture is understood as the sum of the features of a particular society, which enable it to separate from the rest and experience growth. On the other hand, there are the followers of political economy, who, influenced by the criticism of Marx, deemed culture as a feature of the ruling class (Beugelsdijk and Maseland 2011). To these theorists, the state is an extension of the capitalist class, protecting interests of capital. The development of the productive process is based on changes to institutions, values and beliefs (Marx 1978 [1867]). This standard constitutes the beginning of "historical materialism" (De Jong 2009). According to Marx, and more so Smith, values and institutions constitute a part of the economic system and therefore economic analysis. It should be noted however that no specific reference to the relationship between culture and economy was made in their texts, given that they both considered the two concepts to be inherent and mutually complementary to each other.

4.2 The Separation of Culture and Economics

During the nineteenth century, there were a number of events in Europe that had a universal impact. It was during this period that the endless quest for national supremacy and consolidation at an international level began. As far as Europe was concerned, culture was used to establish a conceptual framework in an attempt to interpret the different rates of growth among states.

In the late nineteenth and early twentieth centuries, the prevalence of expansionary policies (imperialism) soon led to thoughts of expansion beyond Europe. Thus, attempts to expand and strengthen a state were based to a great extent on the concept of culture. Geographical expansion had to be accompanied not only by the exertion of political influence over newly subjugated populations, but also by the provision of education and civilization. Hence, imperialism led to the bisection of the world: the civilized and developed countries of the West and the remainder that lacked such features. Civilization and growth were key factors in the divergence of national states, and caused a change in the way we understood culture as a concept.

With the emergence of imperialism, the idea that culture was the sum of the particular features of a society and a form of progress lost traction. Culture was limited to the narrow notion of civilization, by expressing the intellectual cultivation of the individual. With the trend for global sovereignty and the global modernization of societies, the new view of culture saw cultural differences as the outcome of under-development and a commitment to tradition. These cultural differences were considered as trammels to social progress and were not associated with developed countries in the West. The Western world represented societies with high levels of education and prosperity, contrary to societies characterized with irrational behaviors, traditionalism and adherence to stability. Hence, culture started to reflect, as well as to establish, the distribution of the power of the mighty around the world. In other words, the power of the West could legitimize its sovereignty over the others by pleading a rational way of thinking and behavior, which was universally acceptable. Therefore, the concept of culture at that time was considered a relic that societies should get rid of to regain their international footing.

Divergence over the concept of culture, which started to emerge in the late nineteenth century, also acted to gradually remove it from economic analysis. Thus, the need to study the relationship between economics and cultural background as two separate entities emerged for the first time.

The separation of economic science from social sciences and its elevation to an independent science was the result of pertinacious processes. The starting point of the separation was the emergence of the neoclassical model of marginal utility. The view that utility was a determinative factor for economic behavior was first opposed by the supporters of the "institutional approach", such as Veblen and Commons, and by sociologists like Weber. These theorists focused on the role of institutions in economics. By the end of World War II, the neoclassical model was the dominant approach.

According to economists, the focal point of economic science is the maximization of an individual's benefit, meaning that the individual makes the right decisions for the satisfaction of his/her needs. Hence, it is understood that in this form, economic science does not examine the relationships between production and consumption, but instead turns its interest to the individual and the balancing of benefits and costs for the maximization of subjective value.

The key supporters of the new form of economic science were Menger (1871), Walras (1954) and Edgeworth (1881). According to Menger (1871), economic activity should be examined as a result of the rational decisions of the individual. Following the same path, Edgeworth (1881) considered the individual to be constantly searching gratification, but not all, however, will make the right decisions to maximize their benefits. Edgeworth (1881) introduced the rational maximization of benefit as a behavioral standard. Therefore, rationalism constituted the basic view of the neoclassical model.

The intense criticism against the neoclassical model derived from the fact that it was not possible to interpret the operation of an economy based on personal motives. The dispute between Menger (1871) and supporters of the German Historical School, also known as *Methodenstreit*, received much attention circa 1880. According to Schmoller (1901), the main supporter of this school of thought, economists should study historical documents and statistical data to indentify the features that motivate the economic mechanism. In contrast, Menger (1871) viewed economic science as an autonomous science, based on the maximization of benefit and knowledge. Mathematical models on the development of economic theory were also introduced at that time.

Thanks to writers who were not influenced by the Historical School, such as Max Weber (1864–1920), economic theory was not yet limited to the narrow limits of the marginal approach (early twentieth century). In his book *The Protestant Ethic and the Ethic of Capitalism* (1905), Weber linked the capitalist system to Protestant ethics and values. The Protestant ethic, which was based on hard work and the allocation of roles to all members of society and combined with the incrimination of consumption, favored the accumulation of capital for investments and the further expansion of the economy. Weber also viewed Protestantism as an explanation for the existence of worldwide economic and social inequalities.

The views of Weber were the point of reference for many scholars who continued to identify economy, ethics, values and institutions as integral parts of the same system. However, as time passed, their views were displaced and overtaken by those of the neoclassic movement, such as Menger and Marshall. Irrespective of the course followed around the world, since 1950 onwards, the neoclassical model has been the dominant expression of economic theory.

However, a new school of thought emerged during the same period, known as institutionalism, with a focus on the role of institutions in economics. Its representatives were Thorstein Veblen, John Commons and Wesley Mitchell. This movement was then transformed into the "new institutional economics" and included two discrete intellects: D.C. North and O. Williamson, who were both honored for their contribution with the Nobel Prize. They opposed the neoclassical model and sought a more coherent framework for studying economics, one that was based on both history and cultural values. Veblen (1899) heavily criticized the neoclassical model (and the classical model) for considering an individual's behavior as a given fact and as a point of reference for the real world, instead of dealing with the factors in its formation. Veblen regarded an individual's behavior as the result of the developmental process with psychological and biological aspects. In addition, human behavior forms institutions that affect economic activity. Where economic theory is based on the behavior of the individual it includes human nature and motives in its analysis. However, the extensive reference to psychology and institutions highlighted the need for the divergence of economics from social sciences and the introduction of psychology as an independent variable. Although Smith's contemporaries considered values, ethics and beliefs when interpreting economic activity, Veblen (1899) considered it necessary to remove them from the analysis and to consider them separately. In other words, for the first time the concept of culture was examined within economic theory as something separate and independent. The step was made: culture had its own discrete status, independent from economic analysis, and now viewed as an interpretative variable. Thus, on the one hand the concept of economic science as a whole narrowed somewhat, but on the other hand culture now represented an entire distinct field of research.

4.3 Development Economics

The predominance of the neoclassical economics since 1950 onwards is indisputable. A series of events played primary roles in this development. In the following section we briefly mention the introduction of mathematical models in economic analysis and describe relevant political events.

The starting point for the use of mathematical models in economic science goes back to the two world wars. Large-scale military operations highlighted the imperative need for organization and data processing. For instance, a system was needed to monitor supply stock and foresee the future needs of the army—mathematical and statistical models provided a solution. By the end of World War II, the idea of using mathematics in economic science emerged as a tool for the management and distribution of goods and services.

Globalization and technological developments in transportation have reduced geographical distances and resulted in mass immigration to developed Western countries. However, differences in language, mores, customs and civilization among nations have made mathematics the most commonly acceptable language of communication. This move towards mathematics, however, has limited the interest in culture and civilization, and it been the Achilles' heel of analysis, given that it cannot accurately interpret dominant socio-economic conditions.

The devastation caused by World War II went beyond the millions of casualties and innumerable catastrophes. It also produced many political upheavals at a global level, events that still have global impacts today. Following World War II, the Cold War started between the West and the Soviet Union. This conflict impacted economic science with the emergence of a new trend: the fight against communism. Economists considered Marxism to be the big enemy of the capitalist system. Hence, they started to emphasize the benefits deriving from the market economy. Their central argument was the individual's freedom of choices (based on the maximization of benefits), which they believed favored the function of democracy and the safeguarding of human rights. This ideological approach to individual freedom and the focus on the subject during the decision-making process kept economists away from anything that concerned culture and moral values (De Jong 2009).

The rise and domination of the neoclassical model estranged culture from economic science after 1950. Nevertheless, culture continued to play an important role. The field of development economics studied the development process of Third World countries and interpreted the growth gap between them and developed countries. Economists who focused their research on Western and Eastern European countries had previously dealt with the growth gap.

Development economics began to look to less developed countries to study the struggle for domination between capitalism and communism. The two systems tried to consolidate at a global level and attempted to use Third World countries as the means for achieving their goal. Therefore, both sides introduced extensive development programs in undeveloped countries.

The development models of high-income countries could be applied in such countries. However, this might not have the anticipated results given the particular features of Third World nations. In other words, the developing countries need to resolve various issues and their differences with Western countries to look more like them. At this point, cultural background makes its appearance and is used to interpret differences in the mechanisms and principles governing the economies of such countries.

According to development economics, developing countries should eliminate all features that hinder their economic growth. In other words, they should form a rational behavior, based on the sum of values and perceptions. Tradition and cultural background play an important role. Nevertheless, despite the fact that the economic model of rational expectations was capable of studying Western behavior, and by extension the developed world, it could not be applied to the rest of the world. Thus, such ideas were integrated in the economics of development, together with questions regarding production and consumption.

In the decades that followed World War II, economics of development only existed in the field of economic science, which took a broad view of economics, contrary to the dominant view. Within such framework, the Third World was the connecting link between economy and culture. Economics the development, which integrated bureaucratic structures and democracy as economic behavior tools, are referenced in the literature as the "modernization theory".

4.4 The Reemergence of Culture in Economics

From the late twentieth century, theories based on cultural background were gradually starting to appear. The majority of studies, where quantitative methods were used, attempted to interpret the repercussions of the differences between cultural background and the economics of development (Hofstede and Bond 1991; Harrison 1992; Swank 1996; Noland 2005; Pryor 2005).

The reappearance of culture in economics may be explained with two basic axes: a) the failure of the dominant theory to provide convincing answers to many problems, and b) the political developments that occurred because of the Cold War climate, with the climax being the fall of the Berlin Wall in 1989. The end of the Cold War had two significant repercussions. First, the dispute between market economies and centrally planned economies came to an end, and second, the debate on the consolidation of the market economy commenced (De Jong 2009).

The end of World War II represented significant upheaval within economic science, which led to various divergences. Samuelson's (1947) *Foundations of Economic Analysis*, which outlined his approach to optimization under limited conditions, signified a point of reference for understanding most economic problems. However, there still remained a series of theoretical problems due to the fact that certain individual behaviors could not be explained.

Samuelson (1947) created supply and demand curves to determine an economy's point of equilibrium through the maximization of consumers' and producers' benefits under income constraints. This approach raised certain issues. First, there was the question as to whether such curves, which are extracted from the individual decisions of consumers and producers, can lead to general equilibrium in an economy. Views on this issue are conflicting because although in a fully competitive economy economic equilibrium can occur, it is not possible to clarify whether there is just one unique solution to which an economy converges with all other factors remaining constant (ceteris paribus). Another issue concerned whether the model could be used in imperfect markets and applied in the making of macroeconomic policies. During the 1970s and 1980s, many economists suggested that macroeconomics was based on microeconomic analysis. However, reaching certain conclusions regarding the operation of the economy as a whole was impossible given that the models were characterized by representative behaviors, and any shift from the individual to the aggregate level would be arbitrary.

The weaknesses of the model of general equilibria quickly led economists in other directions to study the operation of the market. The game theory was the first attempt to tackle the aforementioned weaknesses. It was through this that the study of strategic interactions among economic agents and the means to address the problem of imperfect competition became possible. Unfortunately though, game theory relied on rational behaviors and players with perfect information, which is not realistic. If all the players of the game are perfectly informed and know that their opponent acts rationally, then there is no motivation for the conduct of transactions. A motivation would exist only in the case of information asymmetry.

In the early 1970s there were attempts to develop the game theory with the focal point being a model of rational expectations. According to this particular model, economic activity agents avoid repeating the same errors in their forecast, and all errors are random. The lack of a systematic forecast error and stochastic risk enables the perfect forecast in rational expectations models. Equilibrium depends on external risks—each time a shock occurs, a new equilibrium comes to the model.

Among the plentitude of equilibria, however, financial activity agents should choose the steadiest equilibrium by relying on their forecasts for the future.

The advantage of rational expectations lies in making decisions with an orientation towards the future. Forecasts are based on future events, such as announcements by central government with regard to its economic planning or the future results of a company's operations. However, the assumption that economic activity agents are aware of all the parameters of an economy and can fully understand its mechanisms is unrealistic because this exceeds the real mental and cognitive powers of individuals.

Together with rational expectations models, some writers have gone on to examine the role of human behavior and psychology to better understand the economic decisions of individuals. By using the dominant economic theory as a point of reference, they attempted to give a new perspective to the decision-making processes of individuals. For example, Kahneman and Tversky (1979) found that uncertainty often leads decision makers to use poor judgment.

Williamson (1975) coined the term "new institutional economics" in an attempt to stress the importance of institutional frameworks in the decision-making process. The neoclassical model does not take into account those factors that form human behavior, but instead assumes a universal structure. According to North (1990), institutions constitute all the restrictions that form human interactions. Such restrictions may be formal or informal. Formal restrictions include legislation and written rules, whereas informal ones concern the codes of behavior of social groups and are connected to the concept of culture.

The importance of institutions in economic activity, according to new institutional economics, lies in the decrease of uncertainty. Through a legal framework, which provides guarantees and determines behavior, uncertainty is diminished and trust towards economic agents is strengthened. A decrease in uncertainty means a decrease in the cost of transactions due to an increase in information and a decrease in the necessary contracts between contracting parties. Therefore, the establishment of institutions leads to greater economic activity.

To summarize, following the period (1950–1980) when economic science separated from the other social sciences and was limited to the marginal analysis of individual decisions, the last decades of the twentieth century saw an attempt to integrate elements from cultural background. The key causes for this shift were the failure of the neoclassical model to provide answers to many problems and the complexity of the mathematical models.

During the Cold War, the key discussion focused on the dispute regarding which system, market economies or centrally planned economies, would produce the best results. During the same period, there was also intense debate with regard the role of rules and restrictions in economic activity. Developed countries were following policies to decrease imports, and were characterized by a strict regulatory framework. Developed European countries were operating under a narrow regulatory framework, which limited the free formation of prices by imposing a maximum limit on wages and primary goods. From this, an ideological discussion emerged between the free market and the imposition of state rules. No attention was paid to the relationship among values, institutions and economic performances within economic science. This task was instead undertaken by fields (especially those in social sciences) with a similar subject matter.

The Asian Miracle can be considered as the causa causans for the post-war examination of the relationship between values and economic development. The spectacular progress of certain countries in Eastern Asia prompted much research and resulted in intense discussion. Countries such as South Korea, Hong Kong, Thailand, Indonesia and Taiwan experienced impressive economic growth rates from the mid-1960s to the mid-1990s. In contrast, countries with a high standard of living and growth prospects followed the opposite path (e.g., Sri Lanka). Finally, rapidly developing countries or NICs (New Industrialized Countries) as they are referred to in the literature, followed policies that prepared their industrial production to face international competition.

Attempts to identify the determining factors of the economic growth of successful Asian countries led economists to a multitude of presumptions. One explanation regarding the determination of growth focused on the widening of the markets. Asian governments had prepared their industries against global competition, by initially imposing policies to protect domestic production. The end target of this undertaking was to place domestic industries under the pressure of global competition and to thereby make competition the means of success. A further explanation concerned the role of the state in these countries. More specifically, states offered incentives for increases in exports, whilst also owning many export businesses.

The search for a convincing explanation for the Asian Miracle was suitable for the emergence of a different suggestion, one that connected values and culture to the economics of development. According to the "Asian values", as the approach was named, Asian countries were characterized by particular values that boost economic growth. Hence, values like team spirit, solidarity, devotion to a target and austerity offered the right incentives for the economics of development. Care for others, collectivism, unanimity and respect for values and institutions can also be added to the list above.

Many have suggested that "Asian values" derive from the philosophy of Confucianism that is predominant in many areas of Asia. According to Hill (2000), the debate on "Asian values" was started by Western scientists in the late 1960s. Initially, many papers (Levy 1962; Dore 1967; Kahn 1979) tried to correlate the economics of development of Japan with Confucianism, and such papers were extended to the other Asian countries over the following decades. During the 1980s, many Asian governments included ethics from Confucianism in their educational system; something similar occurred in Malaysia with Islam (Lee and Ackerman 1997). The Asian financial crisis in 1997 diminished interest in "Asian values", but nonetheless, it had boosted the revival of culture in economic science.

The fall of the Berlin Wall and the end of the Cold War in 1989 suggested a possible relationship between culture and economy. The predominance of the capitalist system over communism was a given fact, however, concern soon grew as to how the capitalist system would be applied to former Communist countries. The views expressed were many and varied. Among these there were supporters of the view that the citizens of the former Communist countries should adapt to the rules and institutions of the market economy. A lack of individual incentives and the settled view that the state ought to take care of and control every aspect of a citizen's life highlighted the imperative need for a complete change in the dominant culture of those peoples. A change in culture and familiarization with institutions were the key to the consolidation of capitalism.

Finally, the policy applied by the World Bank was heavily criticized during the 1990s. The developmental models it used in Third World countries led to failure. The World Bank, as well as other international organizations, attempted to apply one-dimensional development models that did not consider the particular features of the countries receiving finance. For these programs to be effectively applied, they should have understood the cultures of such countries because culture forms behavior as well as reaction to change.

4.5 Culture in the Neoclassical Model

One of the most widespread theories on human activity in economic science is the expected utility theory. In his paper *Exposition of a New Theory on the Measurement of Risk*, the French–Swedish mathematician Bernoulli (1738) established foundations for the development of the utility theory. Two centuries later, Neumann and Morgenstern (1947) developed the theory of utility (VNM-utility), which is based on rational choice, and today constitutes the rational classical theory of human behavior in economic science. To determine the rational man (homo economicus) and rational behavior, they created "the four rationality axioms" as follows:

(a) Completeness: Every individual is clearly aware of his/her needs and preferences.
(b) Transitivity: Preferences are transferred logically.
(c) Continuity: There is a "borderline point" between someone being better or worse than the average choice.
(d) Independence: A choice is realized irrespective of the possibility that a third choice will emerge.

According to this theory, every rational individual is distinguished by a utility function, which includes all the choices, as well as a series of possibilities on the basis of which an individual has chosen to realize the four axioms. In doing so the individual satisfies his/her needs at any given time. This can be illustrated using the following formula:

$$\mathrm{U} = \sum pi \cdot Ai$$

where U is the utility and *pi* is the possibility an individual will choose and realize choice *Ai*.

INDIVIDUAL PREFERENCES + LIMITATIONS = RESULTS

Fig. 4.1 Structure of the neoclassical model. *Source*: Beugelsdijk and Maseland (2011)

Therefore, according to the neoclassical theory, every individual knows exactly what his/her needs are at any given time, as well as what choices he/she has to satisfy them, which, as a whole, form his/her utility. In addition, he/she has the mental ability to choose the best option from the available choices; these options are taken for granted by his/her external environment and therefore the individual can act in the best possible rational way to achieve just one target—the maximization of his/her utility (max U).

Such rational considerations of human behavior, which were the core of classical economic thinking for many years, deems the satisfaction of human needs as the basic motivating factor for human activity. This view has helped economic science to determine the motivation of human activity using this mathematical model. Nevertheless, one key disadvantage is that it is based on a rather simplified form of reality that ignores many important variables of social and psychological interest, including the role of a society's cultural and institutional background.

According to the neoclassical model, the individual has certain preferences and needs, which he/she tries to satisfy by facing certain restrictions (limited available resources). The right choice and the hierarchical classification of the needs an individual must satisfy occur under the prism of rational behavior. However, often the individual is not fully informed of the result and the decisions are made under a state of uncertainty.

Fig. 4.1 shows how the neoclassical model conceptualizes culture. Thus, culture may enter as an extraneous factor in three ways: as a source of preferences, limitations or as a deviation from the model. The common element of the approaches mentioned above is the presumption (either directly or indirectly) that the human mind has finite cognitive powers.

Although neoclassical model examines decision-making based on individual choices, it does look at how such choices are formed. By considering the choices and values of the individual as exogenous variables in the neoclassical model, a pathway towards culture emerges. All versions of culture as a source of preferences state that social groups and individuals have different beliefs and preferences. Such differences lead to a divergence in the performance of the groups (or individuals).

A multitude of definitions of culture may be extracted by considering it as a source of preferences. Fernandez and Fogli (2007) defined culture as "the systematic variation in preferences or beliefs". Hofstede (2001) described it as "the collective programming of the mind", and Inglehart (1997) labeled culture a "system of attitudes, values and knowledge that is widely shared within a society and is transmitted from generation to generation".

In his analysis, De Jong (2009) explained how culture influences economic activity. Culture may be considered as the sum of the values and perceptions dominating a group of people. Whether directly or indirectly, culture influences the outcome of economic processes. The formed views of people and the grid of values influence the organization and operation of institutions and, ultimately, the distribution of available resources. Many writers claim the opposite too. Though indirectly, they consider that it is economic outcome and institutions that influence the way individuals think, the total of the values and, by extension, culture.

The view of culture as a choice does not develop the neoclassical model, but merely completes it by attempting to provide answers to various empirical questions. It must also be clarified which choices are associated with culture and which are not. By embracing Schein's (1985) definition of culture, we can describe culture as a structured pattern of assumptions that are derived from a collective social process. Any preference that is not a result of this process is not characterized as culture but as individual choice.

The literature on culture as a choice is limited. We can however refer to the analysis of Wildavsky (1987) regarding the formation of choices through social relationships and the organization of society. Tabellini (2008) mentioned that differences between institutions and technology determine the differences in values among groups. The better institutions are organized, the easier they spread through the members of the group, as well as from generation to generation.

Some writers have deviated from the dominant trend by trying to identify the ways in which choices and values are formed. Although the structure of an individual's thinking and his/her stimuli are determined to a certain extent by genetics, experiences and consociations with other people play the most important roles (Inglehart 1997; Hofstede and Hofstede 2005; Fernandez and Fogli 2007).

The second approach regarding culture in the neoclassical model of behavior presents it as a source of limitations to the rational choices of the individual. This particular approach is rooted in new institutional economics. The basic idea of new institutional economics is that the individual is not perfectly informed and, thus, faces uncertainty in his/her decisions. To tackle uncertainty, institutions were invented. Institutions are a "system of established and prevalent social rules that structure social interactions" (Hodgson 2006). Through institutions, rules and the actions of individuals are established, behaviors become more predictable and uncertainty is reduced. Therefore, apart from the fact that they reduce uncertainty, institutions also limit the sum of the available choices to the individual (North 1990). In other words, they restrict an individual's choices, and in this way culture is referenced as a source of limitations.

North (1990) divided institutions in two categories: formal institutions (written rules and laws) and informal institutions (unwritten rules and customary law). The way in which individuals manage information and the criteria with which they make their choices are determined by mental models, i.e., by culture. Furthermore, North suggested that the quality of the institutions determines economic growth and acts to limit transaction costs. Therefore, the question arises as to why countries with ineffective institutions do not "copy" the institutions of developed countries.

New institutional economics provides two answers to this question, and these are directly linked to culture. The first mentions that the development of institutions is limited by history, i.e., the choices of the past influence the present and change occurs over long periods of time. Williamson (2000) considered that it takes 10 to 100 years for formal institutions to be changed, and 100 to 1,000 years for informal ones. The second explanation states that informal institutions are human creations that reflect the values, ideas and perceptions of their creators, resulting in the fact that any changes (if any at all) are limited.

Some writers have attempted to extend the debate around culture by citing the concept as a source of limitations. For example, Williamson (2000) presented an economy as a system of four levels: resource management, the state, institutions and informal institutions. In the first level, informal institutions (customs, traditions, folkways) are created spontaneously though social upheaval and over long periods of time. The second level, formal institutions (laws, rules, property rights), has been designed to enable the proper operation of and the allocation of power from the third level, i.e., the state. Finally, the fourth level concerns the price adjustment and market equilibrium in terms of quantity.

The approach where culture deviates from the economic model does not increase the model's explanatory power, but it does try to offer explanations for results the model cannot interpret. The differences between theory and reality can be attributed to non-rational factors such as culture (De Jong 2009).

By studying the employment rates in various countries, Clark (1988) found that those differences did not derive from training, experiences, education, nutrition or employment organization. He reached the conclusion that differences among cultures must result from just one factor. The high savings rate, entrepreneurship and the economics of development of Asian countries cannot be interpreted by existent theory. The explanation given by many writers focused on differences in culture (Daly 1998; Dore 1990). Lincoln et al. (1978) revealed that culture had an influence on the organization of businesses, supported by the fact that businesses with a large number of Japanese workers tend to behave differently than similar companies with US employees.

An awareness of the limits of the economic model soon forced researchers to search for solutions. As expected, culture played a determinative role. However, there were features of societies that the economic theory could not explain; these were characterized as cultural remnants and discouraged further scientific research. Clark (1988) also noted this point and stressed that if culture is treated as a remnant, it will not be able to explain anything.

4.6 Culture in the Post-Keynesian/Institutional Model

Since 1975, a post-Keynesian school of thought has developed in the field of economic science, rooted in the "general theory" of Keynes (1937). Over the last decade, many post-Keynesian scholars have turned to the creation of a new model, scientifically framing and explaining human behavior and being less limitative than that of orthodox thinking. Thus, the so-called post-Keynesian model of human behavior was created.

According to this model, an individual is constantly receiving large quantities of data from his/her external environment, where data has no meaning on its own (Hodgson 1988; Kaufman 1989). Therefore, the individual is asked to give meaning and sense to data by converting it to useful information and creating a cognitive background. Following this, the background will affect his/her reasoning ability when making decisions that will determine his/her actions. The purpose of the individual's action will be the satisfaction of his/her needs and wishes at any given point in time.

Contrary to the neoclassical view, it is suggested in this model that an individual does not clearly and fully know at any given time what his/her needs are and what choices he/she has to satisfy those needs. The post-Keynesian view suggests that the cognitive level of each individual possesses at any given point in time is the one that shapes his/her needs and wishes at that same point in time. Regarding reasoning ability, he/she tries to identify the choices available to him/her to satisfy his/her needs. Therefore, for human activity to be interpreted, the factors that affect and shape the cognitive and reasoning ability of an individual within a period of time need to be examined.

Table 4.1 outlines the key differences of the two models in terms of the motivation of human behavior, knowledge of the environment and the decision-making process.

It is clear from Table 4.1 that the differences between the two models are significant and fundamental. According to the neoclassical model, the basic setsquare for the individual's behavior is the maximization of his/her benefits, and he/she has placed his/her preferences in a hierarchy on the basis of his/her cognitive ability. In contrast, the post-Keynesian/institutional model gives a different tincture to motivation, because aside from an increase in benefit, human behavior also pursues a series of individual needs and wishes.

Regarding perceptions and knowledge of the environment, the neoclassical model considers that an individual is fully aware of reality from a cognizance point of view, and that he/she has the ability to tackle multiplex problems. In contrast, the post-Keynesian/institutional model considers that an individual has limited cognitive ability with creative abilities.

Whereas in the neoclassical model rationalism is connected to the maximization of benefits, in the post-Keynesian/institutional model it is connected to elements of emotional, procedural and creative logic, affecting the decision-taking process.

Hence, within the framework of human behavior processes from an economic perspective, two significant models have been created. First, the neoclassical model produces a model that links economic science to an organized way of thinking, which at a micro level is presented as "rational choice" and at a macro level as "rational expectations". Second, the post-Keynesian model links economic science to social sciences, and with politics and psychology.

It becomes clear that when the post-Keynesian model is examined with the analytical tools of the neo-institutionalists, it has a greater potential to accept cultural elements. In this manner, it presents a more integrated analytical framework. Ultimately, it is "rigidity" that offers "resistance" to cultural analysis.

Table 4.1 Neoclassical model and Post-Keynesian/Institutional model

Neoclassical model	Post-Keynesian/institutional model
Motivation (Motives)	
The individual's behavior is guided by aiming at the maximization of utility	Behavior aims at realizing a series of individual targets (needs and wishes)
All wishes are comparable on a person-by-person basis, according to that person's ability to gain benefit	There is a differentiation of targets among individuals
Preferences are placed in hierarchy	There is a complex grid of needs and wishes with a basic series of priorities
The placement of preferences in a hierarchy constitutes an extraneous procedure for each individual	The acknowledgment of the hierarchical structure of the needs and the wishes is the outcome of a cognitive procedure
The placement of preferences in a hierarchy is complete, steady, consistent and separate for each individual. It has additional characteristics, such as transitivity, continuity and repletion	Other characteristics of the placement of the needs and the wishes in a hierarchy include the repletion and the increase of the needs and the dependence of the targets set
Maximization is the basic motive	Motives constitute a search engine for the various needs and wishes
Perception and knowledge of the environment	
Individuals have sufficient cognitive ability to face reality's complexity	Individuals have limited cognitive ability and are potential creative beings
Knowledge includes the existing information	Knowledge constitutes a social-type action and requires some form of choice, organization and interpretation of the data
The environment is known or capable of being known	Knowledge is subject to uncertainty. This "opens" the door for "uncertain knowledge", which is acquired by means of the continuous procedure of thinking
Causation and decision-making	
Individuals have a developed reasoning ability, which allows them to process and assess all the information they receive	Individuals have limited logical ability, but do have creativity. Their feelings can form the decision-taking procedure
Decision-taking is based on the "essential" or "determinative" rationality	Human rationality includes elements of procedural logic, creativity and emotional logic
Rationalism is connected to the procedure for the maximization of benefit	Rationality is connected to the search for solutions and the idea of satisfaction

Source: Fernandez-Huerga (2008)

Despite these factors, for different reasons and in different fields, both models offer valuable potential for the acknowledgment of the influence of cultural behavior on economic behavior.

4.7 Expectations and Rationality

The use of expectations is one of the economic theory's basic tools. Keynes attributed a central role to the expectations of individuals. Keynes, for example, made reference to waves of optimism and pessimism, which contributed to the shaping of the level of economic activity. The failure of the Keynesian policies (acceleration of inflation, rise of unemployment), though, during the 1960s and the 1970s constituted the signal for the development of the assumption of rational expectations.

The idea of rational expectations was firstly proposed by John Muth in early 1960s. He used the term rational expectations, in order to describe the various economic conditions, whose outcome partly depends on what individuals expect to happen. The assumption of the rational expectations entails that the subjective probability distribution of outcomes, i.e. as far as the same amount of information is concerned, the individuals' or businesses' expectations tend to be consistent with the objective distribution of probabilities of the results, i.e. consistent with the forecasts of the theory (Muth 1961).

The implementation of the assumption of rational expectations to macroeconomics was conducted by Robert Lucas. In this manner, the notion of uncertainty and stochastic risk, which was developed by Keynes (1921) and Knight (1921), was converted to a notion of risk which could be quantified within the context of neoclassical economics. The alternative assumptions regarding the shaping of expectations (e.g. adaptive expectations) take the existence of some particular pattern of systematic expectational error for granted. On the contrary, the theory of rational expectations claims that the results are not systematically different than those expected by the individuals, given that it is based on the assumption that individuals behave in such a manner so as to maximize their benefit or their profits. Individuals compose all the information available to them at that particular point in time in an effective manner and, consequently, achieve optimum forecasts.

The theory in question becomes particularly important when it comes to the analysis and the planning of macroeconomic stabilizing policies, given that such policies are by nature forward-looking. The assessment of the policies on the basis of the Keynesian econometric models relies on the presumption that the assessment of the parameters of the equations of the model, which have been assessed by past data, do not change when the macroeconomic policy changes. Therefore, while such models may provide satisfactory forecasts regarding future conditions of the economy, conditional on a given government policy rule, their results, nonetheless, will be false when the repercussions of a change in the governmental economic policy are analyzed, by ultimately disorientating policymakers with regard to the effectiveness and the desirability of their policy rules.

On the contrary, in accordance with the axiom distinguishing rational expectations, the way expectations are formed, i.e. the relationship between expectations and past information, is changed when the behavior of the forecasted variables is altered. Hence, when the macroeconomic policy changes, the relationship between expectations and past information will also change and, given that expectations affect the behavior of individuals, the relationships in the econometric model cannot remain the same. It should be noted that the assumption of the rational expectations does not entail that all agents have the same expectations. Expectations among individuals may differ. However, according to Muth (1961), such differences will be unconsidered at an aggregate level, unless they are significantly correlated with other cross-sectional differences among agents. Therefore, individuals on average form similar expectations, which will come true.

Despite all these, the assumption of rational expectations could apply only to ergodic processes (Syll 2012), i.e. to a system with a stable structure. Such stable structure allows for the development of a theory and its application in time. However, the economies of the world we live in are in reality non-ergodic, since they constantly change in many respects. The result of such dynamically changing world is that the future is to a great extent unknown and uncertain. The changes concern not only natural changes, but also changes in the social structure and the behavior of individuals. A powerful kind of uncertainty is linked to the possibility of the emergence of unpredictable structural changes in an economy (Lawson 1985; Davidson 1991), which may be of a political or a cultural nature. This kind of changes has, inter alia, a significant impact on the preferences of individuals, on employment relationships, on the bargaining power of employees and on governmental decisions (Dequech 2000).

The existence of uncertainty entails that the future cannot be anticipated in a fully reliable probabilistic estimate, since there is no sufficient information in order to be creditworthy in attributing the probabilities of the realization of the various results. In reality, a big part of the information is not available at the time the decisions are taken. This is also the critical point, on which the criticism to the theory of rational expectations is based (Bausor 1983; Carvalho 1988). Rational expectations make very strict presumptions with regard to information, which presumptions, though, have not been corroborated at an empirical level. The models that are based on rational expectations impute beliefs to individuals, which do not rely on any real information considerations, but are defined in order to make the models mathematically and statistically tractable.

Despite all these, the uncertainty individuals come across is not synonymous with full ignorance, but its extent varies and depends on the existence and the range of institutions (Dequech 2000). In case uncertainty entailed full ignorance, then policymakers would not have a basis to rely on, in order to shape expectations with regard to the reaction of individuals to their policies each time and, consequently, it could be difficult to label some policies as more preferable than others. The existence of social practices (i.e. laws, conventions, customs) tends to ensure some sort of stability on a diachronic basis. For example, legal institutions are related to the existence of another institution, i.e. the state, which has the ability to enforce contracts. Through their influence on prices and the level of economic activity in general, other public institutions, such as the central bank, provide a more concrete basis for people's expectations, by contributing to the mitigation of uncertainty. Furthermore, one can refer to the stabilizing role of institutions in the sense of socially shared and prescribed standards of thought and behavior.

Institutions serve an important cognitive function. Through such cognitive function, institutions provide information to individuals on the one hand, whereas on the other hand they influence the way in which individuals organize and translate such information and, ultimately, the way in which they make their choices. Conclusively, if individuals believe in the enduring nature of these institutions, they may consider that they possess a certain amount of knowledge, with regard to the possible future results.

Contrary to the theory of rational expectations, which presupposes that all agents are fully aware of all the relevant probability distribution functions, the Keynesian theory claims that expectations are the outcome of the confidence and the weighting individuals are attributing to the various results and their alternatives. Therefore, to Keynes expectations are an issue of weighting probabilities by "degrees of belief". In that case, beliefs have little to do with the kind of stochastic probabilistic calculations made by the rational expectations agents modeled by Lucas. Furthermore, according to Keynes it is possible for individuals to have different expectations and information. The central role in the shaping of the preferences and the beliefs, as it has already been noted, is played by culture, whose changes influence human behavior through preferences and beliefs.

References

Bausor R (1983) The rational expectations hypothesis and the epistemics of time. Camb J Econ 7 (1):1–10

Bernoulli D. (1738) Exposition of a new theory on the measurement of risk. Econometrica 22(1): 22–36

Beugelsdijk S, Maseland R (2011) Culture in economics: History, methodological reflections, and contemporary applications. Cambridge University Press, Cambridge

Carvalho F (1988) Keynes on probability, uncertainty and decision making. J Post Keynesian Econ 11(1):66–81

Clark G (1988) Economists in search of culture: the unspeakable in pursuit of the inedible? Hist Meth 21:161–164

Daly GG (1998) Entrepreneurship and business culture in Japan and the U.S. Jpn World Econ 10:487–494

Davidson P (1991) Is probability theory relevant for uncertainty? A Post-Keynesian perspective. J Econ Perspect 5(1):129–143

Dequech D (2000) Fundamental uncertainty and ambiguity. E Econ J 26(1):41–60

De Jong E (2009) Culture and economics: On values, economics and international business. Routledge

Dore R (1967) Aspects of social change in modern Japan. Princeton University Press, Princeton, NJ

Dore R (1990) Reflections on culture and social change. In: Gereffi G, Wyman DL (eds) Manufacturing Miracles. Princeton University Press, Princeton, NJ, pp 353–367

Edgeworth FY (1881) Mathematical psychics: an essay on the application of mathematics to the moral sciences. C.K. Paul, London

Fernandez-Huerga E (2008) The economic behavior of human beings: The institutionalist/post-keynesian model. J Econ Issues 42(3)

Fernandez R, Fogli A (2007) Culture: an empirical investigation of beliefs work and fertility. Unpublished Manuscript

Harrison LE (1992) Who prospers? How cultural values shape economic and political success. HarperCollins Basic Books, New York, NY
Hill M (2000) Asian values' as reverse orientalism: Singapore. Asian Pacific Viewpoint 41:177–190
Hodgson GM (1988) Economics and institutions. A manifesto for a modern institutional economics. Polity Press, Cambridge
Hodgson GM (2006) Institutions, recessions, and recovery in transitional economies. J Econ Issues 40(4):875–894
Hofstede G (2001) Culture's consequences: comparing values, behaviors, institutions and organizations across nations. Sage Publications, Beverly Hills, CA
Hofstede G, Bond H (1991) Cultural roots of economic performance: a research note. Strat Manage J 12:165–173
Hofstede G, Hofstede GJ (2005) Cultures and organizations: software of the mind. McGraw-Hill, New York, NY
Inglehart R (1997) Modernization and postmodernization: Cultural, economic and political change in 43 Societies. Princeton University Press, Princeton, NJ
Kahn H (1979) World economic development: 1979 and beyond. Westview Press, Boulder, CO
Kahneman D, Tversky A (1979) Prospect theory, an analysis of decision under risk. Econometrica 47:263–291
Kaufman BE (1989) Models of man in industrial relations research. Ind Labor Relat Rev 43(1):72–88
Keynes JM (1921) A treatise on probability. Macmillan, London
Keynes JM (1937) The general theory of employment. Quart J Econ 51:209–223
Knight F (1921) Risk, uncertainty and profit. Houghton Mifflin, Boston, MA
Lawson T (1985) Uncertainty and economic analysis. Economic Journa95(4): 909–27
Lee R, Ackerman S (1997) Sacred tensions: modernity and religious transformation in Malaysia. University of South Caroline Press, Columbia, SC
Levy M Jr (1962) Some aspects of 'individualism' and the problem of modernization in China and Japan. Econ Develop Cult Change 10(3):225–240
Lincoln J, Olson J, Hanada M (1978) Cultural effects on organizational structure: the case of Japanese firms in the United States. Am Sociol Rev 43(6):829–847
Marx K (1867) Het Kapitaal. Vol. 1. English edition: Lipschitz I (1978) Haarlem: De Haan
Menger C (1871) Principles of economics. New York University Press, New York, NY
Muth JA (1961) Rational expectations and the theory of price movements. Econometrica 29 (6):315–335
Neumann J, Morgenstern O (1947) Theory of games and economic behavior. Princeton University Press, Princeton, NJ
Noland M (2005) Religion and economic performance. World Dev 33(8):1215–1232
North DC (1990) Institutions, institutional change and economic performance. Cambridge University Press, Cambridge
Pryor FL (2005) National values and economic growth. Am J Econ Sociol 64(2):451–483
Samuelson PA (1947) Foundations of economic analysis. Harvard University Press
Schmoller G (1901) Grundriss der allgemeinen Volkswirtschaftslehre. Duncker & Humblot
Smith A (1759) The theory of Moral Sentiments. Raphael DD, Macfie MA (1981) eds. Liberty Fund, Indianapolis
Smith A (1776) An Inquiry into the Nature and Causes of the Wealth of Nations, Vol I and II. Campbell RH, Skinner AS (1981) eds. Liberty Fund, Indianapolis
Swank D (1996) Culture, institutions, and economic growth: theory, recent evidence, and the role of communitarian polities. Am J Polit Sci 40(3):660–679
Schein EH (1985) Organizational culture and leadership: a dynamic view. Jossey-Bass Publishers, San Francisco, CA
Syll PL (2012) Rational expectations: A fallacious foundation for macroeconomics in a non-ergodic world. Real-World Econ Rev 62

Tabellini G (2008) Institutions and culture. J Eur Econ Assoc 6(23):255–294
Veblen T (1899) The theory of the leisure class: An economic study of institutions. Macmillan Company, New York, NY
Walras L (1954) Elements of Pure Economics. Routledge, London
Weber M (1958) [1905] The Protestant ethic and the spirit of capitalism. Free Press, New York
Wildavsky A (1987) Choosing preferences by constructing institutions: a cultural theory of preference formation. Am Polit Sci Rev 81(1):4–21
Williamson OE (1975) Markets and hierarchies: analysis and antitrust implications. Free Press, New York, NY
Williamson OE (2000) The new institutional economics: taking stock, looking ahead. J Econ Liter 38:595–613

5 Cultural Background and Economic System

The relationship between cultural background and economic system is presented in detail in this chapter. The chapter is structured as follows. Section 5.1 provides macro reflections of cultural background in order to identify the relationships governing economic system and the cultural traits of societies. Section 5.2 presents political institutions as a first-round effect and in Sect. 5.3 we introduce a second-round effect, economic institutions, which can be divided into structures and incentives. Structures as the first dimension of economic institutions are presented in Sect. 5.4.

5.1 Cultural Background and Economic System

Cultural background and the values within are linked to, and interact with, economic systems in a complex manner. The term economic system refers to a network of human institutions (North 1990) and incentives shaping two key variables: growth rate and the distribution of income and wealth. These in turn influence economic result within a society (Fig. 5.1).

Various aspects of cultural background can be seen in both economic and political institutions. First, cultural background influences the quality and operation of political institutions (first-round effects). To follow, political institutions then shape economic institutions (second-round effects), which in turn create structures and action incentives for individuals. Dominant economic institutions ultimately shape the distribution of wealth and the extent of economic growth (third-round effects). Aside from indirect interaction relationships, there are also direct relationships among cultural background, economic institutions and the way in which society decides how it should distribute its wealth and direct its productive forces.

Three consecutive levels of interaction can be observed in the Fig. 5.1. Hence, cultural background first influences political institutions, which shape economic institutions through an on-going process of inter-influence.

P.E. Petrakis, *Culture, Growth and Economic Policy*,
DOI 10.1007/978-3-642-41440-4_5, © Springer-Verlag Berlin Heidelberg 2014

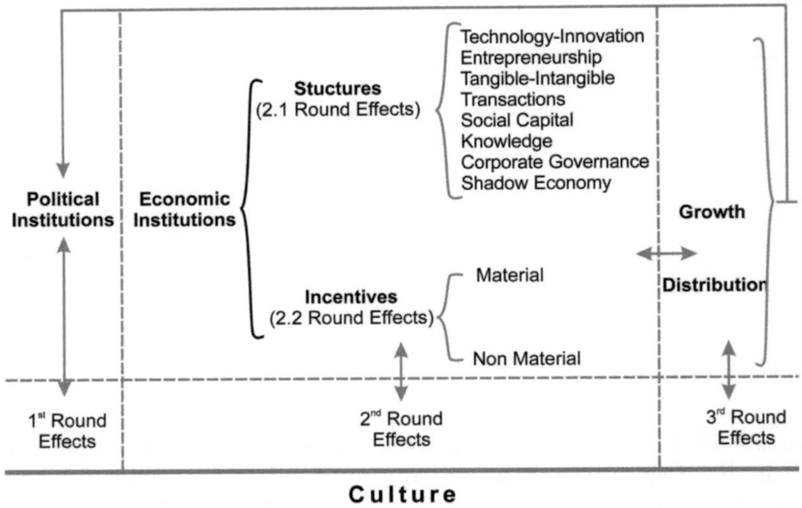

Fig. 5.1 Cultural background and economic system

The first and crucial level of interactions can be identified between cultural background and political institutions. When different portfolios of cultural values and practices are prevalent in a society, the result is the formation of different political institutions. For example, societies with a strong emphasis on the concepts espoused by collectivism are naturally expected to shape participation institutions to the various levels of organization within that society. If, on the other hand, the concepts of economic output are dominant in social cultural organization, then society itself, and particularly during a period of crisis, will more easily accept authoritarian governance solutions.

Political institutions are the most important factor affecting the form of economic institutions. Economic institutions comprise structures and human incentives, which are either material or non-material in nature. The most important factors for the establishment of structures in society can be summarized as follows: Level of technology and opportunities for innovation in the way that entrepreneurship is cultivated, developed and expressed; Tangible and intangible investments in society; Characteristics of the method of transactions facilitating the operation network of the economic system; Social capital of society; Level and content of knowledge; The manner in which companies are governed (corporate governance); and The relationship between the economy's official and shadow sectors.

Therefore, cultural background influences political institutions, which in turn shape structures and incentives. Nevertheless, as we will observe in the following chapter, aside from this indirect process, the secondary elements of economic institutions are also directly influenced by cultural background. Thus, economic institutions ultimately shape conditions for growth and the distribution of income and wealth. These variables also directly depend on cultural values, as is the case for the other elements of economic institutions. In other words, the extent to which the goals to be achieved (which are set by a society) are linked to the per capita product, income or happiness enjoyed by its members, depends on its culture. At the same time, the distribution of income and wealth may be the result of the operation of economic institutions, but is nonetheless directly linked to a society's values and, more particularly, whether a greater or lesser degree of redistribution is a desirable goal. Finally, it should also be noted that growth rate and wealth and income distribution influence political institutions.

5.2 Political Institutions

First-round effects include political institutions, which are shaped by the existing cultural background. Cultural background is deeply rooted in the subconscious of individuals and is responsible for shaping human behavior to deal with various aspects of daily life. Its shaping is essentially based on the historical and cultural heritage of each nation. It is assumed that cultural background is forged via a neutral process that involves no intervention.

Nevertheless, certain writers consider that the formation of cultural background is not a neutral process but rather the result, in part, of political processes. Inglehart (1997) claimed that "it is stupid to believe that culture is neutral: every society legalizes the establishment of a social class—partly because the ruling class attempts to shape the values that will help it exist eternally". Alesina and Glaeser (2004) stated that for one to identify the forces that have shaped society as it is today, one should also include a historical review in the analysis, and attention should be paid to the interests served by the dominant cultural background. At the same time, they make reference to the Western world and, more particularly, to the way in which the political leaderships in question have managed to manipulate the public to obtain support for their ideas and stances.

The foremost question then is, why do societies not opt for the most efficient political institutions and the most effective policies? Three key answers have been suggested (Acemoglu 2009):

(a) There is an intense social conflict, creating losers and winners;
(b) There is a problem of engaged obligations; and
(c) Those with political authority consciously form institutions and make political decisions that do not represent an optimal resource distribution, favoring or displeasing certain groups of individuals.

Institutional weakness is considered to result from strangleholds by the elite and conflict brought about by pressure groups. The elite include large industrial and financial organizations, and pressure groups include trade unions, industrial confederations and professional unions. Both groups affect society's performance and its capacity for adjustment. In this way, the strong influence of pressure groups contributes to reducing the ability of both society and the economy to adjust to external stimuli. The impact of pressure groups on the adjustment capacity mainly derives from their influence on the economy's operational systems, principally affecting the cost of transactions.

Recent studies focusing on the role of politics in cultural background and economic growth are particularly interesting. The term politicized culture refers to an aspect of cultural background deliberately created by political leaders to manipulate groups of people. There are many examples of leaders who, in their attempt to drive their country to economic growth, have followed developmental programs by relying on values of other countries or religions. In early 1980, when Malaysia was facing a significant recession, it adopted a campaign that presented Japan and Korea as models of economic growth. Values such as hard work, austerity and patience were considered driving forces for growth, and Malaysians were encouraged to embrace them. However, in the 1980s and 1990s, when pronounced economic growth had been achieved, the country's government attempted to usurp the aforementioned values and convince people that they were inherent in Islam and were therefore part of their cultural heritage. The government's goal was to promote Islam by stressing that values such as industriousness, austerity and the search for knowledge were distinctive Islamic features. Thus, we have historical examples of how cultural background can be used to promote political goals.

Another example of the use of cultural background by politicians is that of the "African renaissance", a term created by South African president Thabo Mbeki in his attempts to rebuild his nation and boost the pride of the people. Together with his supporters, he attempted to re-establish the state and the economy, and to implement a democratic regime. Ultimately, the adoption of the values and beliefs of the Western world had little impact on the whole undertaking.

A cultural background that is dominated by collectivism and ignores individualism will develop processes that enable high levels of state intervention. However, a cultural background that is dominated by traits that promote individualism develops a very different environment, where the two political institutions co-exist in a framework that is similar to that of Northern Europe. A cultural background that is dominated by uncertainty will establish a large number of complex laws and norms, as is the case in southern European countries. In contrast, a cultural background that is dominated by trust and certainty, e.g., as with Great Britain, can organize a society's functioning using simple customary processes. It should be noted, however, that the volume and complexity of the legal framework do not necessarily ensure effectiveness.

Hence, by summarizing the views stated above, cultural background does influence the design of political institutions and resulting policy; however, at the same time, the political field also influences the shaping of cultural background.

5.3 Economic Institutions

Via second-round effects, economic institutions are shaped by political institutions and cultural background. Capital, labor, technology (Solow 1957; Romer 1986) and institutions (North 1990) are the main factors that generate development and growth in an economy. However, emphasis is often placed on capital, labor and technology while ignoring the importance of institutions. Such an omission should only occur when the institutional framework, including incentives, play a minor role or remain stable over time, both of which are unlikely.

Institutions in society and economy are human constructions that function as rules and restrictions for human, economic and social behavior (Berger and Luckmann 1966; Schotter 1981; North 1990; Greif 2006; Chang 2007). They are influenced by a society's cultural background.

Institutions organize the incentive framework for human transactions, regardless of whether such transactions occur at a political, social or economic level. In fact, institutional frameworks reduce the uncertainty that is inherent in everyday life, offering an operational structure (however, this structure is not necessarily effective). In addition, because of the fact that institutions remain stable for long periods, they are responsible for the historical evolution of societies and economies. The protection of property rights appears fundamental to economic growth (North 1981; Rodrik et al. 2004; Acemoglu et al. 2005). Consequently, the ambiguous nature and thus the ownership of property rights is a central feature of the quality of economic institutions. Fundamentally, there is confusion in many sectors of economic activity as to who is entitled to the property rights of certain assets.

The relationship between institutions and economic growth stems from four sources as follows:

(a) Institutions are a dominant source in defining individuals' incentives in an economy or society in terms of economic development and growth (Hessels et al. 2006; Parker 2007; van Stel et al. 2007), and influence the degree in which these individuals innovate and invest (Wennekers and Thurik 1999; Bowen and De Clercq 2008; Sobel 2008);
(b) Their contribution to coordination and governance;
(c) Their influence on the process of knowledge development and innovation; and
(d) Their effect on income distribution and the development of social coherence (Easterly et al. 2006).

The importance of institutional changes is even more critical today (Carlin and Soskice 2009; Hall and Thelen 2009; Koreh and Shalev 2009; Block 2011; Portes and Smith 2011) because it is acknowledged that in most of the developed world, the process of accumulating basic growth factors has been significantly disrupted. Consequently, institutions remain a promising source for growth revitalization.

5.4 Macro Reflections of Cultural Background: Structures

The most important structures concern technology and innovation, tangibles and intangibles, shadow economy, social capital, knowledge, corporate governance, entrepreneurship and transactions.

5.4.1 Transactions and Entrepreneurship

The existence of cultural differences in societies with respect to perceptions of transaction costs provides an important extension of the transaction cost theory. Economic institutions, in the form of property rights and contractualization, are influenced by the characteristics of trade, cultural stereotypes (Boyer and Petersen 2012) and elements of human behavior. Furthermore, institutions shape the action of every agent (Hédoin 2012). Cultural background is a determinant of consumer behavior (Cleveland and Laroche 2007), and the study of this relationship is particularly important when choosing a strategy for the international expansion of activities and transactions. Different cultural values lead to different types of social structures in economic relationships (Greif 1994). Shane (1992, 1993) sought to connect the effects of cultural differences in the perceptions of transaction costs observed between societies, and the differences in societies' preferences for licensing and international joint ventures. In their attempt to include cultural characteristics in the transaction cost theory, Chen et al. (2002b) concluded that cultures characterized by privacy display more opportunistic behavior in transactions within the same group (whether including individuals or organizations) compared with those characterized by collectivism. Collectivists display greater opportunistic behavior in transactions with other groups.

Hofstede et al. (2008a) focused on the influence of a society's cultural traits on the choices made in transactions. The transactions model in that study was based on the transaction cost theory and included procedures for searching, bargaining, contracting, monitoring and enforcing contracts. Hofstede et al. (2008b) focused on the cultural variable "uncertainty avoidance", as interpreted by Hofstede (1980), and concluded that individuals in societies with low scores for this variable interact more easily with strangers. Furthermore, in societies with dominant elements of either individualism or collectivism, the value of transactions is relatively high. However, in societies where privacy and collectivism co-exist, the value of transactions is lower, as collectivists end up transacting with members of groups to which they belong.

In response to the criticism leveled against transaction cost economics regarding an individual's natural propensity for opportunism, Chen et al. (2002a) attempted to identify those factors that shape opportunistic behaviors. The authors regarded the role of culture as an important factor influencing human behavior. Based on data from sociology and psychology, they suggested that an individual's acts of opportunism are affected by the degree of privacy/collectivism and their moral barriers. However, this opportunistic propensity does not mean that a person with such a propensity will routinely behave opportunistically in all transactions (Ghoshal and Moran 1996).

The basic values of the society, together with its cultural background, can contribute to the emergence of entrepreneurial activity. A clear example is the economy of the United States, where entrepreneurship is particularly developed. The dominant values of this economy are freedom, independence, individualism and the achievement of goals (Morris et al. 1994; Spence 1985). Nevertheless, entrepreneurship is different among countries and for different periods of time because societies have embraced it to various degrees. Therefore, some countries have high entrepreneurial activity (such as the United States), whereas others are in disadvantaged positions (Reynolds et al. 2002; Freytag and Thurik 2007).

The definitions attributed to entrepreneurship also vary. In addition to the establishment of new businesses, entrepreneurship is linked to those actions required to start up something new and to innovative. It is the process that leads to new entrepreneurial forms and it can also integrate innovation and entrepreneurial conduct to existing businesses (Cromie 2000). In this manner, entrepreneurship contributes to the strategic renewal of existing businesses, as well as being associated with the provision of new products (Wennekers and Thurik 1999). By offering vision and prospect, entrepreneurs help to develop businesses (Penrose 1959; Casson 2003) by enhancing their competitiveness on a long-term basis (Leibenstein 1968).

The allegation that divergence in economic growth among countries derives from a lack of entrepreneurship is commonplace (Hoselitz 1957; Soltow 1968). Nevertheless, despite the fact that many associate entrepreneurial culture with economic growth (either directly or indirectly), no particular theory explaining the process and the way this occurs has been formed. Economists have attempted many times to integrate entrepreneurship in an economic model (Lucas 1978; Schmitz 1989; Jovanovic 1994; Braunerhjelm et al. 2010) or to provide a conceptual framework (Leibenstein 1968; Kirzner 1997). Empirical studies that examine specific cases thereby limit the research field and the generalization of results, and in certain cases entrepreneurship is considered as residual of regression. At the same time, efforts have been made to measure entrepreneurial culture.

Why is it that no clear-cut conceptual framework has been developed to examine the relationship between entrepreneurship and economic growth? One explanation is that it is rooted in the neoclassical theory, which does not leave entrepreneurship any margin to be examined as a separate variable in the model. The main reason why entrepreneurship cannot be integrated with neoclassical thinking lies with the production function, in which all of the variables are predetermined and establishes a particular relationship with the outcome (Leibenstein 1968). Entrepreneurs widen the production function by increasing the total number of variables. They should also take into account business risk to ensure that they use and combine available resources in an effective way. Such processes are necessary in economic growth (Leibenstein 1968).

In their research on the comparative study of economic growth standards between 1850 and 1914, Morris and Adelman (1988) created an index reflecting the acceptance of entrepreneurs based on public opinion. Hence, they created a classification system using six categories, ranging from A to Z to describe the degree of acceptance of entrepreneurship. Category A includes countries where entrepreneurs are socially recognized for their entrepreneurial success. In contrast, category Z includes countries where the social recognition of capital's functions is not accepted by the ruling social class. Hence, countries such as Australia, Sweden, Switzerland and the United States belong to category A, whereas countries such as Spain, China, Egypt and India belong to category Z. Countries were classified according to the judgments and behaviors of the social elite with regard to entrepreneurial success. Morris and Adelman (1988) found that entrepreneurial culture plays an important role in growth, though exactly how depends on the economic analysis model used.

Although the scientific community is interested in empirical surveys that examine the relationship between entrepreneurial culture and economic growth, there are a limited number of such surveys. Lynn (1991) conducted a survey of students from 41 countries and created a national entrepreneurial behavior index. He then compared his results with similar papers. The main conclusion reached was that societies' different approaches toward entrepreneurship may explain different growth rates.

Finally, Beugelsdijk (2007) calculated entrepreneurial culture in 54 European countries using the European Values Survey. His results showed that entrepreneurial culture influences and shapes standards by ultimately impacting on economic growth. His observation that entrepreneurial culture is indirectly linked to economic growth is worthy of comment. A society characterized by entrepreneurial culture might be led to achieve higher levels of entrepreneurship (Suddle et al. 2006) and ultimately to a process that strengthens both the economy and economic growth (Carree and Thurik 2003).

5.4.2 Technology and Innovation

The various dominant cultural backgrounds of different societies act to create differences in levels of technological development and investment capacity. A society's network of values either encourages or deters its members from undertaking innovative initiatives. The network mainly concerns a society's levels of individualism/collectivism, the extent of risk aversion, future orientation and planning, the acceptance of inequalities, the importance attached to the education system and attitudes toward science.

Aside from cultural traits, other obstacles to technological progress include certain social factors such as a group's social structure, family structure, interpersonal relationships, incentives offered to group members and the teaching process (Foster 1962). Cultures that reward creativity and encourage their members to achieve individual advancement tend to achieve better results in innovation. At the same time, the extent of innovation is directly linked to the extent that entrepreneurship is accepted in that society.

Societies that avoid risk are willing to invest in new technologies and undertake innovative activity and hence there is a negative relationship between the acceptance of uncertainty and the rate of innovation (Shane 1993, 1995; Hofstede 1980). A willingness to undertake business risk, long-term planning and the acceptance of changes are key cultural traits that encourage innovation (Rothwell and Wissema 1986).

In addition, different cultural behaviors have been observed regarding business formation (Shapero and Sokol 1982). A positive association between individualism and innovation potential has been identified, as the greater the freedom of individuals to express their views, the higher the possibility of the exploration of new ideas (Barnett 1953). Individualistic societies are more likely to encourage their members to express their opinions, and such freedom is necessary for creativity. Furthermore, a weak bond among members in individualistic societies can more easily promote the diffusion of information, as opposed to collectivist societies where members utilize such information at an in-group level and create obstacles in its effusion. Certain characteristics of an individual's psychosynthesis, such as independence, achievement and innovation encouragement, are commonly found in individualistic societies (Shane 1992).

Weak power distance and strong individualism are also related to innovation. Societies that have a high level of individualism and a low power distance score achieve higher growth rates and have a stronger likelihood of innovation (Hofstede 1984). Societies with high power distance scores are more likely to have centralized governance structures, as opposed to low power distance societies where decentralized hierarchical structures are preferred; the latter climate contributes to the undertaking of innovative action.

A diversity of cultural traits also stimulates innovation (Majidi 2010). The ability of businesses to cope with different cultural aspects to achieve better results is a crucial issue. Culture can encourage innovation and creativity. It urges the individual or the group to foster an entrepreneurial spirit. Different cultural traits help the team to adopt new points of view, in contrast to groups with similar characteristics.

Finally, the role of education in innovation has been proven to be significant. High levels of innovation are linked to high levels of education and positive attitudes toward science (Lee 1998). The significance of education lies with the fact that it encourages individuals from an early age to think in a specific manner, equipping them with the necessary tools to become productive and develop innovative ideas in the future.

5.4.3 Tangibles and Intangibles

Tangibles and intangibles are the inputs of the production process. Tangible things are those that are easy to quantify, whereas intangible ones (values, vision, inspiration, recognition, motivation) are elements that are difficult to quantify but whose contribution to organizational success is nonetheless very important. The output of tangibles is products and profits, whereas culture is the output of intangible assets.

The inclusion of intangibles as a sector with cultural reflections may come as a surprise. It represents, however, one of the most important sectors where culture shapes structures. Furthermore, it would be very difficult to change such structures.

Typical examples of the influence of cultural background on the development of traditional investments are town planning, transportation and the environment. A society that strongly favors the present rather than the future would find it difficult to implement town planning and environmental planning schemes with the aim to serving the interests of future generations. In such a situation, towns and infrastructure are not planned, and if they are, then they have a tight time frame for development due to a key reliance on short-term profit maximization. However, town planning is by nature a serious obligation for the actual structures of the economy, and dramatically influences the way in which it can grow. Hence, if investments in large-scale traditional assets (e.g., ports and airports) are not properly realized and lack foresight, they can easily lose their value and be difficult to replace.

Yet another example of the influence of cultural background is that of human capital—it influences its characteristics and accumulation. A crucial issue regarding the qualitative formation of human capital and its effectiveness as a growth factor is preschool education (Mincer 1974; Psacharopoulos 1994; Dickens et al. 2006). However, when elements for the development of close interpersonal relationships to "provide" preschool care are included in cultural background (Magnuson et al. 2004), then not only is society not oriented toward providing resources to develop preschool care but similar services are also not requested by the society.

The specialization offered by higher education is another area that influences the quality of human capital. It is obvious that growth-"friendly" higher education organizations require courses in, for example, IT, sciences and applied mathematics. However, a socioeconomic formation with high uncertainty, an orientation toward the present and an emphasis on collectivism produce specializations linked to the management and utilization of small-scale property (e.g., lawyers and engineers). Higher education structures in general are not easily changed. This element is even stronger in cases where cultural background includes a lack of flexibility and adaptability. Hence, situations where there is discordance between productive needs and the offer of specialization are eternalized.

5.4.4 Shadow Economy

Participation in shadow economy activities is largely influenced by the following factors:

(a) Surcharges from taxes and social security contributions: The relationship between the size of the shadow economy and the amount of social surcharges derived from taxes and social security contributions is positive (Thomas 1992; Lippert and Walker 1997; Schneider 1994, 1997, 1998, 2000). Cultural background influences the relationship between surcharges and a shadow economy. When individualism is dominant, then a society has the tendency to increase its shadow economy by not enforcing the "disclosure" of transactions.

(b) Inflexible regulatory framework: An (qualitative) increase in the legislative regulations of the market, as well as accompanying bureaucracy, acts to increase the size of a shadow economy. Such regulations can include labor market regulations, obstacles to commercial transactions, employment restrictions to foreigners, and regulations concerning the licensing of new businesses (Johnson et al. 1998). If society is oriented toward the achievement of maximum results, then the preservation of the social status-quos does not constitute an end in itself. Hence, it is more efficient for society to seek the best regulatory solutions.

(c) The likelihood of getting caught and the gravity of the penalty: The likelihood of a tax evader (legal or natural) being caught as well as the penalty imposed constitute critical determinative factors in the size of a shadow economy. The relationship between these two factors is interrelated because the effectiveness of one relies on the existence of the other. When society is dominated by masculinity vs. feminism, i.e., a situation where the role of personal prevalence and sovereignty is enlarged in comparison to the respect shown toward procedures, this factor does not play the anticipated role with regard to the reduction of the shadow economy.

(d) Level of unemployment: Unemployment, and particularly long-term unemployment, plays an important role in the size of shadow economy. The inability of individuals to find jobs in the formal economy leads them to the shadow economy, where they are usually employed under poor employment terms (e.g., non-payment of social security contributions).

The ambiguous nature of property rights favors informal economic activities and encourages the growth of the shadow economy because most transactions related to similar rights begin in the official economy and end up in the shadow economy.

Other possible reasons for the expansion of an informal economy are as follows:

(a) High transaction costs;
(b) The basic features of cultural background with an emphasis on the prevalence of high uncertainty, faith in in-group collectivism and lack of future orientation; and
(c) High tax and insurance rates that inevitably become higher and higher as the informal economy and tax evasion grow.

The issue of connecting property rights with the shadow economy is a renowned and theoretically founded view (Torgler and Schneider 2009). The most common example is, of course, the frequent (and almost always increasing) change in tax and insurance coefficients that result in the expansion of the parallel economy. The above is also valid for the additional reason that ambiguity is usually based on the existence of "semi-illegal" procedures and markets that could in no way be part of a formal economy. Under these circumstances, a large part of intellectual creation (which is the cornerstone of productive innovation) is traded in the shadow economy rather than in the official one. In addition, according to the evidence, this allows for the exclusive preservation and management (by the holder) of the property rights deriving thereof. When transactions relate to non-specified property rights, the operation of both formal and parallel economies is affected.

However, precisely because of the cloudy nature of intellectual rights, peculiar transactions with very low repeatability are developed. In addition, repeatability also leads to a better description of property rights that shed light on their exact nature. Therefore, those that perform transactions are aiming to minimize precision repeatability and this is usually assisted by the single-sided structure of transactions in a non-rational way (e.g., multiple overlapping laws), ensuring the preservation of obscure property rights. The above conditions obviously increase uncertainty in transactions, add uncertainty and risk premiums and, obviously, favor corruption. It is very difficult under these circumstances to discuss the consolidation of innovation and the promotion of intellectual property production.

5.4.5 Social Capital

The smooth and effective operation of modern economies and democracy rely to a great extent on social capital. Social capital is an instantiated informal norm that promotes cooperation between two or more individuals (Fukuyama 1999). Social capital reflects the cultural elements of modern economies (Fukuyama 1999) in conjunction with a network of economic and political institutions, feelings of fairness and rationality within a society.

The concept of social capital was originally used as an individual-specific variable to express an individual's ability to do well in social situations (James 1904; Loury 1977). As the concept developed it began to reflect group-level attributes, such as the existence of social networks among groups of people (Coleman 1990; Putnam 1993).

Numerous studies underline the importance of social capital in shaping economic and political institutions. Both Arrow (1972) and Fukuyama (1995) considered that the level of trust in a society, which is a basic component of social capital, can predict economic result. Using Italian cross-regional data, Putnam (1993) showed that increased participation in civics is positively associated with the effective operation of institutions.

The contribution of social capital can be understood both at an economic and political level, given that it constitutes a key element that shapes the effective operation of the free market and the smooth operation of democratic regimes.

From an economic perspective, social capital tends to decrease the transaction costs linked to the official mechanisms of economic transactions, such as contracts, hierarchies and norms. Individuals in societies with high levels of trust spend less to protect themselves from a possible breach in their economic transactions. The accumulation of social capital ensures trust between the contracting parties, resulting in the minimization of resources required to monitor, negotiate and enforce agreements. As the nature of economic activity becomes more complex, the trust relationships that are developed between the contracting parties become very important.

In addition, social capital can also indirectly influence economic activity because trust and civic norms can improve economic result through political channels (Knack and Keefer 1997). A large stock of social capital is a prerequisite for a civil society, which is a necessary convention in a modern democracy (Gellner 1994). A civil society tends to restrain the state's power and to protect citizens from it. A lack of social capital leads to political dysfunction because decreased trust in political institutions and the absence of citizens from civics restrains the effectiveness of democracy. However, it also facilitates the spread of corruption as a way of protecting the social networks of individuals.

5.4.6 Knowledge

There are two approaches to the influence of cultural differences on business operation and, consequently, economic result. According to the traditional approach, culture operates as an obstacle among groups of people with different cultural traits, in which case such differences will have to be eliminated. The second approach, however, understands culture as a source of knowledge and interaction among individuals. The outcome of this process can influence business operation. In this way, culture can be considered a knowledge management resource (Holden 2010) and constitutes a basic instrument for managers rather than an obstacle.

Knowledge is also viewed as an asset for businesses and a comparative advantage against their competitors. Performance differences among businesses are caused largely by different knowledge bases (DeCarolis and Deeds 1999). Knowledge can be considered as the basic component of strategic planning for businesses (Grant 1996; Hill and Deeds 1996; Kogut and Zander 1992), although its transfer and reproduction is not easy (Grant 2002).

At a corporate level, knowledge can take two basic forms: explicit knowledge and tacit knowledge (Polanyi 1966). Explicit knowledge within an organization can be codified and diffused to all members through channels, tools and official procedures. In contrast, tacit knowledge is the sum of the knowledge acquired by members through experience and can be diffused via various activities (Nonaka and Takeuchi 1995). Tacit knowledge is directly connected with knowledge. Not only does it determine behavior and communication among people, but its cross-cultural acceptance also favors the exchange of views and the creation of new knowledge.

Organizational culture is a key factor in the process of knowledge diffusion at the firm level (Davenport et al. 1998; DeLong and Fahey 2000) because it can encourage or hinder effective knowledge management. Culture can be defined as a set of implicit assumptions possessed by a group, which then determines the way the group behaves and reacts to its environment (Schein 1985). A set of values and beliefs coexist by determining the organization's aims and how they should be achieved (DeLong and Fahey 2000). Organizational changes encouraging knowledge management for strategic changes to be applied (e.g., the introduction of new technologies) are influenced by the existence of cultural values, which can either contribute or hinder such change.

Cultures that emphasize values related to encouragement, affiliation and achievement tend to achieve better knowledge management (Baltahazard and Cooke 2003), and also positively influence the creation of structures for the diffusion of knowledge (Gold et al. 2001).

Existing cultural values, beliefs and stereotypes affect the shaping of social context (norms and practices), which in turn provide the means for their integration with knowledge management behaviors. As such, the dominant organizational culture can influence knowledge management and create appropriate incentives for group members with regard to the production and diffusion of knowledge. Furthermore, knowledge management can become a part of organizational culture because it mirrors the values of organization.

5.4.7 Corporate Governance

Corporate governance concerns the entire legislative framework, culture and the institutional regulations that determine the actions of businesses, who controls them, how such control is exercised and how the risks and performances are managed (Blair 1995). The most important aspects of corporate governance are as follows:

(a) Decision systems and the distinction between managers and ownership (Fama and Jensen 1983a, b);
(b) Performance, management and employees control systems (Jensen and Meckling 1976);
(c) Reward systems (Hart and Holmstrom 1987);
(d) Insolvency systems (Smith and Warner 1979);
(e) Ownership organization and structuring systems (Stulz 1988);
(f) Systems regarding creditors, capital structure and control mechanisms (Jensen and Ruback 1983); and
(g) Market competition systems.

Each of these factors is influenced differently by cultural background, and the influence may be stronger for particular sectors (e.g., rewarding, salaries and compensation systems or insolvency systems). The analysis of corporate governance systems sheds light on the paths through which cultural background influences corporate governance.

In the field of financial economics, corporate governance deals mainly with the principle-agent problem. Principle-agent problem faced by businesses whereby the distinction between ownership and administration is strong and is one commonly observed in modern businesses where ownership is not always with the decision-makers. Many times such officers act for the benefit of their own personal interest and not to maximize the wealth of the shareholders. Hence, there is no matching of interests between the principal and agent. In cases where there is no appropriate legislative framework for the protection of investors, administrators can usurp the company's profits. This fact restrains potential investors from funding in such companies (LaPorta et al. 2000).

The basic concern of corporate governance is the protection of investors and the establishment of an appropriate legislative framework to prevent administrators from engaging in exploitative behavior. Consequently, the legislative framework is important in the relationship between investors and administrators. Legal shelters constitute an important step toward the development of economic and, more specifically, financial systems (LaPorta et al. 2000, 2008). The establishment and the proper implementation of a legislative framework that sets rules of behavior for participants have significant consequences for an economy.

At this point, cultural background enters the analysis, and we argue that it shapes the legislative system. Legislative tradition recognizes the relationship between the legal system and culture (Merryman 1985). Nevertheless, legislative and regulatory frameworks are not the only entry points for cultural background in terms of corporate governance. The traditional organization of the most important expressions of corporate governance is of equal importance.

References

Acemoglu D (2009) Introduction to modern economic growth. Princeton University Press, Princeton, NJ

Acemoglu D, Johnson S, Robinson JA (2005) The rise of Europe: Atlantic trade, institutional change, and economic growth. Am Econ Rev 95(3):546–579

Alesina A, Glaeser E (2004) Fighting poverty in the US and Europe: a world of difference. Oxford University Press, Oxford

Arrow K (1972) Gifts and exchanges. Philos Public Aff 1:343–362

Baltahazard PA, Cooke RA (2003) Organizational culture and knowledge management success: assessing the behavior-performance continuum (Working Paper). Arizona State University West

Barnett HG (1953) Innovation: the basis of cultural change. McGraw Hill, New York, NY

Berger PL, Luckmann T (1966) The social construction of reality: a treatise in the sociology of knowledge. Anchor Books, Garden City, NY

Beugelsdijk S (2007) Entrepreneurial culture, regional innovativeness and economic growth. J Evol Econ 17(2):187–210

Blair M (1995) Ownership and control: re-thinking corporate governance for the 21st century. Brookings Institution Press, Washington, DC

Block F (2011) Crisis and renewal: the outlines of a twenty-first century new deal. Socioecon Rev 9(1):31–57

Bowen HP, De Clercq D (2008) Institutional context and the allocation of entrepreneurial effort. J Int Bus Stud 39:747–767

Boyer P, Petersen M (2012) The naturalness of (many) social institutions: evolved cognition as their foundation. J Inst Econ 8(1):1–25

Braunerhjelm P, Acs ZJ, Audretsch DA, Carlsson B (2010) The missing link: knowledge diffusion and entrepreneurship in endogenous growth. Small Bus Econ 34(2):105–125

Carlin W, Soskice D (2009) German economic performance: disentangling the role of supply-side reforms, macroeconomic policy and coordinated economy institutions. Socioecon Rev 7 (1):67–99

Carree M, Thurik R (2003) The impact of entrepreneurship on economic growth. In: Acs Z, Audretsch D (eds) Handbook of entrepreneurship research. Kluwer Academic Publishers, Boston, pp 437–471
Casson M (2003) [1982] The entrepreneur, an economic theory. Edward Elgar, Aldershot
Chang H-J (ed) (2007) Institutional change and economic development. Anthem, London
Chen C, Peng MW, Saparito PA (2002a) Individualism, collectivism, and opportunism: a cultural perspective on transaction cost economics. J Manag 28(4):567–583
Chen M, Lapaugh AS, Singh JP (2002) Predicting category accesses for a user in a structured information space. Paper presented at the 25th annual international ACM SIGIR conference on research and development in information retrieval, Sigir.
Cleveland M, Laroche M (2007) Acculturation to the global consumer culture: scale development and research paradigm. J Bus Res 60(3):249–260
Coleman J (1990) Foundations of social theory. Harvard University Press, Cambridge, MA
Cromie S (2000) Assessing entrepreneurial inclinations: some approaches and empirical evidence. Eur J Work Organ Psychol 9(1):7–30
Davenport T, DeLong D, Beers M (1998) Successful knowledge management projects. Sloan Manage Rev 39:43–57
DeCarolis DM, Deeds D (1999) The impact of stocks and flows of organizational knowledge on firm performance: an empirical investigation of the biotechnology industry. Strateg Manage J 20:953–968
DeLong DW, Fahey L (2000) Diagnosing cultural barriers to knowledge management. Acad Manage Exec 14:113–127
Dickens WT, Sawhill I, Tebbs J (2006) The effects of investing in early childhood education on economic growth. Brookings Institution, Education Resources Information Center, Policy Brief 153
Easterly W, Ritzen J, Woolcock M (2006) Social cohesion, institutions, and growth. Econ Polit 18 (2):103–120
Fama EF, Jensen MC (1983a) Agency problems and residual claims. J Law Econ 26:327–349
Fama EF, Jensen MC (1983b) Separation of ownership and control. J Law Econ 26:301–325
Foster GM (1962) Traditional cultures and the impact of technological change. Harper & Row, New York, NY
Freytag A, Thurik R (2007) Entrepreneurship and its determinants in a cross country setting. J Evol Econ 17:117–131
Fukuyama F (1995) Trust. Free Press, New York, NY
Fukuyama F (1999) Social capital and civil society. Paper presented at IMF conference on second generation reforms, The Institute of Public Policy, George Mason University, 1 October 1999
Gellner E (1994) Conditions of liberty: civil society and its rivals. Hamish Hamilton, London
Ghoshal S, Moran P (1996) Bad for practice: a critique of the transaction cost theory. Acad Manage Rev 21:13–47
Gold AH, Malhotra A, Segars AH (2001) Knowledge management: an organizational capabilities perspective. J Manage Inf Syst 18(1):185–214
Grant RM (1996) Toward a knowledge based theory of the firm. Strateg Manage J 17:109–122
Grant RM (2002) Contemporary strategy analysis. Concepts, techniques and applications. Blackwell, Boston
Greif A (1994) Cultural beliefs and the organization of society: a historical and theoretical reflection on collectivist and individualist societies. J Polit Econ 102:912–950, University of Chicago Press
Greif A (2006) Institutions and the path to the modern economy: lessons from medieval trade. Cambridge University Press, Cambridge
Hall P, Thelen K (2009) Institutional change in varieties of capitalism. Socioecon Rev 7(1):7–34
Hart O, Holmstrom B (1987) The theory of contracts. In: Bewley T (ed) Advances in economic theory. Cambridge University Press, Cambridge, pp 71–155

Hédoin C (2012) Linking institutions to economic performance: the role of macro-structures in micro-explanations. J Inst Econ 8(3):327–349. doi:10.1017/S1744137412000045

Hessels SJ, van Stel AJ, Brouwer P, Wennekers ARM (2006) Social security arrangements and early-stage entrepreneurial activity: an empirical analysis (EIM Scales Paper N200518), EIM, Zoetermeer, The Netherlands

Hill CW, Deeds DL (1996) The importance of the industry structure for the determination of firm profitability: a neo-austrian perspective. J Manage Stud 33:429–451

Hofstede G (1980) Culture's consequences: international differences in work-related values. Sage, Beverly Hills, CA

Hofstede G (1984) Culture's consequences: international differences in work-related values. Sage, Beverly Hills, CA

Hofstede et al (2008a) Announcing a new version of the values survey module: the VSM 08. http://stuwww.uvt.nl/~csmeets/VSM08.html

Hofstede et al (2008b) Values survey module 2008 manual. http://www.geerthofstede.nl/media/229/manualvsm08.doc

Holden N (2010) Culture should be seen as a knowledge management resource. A vision on cultural diversity 6, ADP publication, Rochester, NY

Hoselitz B (1957) Non-economic factors in economic development. Am Econ Rev 47:28–41

Inglehart R (1997) Modernization and postmodernazation: changing values and political styles in advanced industrial society. Princeton University Press, Princeton, NJ

James H (1904) The golden bowl. Scribners, New York, NY

Jensen MC, Meckling WH (1976) Theory of the firm: managerial behavior agency costs and ownership structure. J Financ Econ 3:305–360

Jensen MC, Ruback R (1983) The market for corporate control. J Financ Econ 11:5–50

Johnson S, Kaufmann D, Zoido-Lobatón P (1998) Corruption, public finances and the unofficial economy. Discussion paper, World Bank, Washington

Jovanovic B (1994) Firm formation with heterogeneous management and labour skills. Small Bus Econ 6:185–191

Kirzner I (1997) Entrepreneurial discovery and the competitive market process: an Austrian approach. J Econ Lit 35:60–85

Knack S, Keefer P (1997) Does social capital have a economic payoff? a cross-country comparison. Q Econ J 112:1251–1288

Kogut B, Zander U (1992) Knowledge of the firm, combinative capabilities and replication of technology. Organ Sci 3:383–397

Koreh M, Shalev M (2009) Dialectics of institutional change: the transformation of social insurance financing in Israel. Socio-econ Rev 7(4):553–584. doi:10.1093/ser/mwp018

LaPorta R, Lopez-de-Silanes F, Shleifer A, Vishny R (2000) Investor protection and corporate governance. J Financ Econ 58:3–27

LaPorta R, Lopez-de-Silanes F, Shleifer A (2008) The economic consequences of legal origin. J Econ Lit 46(2):285–332

Lee C (1998) De terminants of national in novativeness and in ternational market segments. Int Market Rev 7(5):39–49

Leibenstein H (1968) Entrepreneurship and development. Am Econ Rev 58:72–83

Lippert O, Walker M (1997) The underground economy: global evidences of its size and impact. The Frazer Institute, Vancouver

Loury G (1977) A dynamic theory of racial income differences. In: Wallace P, LeMund A (eds) Women, minorities and employment discrimination. Lexington Books, Lexington, KY

Lucas RE (1978) On the size distribution of business firms. Bell J Econ 9:508–523

Lynn R (1991) The secret of the miracle economy. Different national attitudes to competitiveness and money. The Social Affairs Unit, London

Magnuson KA, Ruhm CJ, Waldfogel J (2004) Does prekindergarten improve school preparation and performance? National Bureau of Economic Research, Working Paper No. 10452

Majidi M (2010) Invest in diversity as a competitive advantage. A vision on cultural diversity 6, November 2010, ADP publication, Rochester, NY
Merryman JH (1985) The civil law tradition. Stanford University Press, Stanford, CA
Mincer J (1974) Schooling, Earnings and Experience. Columbia University Press, New York, NY
Morris CT, Adelman I (1988) Comparative patterns of economic development 1850–1914. John Hopkins University Press, Baltimore, MD
Morris MH, Davis DL, Allen JW (1994) Fostering corporate entrepreneurship: cross-cultural comparisons of the importance of individualism versus collectivism. J Int Bus Stud 25:65–89
Nonaka I, Takeuchi H (1995) The knowledge creating company: how Japanese companies create the dynamics of innovation. Oxford University Press, New York, NY
North DC (1981) Structure and change in economic history. WW Norton & Company, New York, NY
North DC (1990) Institutions, institutional change and economic performance. Cambridge University Press, Cambridge
Parker S (2007) Policy-makers beware! In: Audretsch D, Grilo I, Thurik R (eds) The handbook of entrepreneurship policy. Edward Elgar, Cheltenham, pp 54–63
Penrose E (1959) The theory of the growth of the firm. Blackwell, Oxford
Polanyi M (1966) The tacit dimension. Anchor Day Books, New York, NY
Portes A, Smith L (2011) Institutions and national development in Latin America: a comparative study. Socio-econ Rev 8(4):585–621. doi:10.1093/ser/mwq018
Psacharopoulos G (1994) Returns to education: a global update. World Dev 22:1325–1343
Putnam R (1993) Making democracy work: civic traditions in modern Italy. Princeton University Press, Princeton, NJ
Reynolds P, Bygrave W, Autio E, Hay M (2002) Global entrepreneurship monitor; executive report. Babson College, Kauffman Foundation and London Business School, Wellesley, MA
Rodrik PD, Subramanian A, Trebbi F (2004) Institutions rule: the primacy of institutions over geography and integration in economic development. J Econ Growth 9:131–165
Romer P (1986) Increasing returns and long-run growth. J Polit Econ 94(5):500–521, 1002–37
Rothwell R, Wissema H (1986) Technology, culture, and public policy. Technovation 4(2):91–115
Schein EH (1985) Organizational culture and leadership. Jossey-Bass, San Francisco, CA
Schmitz JA (1989) Imitation, entrepreneurship, and long-run growth. J Polit Econ 97:721–739
Schneider F (1994) Can the informal economy be reduced through major tax reforms? An empirical investigation for Austria. Public Finance/ Finances Publiques 49:137–152
Schneider F (1997) The informal economies of Western Europe. J Inst Econ Aff 17(3):42–48
Schneider F (1998) Further empirical results of the size of the informal economy of 17 OECD-countries over time. Paper presented at the 54. Congress of the IIPF Cordowa, Argentina and discussion paper, Department of Economics, University of Linz, Linz, Austria
Schneider F (2000) The increase of the size of the informal economy of 18 OECD countries: some preliminary explanations. Paper presented at the annual public choice meet. Charleston, SC
Schotter A (1981) The economic theory of social institutions. Cambridge University Press, Cambridge
Shane SA (1992) Why do some societies invent more than others? Journal of Business Venturing 7:29–46
Shane SA (1993) Cultural influences on national rates of innovation. J Bus Ventur 8(1):59–73
Shane SA (1995) Uncertainty avoidance and the preference for innovation championing role. J Int Bus Stud 26(1):47–68
Shapero A, Sokol L (1982) Social dimensions of entrepreneurship. In: Kent CA, Sexton DL, Vesper KH (eds) Encyclopedia of entrepreneurship. Prentice Hall, Englewood Cliffs, NJ
Smith C, Warner J (1979) On financial contracting: an analysis of bond covenants. J Financ Econ 7:117–161
Sobel RS (2008) Testing baumol: institutional quality and the productivity of entrepreneurship. J Bus Ventur 23(6):641–655

Solow RM (1957) Technical change and the aggregate production function. Rev Econ Stat 39:312–320
Soltow JH (1968) The entrepreneur in economic history. Am Econ Rev 58:84–92
Spence JT (1985) Achievement American style: the rewards and costs of individualism. Am Psychol 40:1285–1295
Stulz R (1988) Managerial control of voting rights: financing policies and the market for corporate control. J Financ Econ 20:25–54
Suddle K, Beugelsdijk S, Wennekers S (2006) Entrepreneurial culture as determinant of nascent entrepreneurship. SCALES paper EIM Zoetermeer
Thomas J (1992) Informal economic activity, LSE, handbooks in economics. Harvester Wheatsheaf, London
Torgler B, Schneider F (2009) The impact of tax morale and institutional quality on the shadow economy. J Econ Psychol 30:228–245
van Stel AJ, Storey DJ, Thurik AR (2007) The effect of business regulations on nascent and young business entrepreneurship. Small Bus Econ 28:171–186
Wennekers ARM, Thurik AR (1999) Linking entrepreneurship and economic growth. Small Bus Econ 13:27–55

The Effect of Cultural Background on Incentives, Growth and Distribution, and Vice Versa

6

The previous chapter presented the structures of the first element of cultural background's second-round effects. The present chapter deals with the second element, incentives (Sect. 6.1). Section 6.2 concerns third-round effects with a focus on the relationship between cultural background and growth, followed by Sect. 6.3 on income and wealth distribution. Finally, the interactions are presented in reverse, i.e., from growth and distribution to cultural background in Sect. 6.4.

6.1 Incentives

Incentives are the second element of economic institutions. There is general agreement that incentives are driven by the purposes set by individuals (Lawler 1994), they shape attempts to pursue such purposes and depend on the external environment. It is also commonly accepted that incentives are not directly observable, do not match satisfaction, are not consciously designed and, finally, are not controlled in a direct and obvious manner.

Incentives, in fact, concern an internal human state, which leads humans to behave in a specific way to achieve specific purposes and goals. In general, we can observe external expressions of incentives but not the incentives themselves. For instance, we can observe the accumulation of wealth without necessarily being able to distinguish the internal processes leading to such achievement.

The theory of incentives is not matched to behavior theories. Incentives are merely one of many factors that shape behavior. Other effects are derived from biology, cultural background and external situations.

Perhaps the simplest way to separate the notion of incentives from that of satisfaction would be to understand that satisfaction refers to the past, whereas incentives to the future. A past satisfactory compensation (satisfaction) may not refer to a particularly positive mood for future work (incentives).

According to Freud, incentives may derive either from an individual's consciousness or subconscious. They are not offered for direct control because they

P.E. Petrakis, *Culture, Growth and Economic Policy*,
DOI 10.1007/978-3-642-41440-4_6,

are purely internal situations, despite the fact that external forces may influence them but not control them.

Generally speaking, we accept the existence of two groups of theories on the formation of incentives. The first theory concerns the content of incentives and supports that everyone shares the same human needs and, hence, is motivated to satisfy such needs. The second group of theories focuses on the logical process of understanding reality and accepts the possibility that needs are similar for most people. Nevertheless, the way in which every human is placed inside such a framework is clearly a subjective issue.

Incentives may also be categorized as either intrinsic incentives or extrinsic incentives. Intrinsic incentives are those for which no other reward exists, apart from the activity itself. Examples of such incentives are hunger and altruism. Extrinsic incentives are those whose control mechanism is very obvious. Intrinsic incentives produce creativity, well-being and impulsiveness. In contrast, extrinsically imposed incentives are the result of pressure and low self-esteem.

Vroom (1964) proposed the famous "expectancy theory", according to which an individual is always trying to foresee the future. Therefore, a new reality is created that takes for granted the costs and benefits of such a process. In this way, three elements surround the process of motivation (instigation): valence, instrumentality and expectation. Valence is merely the desire for an intended outcome. Instrumentality is the belief that when certain intermediate stages are satisfied, the intended outcome will be reached. Finally, expectation is linked to the belief that one can indeed achieve the intended outcome. When those three elements are activated, the individual has the desired mix of incentives.

Adams (1963) proposed a view on "fairness", where humans are largely satisfied with relationships (personal or professional) in which the trade-off is fair. The view on fairness in transactions is formed through socialization. According to this opinion, a lack of fairness in social transactions creates prerequisites and tensions that induce individuals to search for and implement change. Adams proposed six ways to reduce inequity tension and "reinstate justice": (1) the alteration of the tension, (2) the alteration of the intended outcome, (3) the alteration of the way in which individuals think with regard to effort or outcome, (4) quitting that field of effort, (5) attempts to alter the outcome of others, and (6) the alteration of comparison criteria among alternative situations.

Goal setting may operate as a form of incentives. The core of Locke's (1968) suggestion is that when individuals set goals of a "feasible" difficulty that are self-determined, the prerequisites for their motivation are created (Locke 1968).

A purpose or goal is defined as a future situation that one aims at conquering through one's activity (Kruglanski 1996). Purpose is considered as the main pilot of human activity. Two questions are raised in this regard: (1) What are the sources that create purpose? (2) What does it mean when a specific purpose is determined? As far as the first question is concerned, the foundation of purpose is found in needs. Human needs produce desires, which in turn produce incentives and incentives have purpose as their product. Setting a purpose to achieve, however, requires one further step. Individuals ought to devote themselves to achieving such purpose. It is therefore clear that the process of organizing purposes plays an important role in studying incentives (Ford 1992). In contrast, studying purpose and the process of goal setting in general complements the study of incentives. Need and purpose correspond through a logical sequence, which starts at needs, moves to incentives for purposes to be achieved and, finally, for human activity to be activated.

This process raises two further questions. The first refers to whether instigations have an internal or external origin. The second question is whether or not goal setting facilitates the simplest version of needs, i.e., the three basic psychological needs as stated by Ryan (1993). These are autonomy, relatedness and competence, also known as the self-determination theory.

Many purposes are derived from the dominant cultural background. Cultural background may include a variety of purposes (e.g., intellectual and professional achievements and ethical issues) and form the prerequisites (by creating tools and skills) for the successful achievement of such purposes. Individuals, however, are different regarding the purposes they set and their paths to achievement.

This process, through which purposes are transferred to the individual, is mainly realized in two ways: by supporting the "autonomous personality" and by "intervening" in an individual's goal setting. In the first case, people in the individual's close environment (e.g., parents, teachers, and friends) play an important role in setting personal goals and encourage the individual by supporting initiatives and minimizing their control over the individual. In the second case, participation takes the form of spending time with, resources on and paying attention to the individual. When both procedures are applied, intrinsic incentive-formation processes are very likely to appear, which integrate extrinsic influences such as the formation and transfer of extrinsic incentives.

A significant part of human activity is spent achieving purpose. Purpose triggers behavior and drive choices. Failing to achieve purpose causes discontent, whereas success causes pleasure. Thus, purpose gives meaning to human existence, whereas its absence limits life's meaning and integration.

Purpose belongs to a unique category of knowledge that has its own primary characteristics. Thus, the multitude of phenomena linked to purpose setting is related to three levels of readout. The first and most general category refers to the organization of cognitive structures; this may constitute an individual feature but at the same time these structures are diffused through cultural background. Hence, the same principles that govern the accumulation, change and trigger of cognitive structures (and, hence, stereotypes) also apply to purpose. The second level concerns special psychological characteristics and functions. The third concerns special purpose and types of purpose; not all purposes are the same and, hence, they cannot have the same degree of significance.

As a cognitive category, purpose setting is realized through a judgment process, which is influenced by the activation of rational structures, stereotypes existing in the memory and incentives. Organizing purposes, however, do not stem from merely conscious processes but also from subconscious ones. Mental structures are triggered through the process of priming, where a previous stimulus influences

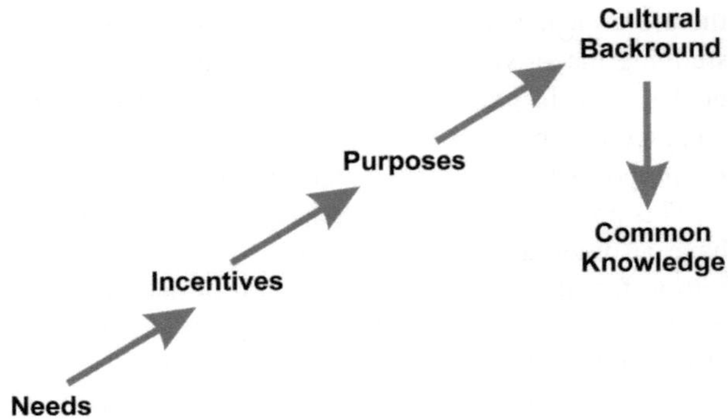

Fig. 6.1 Needs, incentives, purposes and cultural background

an individual's approach to activation. Accordingly, a subsequent purpose influences the following one and so on.

Therefore, despite the fact that incentives constitute an individual state, purpose has a direct relationship with cultural background (in other words, with common knowledge). In essence, purpose links cultural stereotypes to individual behavior. In this sense, it plays a very important role in social and economic processes, economic development and growth.

In addition, purposes are by definition an individual's future states. If there are no future horizons in the functioning of individuals and societies, then the interaction between incentives and cultural background is interrupted, leaving individual needs as the sole producer of incentives and purposes (Fig. 6.1).

As a particular cognitive procedure, purpose setting includes three separate issues: the setting of the purpose, attempting to achieve the purpose and reacting to the results of a specific purpose.

The individual can set purposes on the basis of the degree of their "desirability" and "achievability". Nevertheless, while individuals usually seek information regarding purposes they have set in a systematic manner, either on the basis of their degree of desirability or achievability, these purposes can also be set using a more passive approach. This situation refers to the case where the final choice is made by a third party or is the outcome of the exertion of power (e.g., from parents or employer) over the individual.

When a purpose has been set, it must be achieved through an appropriate activity. The attempt to achieve is considered successful when the mental construction of setting the purpose is sufficiently developed and is accompanied by an appropriate plan. In contrast, it is considered unsuccessful when the construction is not sufficiently developed and, consequently, the individual lacks specific ideas to achieve the purpose.

Of course, approaching purpose requires effort on the part of the individual, which raises issues regarding potency availability. This fact alone raises a "power saving" issue, which becomes particularly important when the purpose is difficult to realize and achieve. Thus, a purpose may be abandoned despite the fact that its degree of desirability and achievability does not lead in that direction.

6.2 Growth

Economic institutions shape conditions for growth and income and wealth distribution through the structures and incentives they create in society. The functioning of economic institutions and an effective political system define the growth prospects of a society, and they also constitute the basic mechanisms for the distribution of the wealth produced. Following that, of course, reverse inter-influence relationships are developed because both growth and politics influence a society's cultural background.

The exact impact of culture on growth, a question posed across the disciplines of economics (Schumpeter 1934), sociology (Weber 1930) and psychology (McClelland 1961), concerns several complex issues attributable to several social characteristics of "culture". The cultural characteristics of societies reflect psychological social stereotypes that have been created over time and are human constructions prior to current transactions and institutions.

Many studies have quantified the "effects" of cultural background and provide data for many countries (Hofstede 1980; House et al. 2004; McClelland 1961). The interrelation of the studies' results with economic growth indices demonstrates that culture can have particular and significant impacts (Minkov and Blagoev 2009).

Since the late twentieth century, we have witnessed the gradual appearance of research using empirical models to explain the impact of cultural background on economic growth (Hofstede and Bond 1988: Marini 2004; Pryor 2005).

Granato et al. (1996) examined the explanatory power of the standard endogenous growth model and compared it to that of two types of cultural values that capture motivational factors—achievement motivation and post-materialistic values. They created an index to measure the extent of incentives achievement using cultural background data from the World Values Survey (WVS). Granato et al. (1996) found that in 25 countries economic growth is influenced not only by economic factors but also by cultural background. They concluded that both economic and cultural factors affect growth and play complementary roles, as both models explain aspects of growth that the other alone cannot.

Marini (2004) attempted to perfect the work of Granato et al. (1996) by constructing a cultural variable for each of the three periods of economic development. The first period, the traditional economy, includes values such as obedience, faith in religion and tolerance. The second period is characterized by personal achievements and general trust in others. Finally, the values linked to the post-modern period are imagination and unselfishness. Using the same countries as Granato et al. (1996), Marini (2004) discovered a negative association between economic growth and the values in traditional economies and a positive association with values such as independence, austerity and diligence. In the third period, the authors found no statistically significant relationship between culture and an economy's development.

Using a set of dummies for "cultural areas", Paldam (2002) argued that the transition from a poor, highly corrupt, traditional country to a wealthy, liberal democracy is influenced by culture. Thus, countries with the same "basic culture" cluster along the transition path. However, he found little basis for the belief that corruption is so deeply embedded in the culture of a society as to be unchangeable. Paldam (2002) concluded that culture is an inferior explanation of the level of corruption because of the fact that countries within the same cultural area are more similar in terms of GDP level than corruption level. Furthermore, it was found that corruption can vary greatly within the same cultural area.

Barro and McCleary (2003) examined religion as a determinant of economic growth. They found that economic growth responds positively to the extent of religious beliefs but negatively to church attendance. They stated that growth depends on the extent of belief relative to belonging. These results accord with the perspective in which religious beliefs influence individual traits that then enhance economic performance.

Tabellini (2005) analyzed 69 regions in eight different European countries by defining cultural background as a result of historical developments and divergences. He looked at the regional variants in trust, belief that personal efforts are rewarded, respect and teaching obedience to children and political institutions between 1,600 and 1,850. Initially, literacy level and political institutions explained cultural background. Tabellini (2005) then used these values in regressions to measure the influence of cultural background on per capita income. The results showed that trust and obedience (as cultural background indices) positively influence per capita income. The current cultural background of every society is the result of a long process and is largely owed to historical factors such as political institutions and illiteracy level. The institutions of each society, which are the outcome of these long progressions, influence economic results through cultural background.

Another controversial issue in the literature lies between the effects of individualistic or collectivistic societies in terms of the economic outcome (Triandis 1995). Collectivism may offer a competitive edge in the production of final goods; however, its connection with tradition creates obstacles in economic growth as well as in decision-making that would otherwise benefit society. In-group collectivism is incompatible with competitiveness and the development of free entrepreneurship because it favors conceptualism and small, low-risk businesses. Furthermore, because of increased responsibilities, individuals lack the necessary energy to innovate and create, thus creating an additional obstacle to wealth accumulation. In contrast, according to Pareek (1968), economic growth is a function of the "need for progress", which is often associated with privacy and competition. The quality of intermediate inputs that lead to final goods is determined by individual effort, which in turn is a function of rewards for innovation.

De Jong (2009) explained how culture affects institutions and economic activity. He did not detect a direct influence by culture on economic results. Regarding wealthier countries, he concluded that the dimension of individualism is negatively associated with economic growth and positively associated with per capita GDP and the Human Development Index, although not statistically significantly. In contrast, uncertainty avoidance is negatively associated with per capita GDP. These results conflict with those of Hofstede (2001), who identified a powerful relationship between per capita GDP and individualism. At the same time, the dimensions of power distance and masculinity can provide significant explanations regarding income divergence among countries. High scores for these two dimensions show large inequalities in the distribution of income. Finally, his regressions corroborated a negative relationship between growth rate of GDP and uncertainty. Hence, values may indeed be significant for the way in which society is organized but they do not necessarily influence the level of income or rate of growth.

More recently, Sacco and Segre (2009) suggested an endogenous growth mechanism sustained by investments in culture, thereby elucidating the factors through which culture may affect economic growth. Bucci and Segre (2011) suggested that in a world where complementarities are important (especially those involving human capital), culture is of particular interest in explaining economic growth. Building a two-sector endogenous growth model where two different types of capital (human and cultural capital) can be accumulated, they argued that investment in culture can affect economic growth in the long run only through the complementarity between the two forms of capital accumulation.

6.3 Distribution

Understanding the contribution of cultural background to determine income distribution is critical. If some societies demonstrate values that favor economic inequality, then such observations may help us understand income difference.

The distribution of income in society and its relationship with current cultural background has troubled social science (Flanagan and Rayner 1988; Leacock 1978). Cultural relationships are crucial determinants for the distribution of income and economic activity (Mushinski and Pickering 2000) and societies with strong hierarchical structures demonstrate higher income inequality (Britan and Cohen 1980). However, it should be noted that economic analysis has many times ignored the contribution of cultural context and social organizations in income distribution.

Despite the fact that income differences are diachronically stable in a society (Li et al. 1998), such differences are derived, in part, from a nation's political economy nation (Bertola 1993). Relying on Hofstede's cultural dimensions, many studies have examined the link between culture and economic variables, like GDP per capita distribution. Tang and Koveos (2008) identified a negative association among GDP per capita and the acceptance of inequalities and long-term orientation. These relationships are due to the fact that hierarchical societies comprise ineffective and bureaucratic procedures, which claim resources and therefore diminish national wealth. Similarly, Dodor and Rana (2007) identified the existence of a negative correlation among acceptance of inequalities, uncertainty avoidance and the Gini coefficient. Risk aversion decreases the undertaking of high-risk investments, resulting in the slowing of economic growth. In contrast, they also identified a positive correlation between individualism and the Gini coefficient, because in societies with a strong degree of individualism, individuals are more likely to focus on their personal interests and be encouraged by the achievement of their personal goals. As a result, national wealth is increased.

6.4 Reverse Causation: Economic Growth, Wealth Distribution and Cultural Background

The way in which income and wealth are distributed in society is an integral part of cultural background. This process in turn shapes political institutions, affecting continuous layers of influence via an on-going process.

Technological and political events may cause changes in the structures of cultural background (Schwartz 1992). However, little has been written on the causation relationships between cultural background and growth because of data limitations (i.e., data cover different time periods).

To obtain relevant results, researchers have used various databases that provide data over a long period of time, and which are appropriate for diachronic analyses: the European Values Survey and the World Values Survey. Relying on the paper by Ng et al. (1982), Allen et al. (2007) studied the changes in the cultural background of nine nations in East Asia and the Pacific over a 20-year period. Allen et al. (2007) created 2002 sample that was equivalent to that created by Ng et al. for 1982, and then compared the two samples. It was observed that during the two last decades of the twentieth century, nations that scored highly for values such as for love of nature and life in 1982, scored even higher values in 2002. Countries with high growth rates were dominated by such values, whereas economies with lower growth rates paid greater attention to politics and issues of national security. At the same time, their results confirmed that an increase in wealth leads to an increase in the level of individualism. In addition, a causation relationship from economic conditions to values was identified in both samples; causation relationships from the opposite direction were also identified. The values of predominance and imposition were positively associated with increases in GDP during the two decades between the two surveys. This fact suggests that the values in question lead to economic growth.

Finally, based on three World Values Survey measurements (1970–1971, 1981 and 1990), Inglehart (1997) attempted to identify possible relationships between cultural background and economic growth. He succeeded in identifying causation relationships in both directions. High incomes meant that the majority now had access to the necessities of life and they were no longer concerned with survival. The security brought about by the materialism of economic growth led to a shift in the priorities of individuals. Individuals were found to be less interested in the accumulation of wealth and now focused on "feminine values" such as quality of life, environment protection, respect towards others and solidarity. Hence, economic growth can lead to a change in values. However, a lack of orientation in the growth of postmodern societies can also lead to reduced growth rates. In other words, as growth influences values, so do values influence performance.

References

Adams JS (1963) Toward an understanding of inequity. J Abnorm Soc Psychol 67:422–436
Allen MW, Ng SH, Ikeda K, Jawan JA, Sufi AH, Wilson M, Yang KS (2007) Two decades of change in cultural values and economic development in eight Asian and Pacific Island nations. J Cross-Cult Psychol 38:247–269
Barro RJ, McCleary RM (2003) Religion and economic growth across countries. Am Sociol Rev 68(5):760–781
Bertola G (1993) Factor share and savings in endogenous growth. Am Econ Rev 83:1184–1198
Britan G, Cohen R (1980) Toward an anthropology of formal organizations. In: Britan GM, Cohen R (eds) Hierarchy and society. Institute for the Study of Human Issues, Philadelphia, PA, pp 9–30
Bucci A, Segre G (2011) Culture and human capital in a two-sector endogenous growth model. Res Econ 65:279–293
De Jong E (2009) Culture and economics: on values, economics, and international business. Routledge, London
Dodor J, Rana D (2007) Culture and economic development: an investigation using Hofstede cultural dimensions. Int J Bus Res 7(2):75–84
Flanagan JG, Rayner S (1988) Rules, decisions, and inequality in egalitarian societies. Avebury, Sydney
Ford ME (1992) Motivating humans: goals, emotions and personal agency beliefs. Sage, Newberry Park, CA
Granato J, Inglehart R, Leblang D (1996) The effect of cultural values on economics development: theory, hypotheses and some empirical tests. Am J Polit Sci 40:607–631
Hofstede G (1980) Culture's consequences: international differences in work-related values. Sage, Beverly Hills, CA
Hofstede G (2001) Culture's consequences—comparing values, behaviours, institutions and organisations across nations, 2nd edn. Sage, London
Hofstede G, Bond HM (1988) The Confucius connection: from cultural roots to economic growth. Organ Dyn 16:4–21
House JR, Hanges JP, Mansour J, Dorfman WP, Gupta V (2004) Culture, leadership and organisations—the GLOBE study of 62 societies. Sage, Thousand Oaks, CA
Inglehart R (1997) Modernization and postmodernization: changing values and political styles in advanced industrial society. Princeton University Press, Princeton, NJ
Kruglanski AW (1996) Motivated social cognition: principles of the interface. In: Higgins ET, Kruglanski AW (eds) Social psychology: handbook of basic principles. Guilford, New York
Lawler EE (1994) Motivation in work organizations. Jossey-Bass Publishers, San Francisco, CA
Leacock E (1978) Women's status in egalitarian society: implications for social evolution. Curr Anthropol 19(2):225–259
Li H, Squire L, Zou H (1998) Explaining international and intertemporal variations in income inequality. Econ J 108(1):26–43
Locke EA (1968) Toward a theory of task motivation and incentives. Organ Behav Hum Perform 3 (2):157–189
Marini M (2004) Cultural evolution and economic growth: a theoretical hypothesis with some empirical evidence. J Socio Econ 33:765–784
McClelland DC (1961) The achieving society. Van Nostrand, Princeton, NJ
Minkov M, Blagoev V (2009) Cultural values predict subsequent economic growth. Int J Cross-Cult Manag 9:5–24
Mushinski D, Pickering K (2000) Inequality in income distributions: does culture matter? an analysis of western native American tribes. J Econ Issues 34(2):403–412
Ng SH, Hossain A, Ball P, Bond MH, Hayaski K, Lim SP, O'Driscoll MP, Shinha D, Yang KS (1982) Human values in nine countries. In: Rath R, Asthana HS, Sinha D, Sinha JBP (eds) Diversity and unity in cross-cultural psychology. Swets and Zeilinger, Lisse, pp 196–205

Paldam M (2002) The cross-country pattern of corruption: economics, culture and the seesaw dynamics. Eur J Polit Econ 18:215–240
Pareek U (1968) A motivational paradigm of development. J Soc Isssues 24:115–122
Pryor F (2005) National values and economic growth. Am J Econ Soc 64(2):451–483
Ryan RM (1993) Agency and organization: intrinsic motivation, autonomy, and the self in psychological development. In: Jacobs JE (ed) Nebraska symposium on motivation: developmental perspectives on motivation. University of Nebraska Press, Lincoln, NE
Sacco PL, Segre G (2009) Creativity, cultural investment and local development: a new theoretical framework for endogenous growth. In: Fratesi U, Senn L (eds) Growth and innovation of competitive regions. Springer, Berlin
Schumpeter J (1934) The theory of economic development. Harvard University Press, Cambridge
Schwartz SH (1992) Universals in the content and structure of values: theoretical advances and empirical tests in 20 countries. Adv Exp Soc Psychol 25(1):1–65
Tabellini G (2005) Culture and institutions: economic development in the regions of Europe. CESifo working paper no. 1492
Tang L, Koveos P (2008) A framework to update Hofstede's cultural value indices: economic dynamics and institutional stability. J Int Bus Stud 39(1):1045–1063
Triandis CH (1995) Individualism and collectivism. Westview Press, Boulder, CO
Vroom VH (1964) Work and motivation. Jossey-Bass, San Francisco, CA
Weber M (1930) The protestant ethic and the spirit of capitalism. Unwin Hyman, London

7 Cultural Background and Rationality

The previous chapters analyzed the relationship between the various dimensions of cultural background and basic structures at a macro level (societies or world level). The present chapter attempts to verify the relationship between cultural particularities and individual economic behavior. In other words, the relevant control is exercised at a micro level.

As a rational being and within the context of rational choice, an individual functions under a network of basic assumptions regarding the sum of the individual's beliefs and preferences, which are generally selfish and materialistic. Nevertheless, the theory of rational expectations does not reveal the nature of the individual on the basis of which such assumptions are made. Consequently, it ignores the way human beliefs and preferences are formed and in which cultural background lies. The present chapter attempts to reveal the relationship between cultural background and rational choice by analyzing the conclusions of certain laboratory experiments that examine whether different cultural dimensions influence rational behavior.

The concept of rational choice as a theory to predict human behavior is presented in Sect. 7.1. Section 7.2 shows the results of an experiment on the behavior of rational choices under the influence of variables such as time preference, trust, uncertainty and social capital.

7.1 Rational Choice

Despite the fact that the rational approach constitutes a theory on the prediction of human behavior, it does not attempt to accurately determine all the possible options—individuals are not always informed of all of their available options and the cognitive capacity of individuals differs. Therefore, irregularities are created, which are connected to individuals' indecisiveness to make rational decisions from a multitude of choices. Thus, individuals are called to make decisions that fully interact with other decisions and have an uncertain duration (Fudenberg and Maskin 1986) or in situations where cooperation is required to achieve the best

P.E. Petrakis, *Culture, Growth and Economic Policy*,
DOI 10.1007/978-3-642-41440-4_7, © Springer-Verlag Berlin Heidelberg 2014

possible result. A further irregularity that appears in conventional theories concerns inaccuracies between anticipated and observed behavior. This is mostly found in social dilemma situations, where despite the fact that cooperation is mutually beneficial, the individual's interests conflict with the interests of the group because of individual reward (Henrich et al. 2004; Gintis et al. 2006).

The individual, as a member of social groups and via external environmental influences, develops action and decision-making mechanisms. The role of culture as the sum of traits that shape preferences and beliefs is introduced at this point. Contrary to the rational choice approach, the cultural approach does not take for granted the fact that human behavior is invariable and independent from internal mechanisms. In contrast, it considers that culture is the outcome of specific attitudes that vary among individuals, groups and societies. The cultural approach is based neither on a specific human behavior prediction model nor on specific assumptions. This may result in uncertain predictions but it also examines how changes in values influence preferences and, consequently, human behavior.

However, the cultural approach has been heavily criticized with regard to its ability to predict human behavior. Those criticizing this specific approach do not consider that it constitutes a theory, but simply offers a set of categories and concepts (Harsanyi 1969; Barry 1970; Gray 1987) that do not share a common deductive base.

Despite these limitations, the cultural approach is now appreciated for its contribution to the interpretation of human behavior in conjunction with the basic assumptions of the rational approach. The individual indeed functions on the basis of benefit maximization, but the assumption that the choices are solely selfish and materialistic does not always apply. The individual's options and the information process converting them to beliefs may differ among people and different time periods and can be the result of social process. Therefore, the rational choice constitutes a theory that links preferences and beliefs to behavior, without determining their content. The contribution of culture at this point is determinative. By being a social-psychological variable, culture forms stances and behaviors that are shaped through social interactions.

Based on this view, culture is not in conflict with rational choice but is instead an essential element in the rational choice analysis of real-world behavior (North 1981, 1990; Kreps 1990; Lane 1992). Thus, while decisions are generally made by rational individuals, people often prefer to sacrifice a part of their anticipated benefit, thus showing a "taste for discrimination" (Becker 1957).

Many of the choices related to culture are based on altruism, whose influence on rational choices has been studied by many scholars (see Phelps 1975; Collard 1978; Taylor 1987). In terms of rational choices, altruism is the degree to which individuals integrate a part of the prosperity of other individuals or groups to their own utility. A high level of altruism and the team spirit it entails favor the creation of cohesive bonds among the members of a group. Individuals with a high sense of altruism tend to show team spirit, whereas a lack of altruism gives rise to aggressive and intensively competitive behavior.

7.2 Cultural Traits and Rational Choice Through Experiments

In our attempt to examine human behavior, we conducted an experiment at the University of Athens to study decisions processes.[1]

To accomplish the aim of the project, a series of experiments and a survey were designed to be conducted in a laboratory setting at the University of Athens, as well as an online experiment/survey using the e-learning mailing list of the university. The laboratory experiment/survey was held between 20 and 22 June 2012 over six sessions (two sessions per day). Eighteen students from the University of Athens participated in each session, with a total of 100 participants. The main objective of this study was to measure the levels of cooperation through a public good game (PGG) and then analyze to what extent cooperation interacted with the cultural and social characteristics of the sample.

Our study comprised two separate but sequential stages. In the first stage, a public good experiment was conducted to measure participants' levels of cooperation or defection with the use of real monetary incentives. The dependent variable was the level of cooperation, based on the percentage of people who contributed to the PGG. It was designed to measure the cooperation and selfishness levels of Greek university students. We ran monetary incentivized PGGs with groups of three or six members and with different marginal return per capita (0.133–0.66) to test for cooperation under different levels of group consistency and public good efficiency.

In the second stage, participants answered a questionnaire on cultural characteristics. The self-reported cultural characteristics were measured either by behavioral type questions or descriptive questions, which directly revealed the scope of the particular question. To avoid any kind of misinterpretation, we also included a short definition of the cultural characteristic under examination in the final section of questions. The main objective of the project was to gain a deeper understanding and interpretation of the interactive relationship between cultural characteristics and rational behavior in Greece.

The questionnaire comprised 127 items in total. It had four main sections: (1) sociodemographics; (2) attitudinal items measuring, for example, social capital, reciprocity, fairness, altruism, distributional preferences and propensity to impose norms; (3) individual characteristics such as risk preferences, time preferences, cognitive abilities, BMI (self-reported); and (4) behaviors observed in three experimental games (five decisions) measuring social preferences (altruism, fairness, negative reciprocity, trust, positive reciprocity and strategic behavior).

The criteria, according to which the individuals who participated in the experiment were chosen, were that they should have no knowledge of economics and that their decisions should not be influenced by decision-making models. At the same time, the goal and content of the experiment were not known to the participants to

[1] The experiment was conducted with the help of the following researchers: Benedikt Herrmann, Antonios Proestakis and Mark Bernard.

fully ensure the project's impartiality and merit. By doing so, we ensured that their behavior would not be influenced by the purpose of the experiment. Finally, the individuals within the group did not know each other, and none knew which group they would belong to. This was done to avoid cooperation phenomena prior to conducting the experiment. After ensuring anonymity and experimental protocols were implemented, we ran a short questionnaire to test the subjects' comprehension level on the specific public good task. The experiment started once all subjects had individually answered all questions regarding the public good test. We conducted a ten-period repeating PGG using a z-tree (Fischbacher 2007) with the subjects remaining in the same group for all periods. We observed the number of subjects who cooperated or defected in each sequential period. People that contributed 3 € were considered as cooperators and people who contributed 0 € were considered as defectors or free riders.

We performed a six-person PGG (see Ledyard 1995) with binary decisions. Each of the six individuals decided on how to spend 10 €. A subject could either keep this amount in their private account or invest it in a so-called common project. The following payoff function was clearly explained to the subjects:

$$P_i = (w - c_i) + 1/6\sum_{j=1}^{6} 2c_j$$

where c_i is the contribution of the i-player (binary decision 0 or 3), w is the endowment of the subject and it is always 10 €. The size of the common project was double the sum of all contributions. Each player's final profit was a 1/6 share of the common project and the money was placed in a private account. The marginal return per capita for this game was 0.33. Hence, under standard game theoretic assumptions the prediction is complete free riding by all subjects.

7.2.1 Cooperation in the Public Good Game and Time Preference

Figure 7.1 shows the contribution probability over the ten periods of the game. The figure shows that the individuals in period 1 show cooperative behavior of rational and selfish individuals. Moreover, the observed cooperation declines over time reaching the lowest level of cooperation in period 10 (only 15.48 %).

For the purposes of the following analysis and to analyze the relationship of our dependent variable (cc) with the corresponding dependent variable in each case, we made a distinction regarding the subjects' contribution levels as follows: (a) during period 1 (c_1); (b) during period 10 (c_10); and (c) during all remaining periods (c_2–9) (the average value for these eight periods). While we essentially looked at the average contribution of the sample, data from periods 1 and 10 were important. Contributions in period 1 were more spontaneous with no learning or experience effect. In contrast, in period 10, the last period, subjects with the highest experience

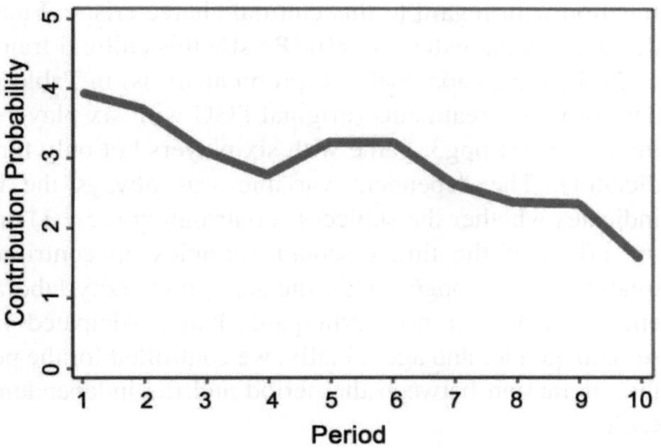

Fig. 7.1 The Contribution probability over the ten periods of the game

level were more likely to free ride as they anticipated that the game would end after this period (end game effect).

We measured cultural characteristics using two different types of questions. The first used behavioral insights and aims to elicit subjects' spontaneous answers without them realizing the true purpose of the question. Under this approach some questions were also analyzed in combination with each other or in parallel. To analyze the participants' time preferences we used two behavioral measures. The first one measured the long-run discount rate by asking subjects to declare the minimum amount of money they would be willing to accept and receive in 1 month instead of waiting for 7 months to receive 200 €.

The second measured the short-run discount rate by asking subjects to declare the minimum amount of money that they would be willing to accept and receive that day instead of waiting for 1 day to receive 10 €.

To perform meaningful comparisons between these two measures, after assuming hyperbolic discounting, we calculated the long-run time discount (ltd) and the short-run time discount (std) parameters in annual terms[2] (the higher the ltd, the more a person discounts the long-run future [more impatient]). In accordance with previous findings in the time preferences literature, we found that people are much more impatient in the short term than in the long term.

The second approach was more straightforward and descriptive. It provided an accurate definition of the question under examination and left no room for spontaneous answers. Subjects were first given a descriptive definition of present- and future-oriented people within a culture. They were then asked to allocate 10 units (PresR) to best describe how they personally function in their everyday life and another 10 units (PresW) to describe how they would like their everyday life to

[2] The ltd in annual terms was calculated by assuming the indifference between the declared amount (time_33) in 1 month and 200 € in 7 months time. By reallocating terms we got $ltd = \frac{2400-12*time_{33}}{7*time_{33}-200}$ and for the short-run time discount $std = \frac{3560}{time_{3.4}} - 365$.

function with regard to this cultural characteristic. Finally, subjects were asked to declare to what extent (0–80) (PresD) this cultural trait influences their lives.

In the regression analysis (probit analysis) in Table A.1 (Appendix A), we used data from all treatments (original PGG with six players: opg6; original PGG with three players: opg3; game with six players but only three players make decisions: dictator). The dependent variable was always the binary variable cc, which indicates whether the subject is contributing (cc = 1) or not (cc = 0). We analyzed the effect of the time-discount variables on contributions after controlling for treatment type (opg6, opg3, dictator), university laboratory, experimental experience (whether or not participants had participated in a previous experiment), session, gender and age. Finally, we controlled for the period and we also examined the interaction between the period and the independent time discount variable in each case.

The long distance variable had a weak positive effect on contributions while the period was always significant and negative. Interactions were not significant for any period. Although weak, the effect of (long-run) time discount was in accordance with experimental findings.

The positive effects of PresR and PresW on the levels of contributions contradicted empirical findings revealing a negative relationship between time discount and cooperation. Nevertheless, when testing the interactions between these two variables and different periods we found that this positive effect is true only in the intermediate periods. As soon as the game reaches its end subjects became less cooperative. Strategic reasoning ("you have to feed the cow if you want to milk") might explain this observation. Finally, in period 10, subjects' present or future orientation had no effect on their contribution choice.

According to the result of the analysis both PresR and PresW were positive and significant. The interactions between PresR and periods 3–8 were significant at the 5 % level (and at the 10 % level between PresR and periods 2, 9 and 10). The interactions between PresW and periods 5–7 were all significant at the 5 % level (and at the 10 % level between PresR and periods 4, 8 and 9).

Thus, the main finding establishes that the more a person considers themselves present orientated or desires to be so, the more cooperative he/she is.

7.2.2 Cooperation in the Public Good Game and Trust

Based on the methodology presented for time preference, a probit analysis for the case of trust was conducted (Table A.2) (Appendix A). The variables used for trust were as follows:

(a) trustR (trust Reality): This concerns subjects' answers to a question on how they truly function in their everyday life, with or without trust. The subjects scored the two notions (with or without trust) from 0 to 10. The sum of the scores equaled 10.

(b) trustW (trust Willingness): This concerns subjects' answers to a question on how they consider their everyday life should or would function with regard to a

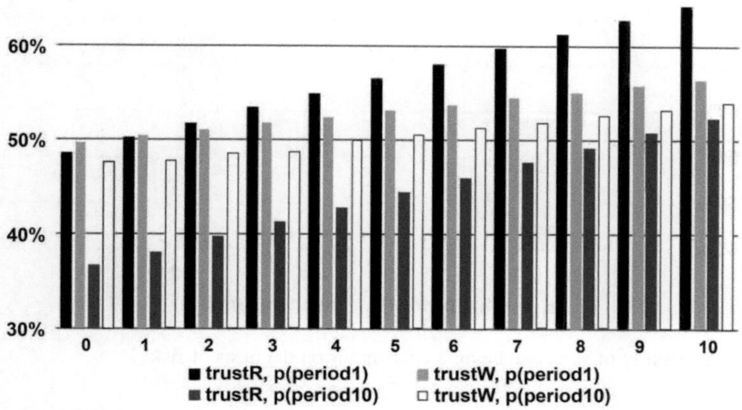

Fig. 7.2 Probability of someone being a contributor according to level of trust. *Note*: 0=Lack of Trust, 10=Full Trust

lack of trust and with trust. Again, the subjects answered the two notions scoring them from 0 to 10. The sum of the scores equaled 10.

Table A.2 (Appendix A) shows the probit analysis using the data from all treatments (opg6, opg3, dictator). The dependent variable was always the binary variable cc, which indicates whether the subject is contributing ($cc = 1$) or not ($cc = 0$).

Furthermore, Fig. 7.2 shows the different probabilities of someone being a contributor or not, according to the level of trust. The probabilities for periods 1 and 10 are shown.

We initially observed that during period 1 the probability of someone being a contributor is higher when there is full trust. This conclusion applies to both trustR and trustW. In other words, the higher the level of trust, the higher the probability of someone being a contributor. Nevertheless, such a tendency is higher for the variable trustR compared with trustW. Thus, despite the fact that higher levels of trust make it more likely that a subject will be a contributor, in this period, subjects do not have a strong desire to do so.

As far as period 10 is concerned, it again emerged that the higher the level of trust, the higher the probability of someone being a contributor; this result was obtained for both trustR and trustW. In addition, such a tendency is again higher for trustR compared with trustW. This suggests that those who participated in the experiment would like for the contribution of others to be more in line with their levels of trust. In fact, it is obvious that—particularly in the lower levels of trust—they wished for their contribution to be much higher.

Regarding the variable trustR (reality), if we compare period 1 and period 10, the contribution probability of the participants is significantly lowered in period 10 for all levels of trust. Nevertheless, as far as the variable trustW (as it should be) is concerned, participants would like the decrease in this level of probability to be much lower for all levels of trust.

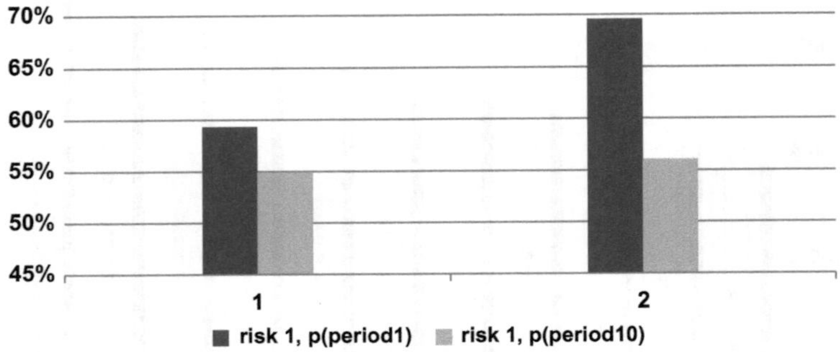

Fig. 7.3 Probability of someone being a contributor on the basis of risk_1

Thus, the main conclusion here is that the higher a person's level of trust towards society, the more cooperative that person is.

7.2.3 Cooperation in the Public Good Game and Uncertainty/Risk

Below we examine the individual's perception of risk to determine human behavior. The questions of the experiment attempted to identify the development of human choices in relation to risk, by categorizing the variables as either behavioral or descriptive variables. We used the following behavioral time variables in the probit analysis (Table A.3, Appendix A):

(a) risk_1: The subject was asked to choose between two options. The first option offered the chance to win 1,000 €, irrespective of whether the coin lands heads or tails up. The second option offered the chance to win 2,000 € if the coin lands heads up or nothing if it is tails. The answer indicates whether the subject is risk neutral or risk lover.
(b) risk_2: Given two choices, the subject was asked to whether they wanted to take a lottery ticket with an 80 % probability of winning 45 € and a 20 % chance of winning nothing or to receive 30 € in cash. If subjects choose the lottery ticket, they are characterized as risky, otherwise as not risky.
(c) risk_3: The subject was asked to state whether or not they would agree to the following arrangement: You toss a coin with somebody. If the coin lands tails up, you win 1,500 €, whereas if it is heads you lose 1,000 €. A positive answer indicates an assumption of risk, whereas a negative answer indicates risk aversion.

The results of the probit analysis for the behavioral variables for uncertainty are shown in Table A.3 (Appendix A).

The degree of risk aversion determines the probabilities of a player being a contributor (Figs. 7.3, 7.4 and 7.5). A risk-neutral individual is less of a contributor compared with a risk-loving individual. Nevertheless, during the experiment, the players limited their participation because they did not believe that they would gain any additional benefit, thus expressing a high degree of selfish behavior.

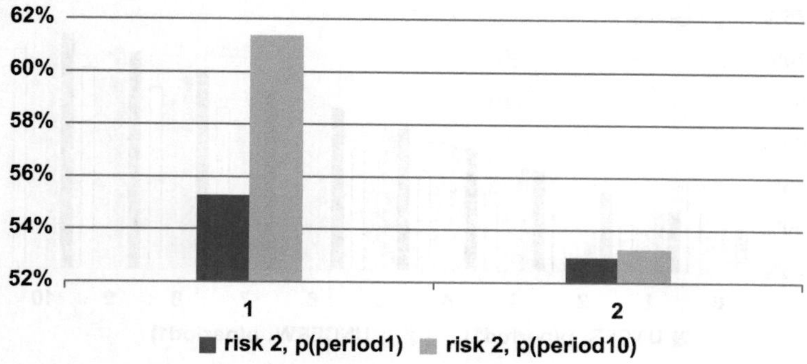

Fig. 7.4 Probability of someone being a contributor on the basis of risk_2

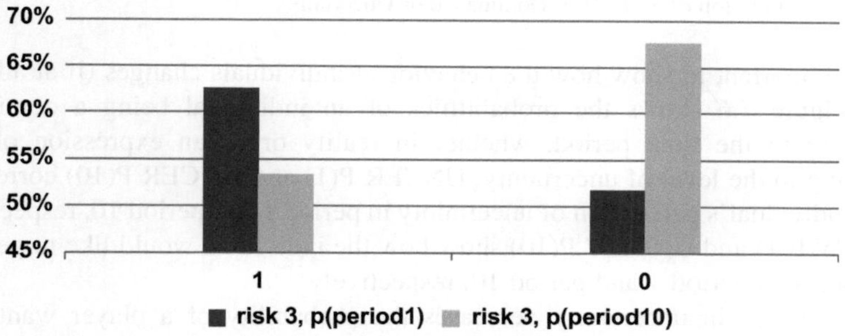

Fig. 7.5 Probability of someone being a contributor on the basis of risk_3

The contribution probability becomes lower as the period changes. However, even in period 10, a risk-lover is more of a contributor compared with a risk-neutral individual. A risk-loving individual is more likely to participate from period 1 compared with risk-neutral and risk-averse individuals.

The period changes the marginal effect of each variable in the individual's probability to contribute. In other words, the individual's preferences are not stable and their perception of risk changes over time. The information acquired by the individual throughout the process of the experiment helps them have a better image of reality and change the way in which they make decisions.

The descriptive approach included two variables:

(a) UNCER: the subject was asked to allocate 10 units to best describe how they understood risk in their everyday life, and
(b) UNCEW: a further 10 units to describe the role they would like risk to play in their everyday life.

The results of the probit analysis for the descriptive variables are presented in Table A.4 (Appendix A). Risk aversion determines whether the player will be a contributor. The more a player avoids risk, the less probable it is to contribute to the group.

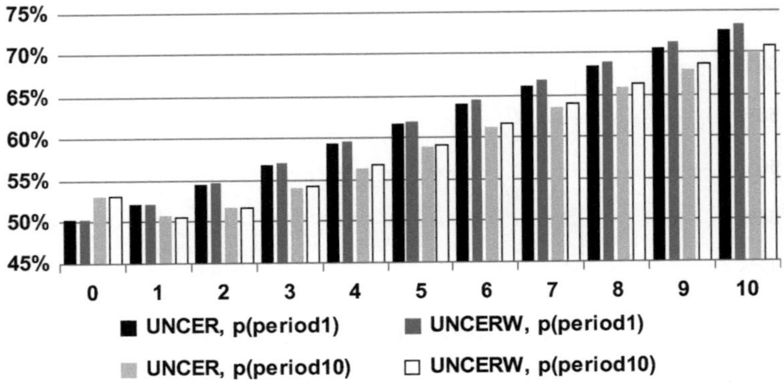

Fig. 7.6 Probability of someone being a contributor on the basis of the Uncertainty/Risk level. *Note*: 0 = Assumption of Risk, 10 = Dominance of Uncertainty

It is important to show how the behavior of individuals changes (if at all) over time. Figure 7.6 shows the probabilities of an individual being a contributor according to the time period, whether in reality or as an expression of will, according to the level of uncertainty. UNCER P(1) and UNCER P(10) correspond to the individual's perception of uncertainty in period 1 and period 10, respectively. UNCEW P(1) and UNCEW P(10) show how the individual would like to perceive uncertainty in period 1 and period 10, respectively.

An increase in uncertainty decreases the probability of a player wanting to contribute to the team, thus expressing selfish behavior. Individuals aim to maximize their own personal benefit. Nevertheless, when the individual become aware of the fact that the marginal utility that may emerge from assuming additional risk is less than the resources that might be sacrificed, then the individual tends to contribute less.

As shown in Fig. 7.6, the actual perception of risk is initially matched to the willingness to accept risk. As time passes however, the willingness for risk is higher than the level of risk the individual actually assumes. Finally, the will to assume risk is restrained as the experiment is underway. Risk acceptance is higher in period 1 and then gradually decreases towards period 10.

Thus, the main finding is that the perception of risk plays an important role in an individual's decision making on whether or not they will be a contributor. The more risk-loving someone is, the more cooperative he/she is.

7.2.4 Cooperation in the Public Good Game and Social Capital

The probit analysis for social capital included the following variables:

(a) SC_1: Whether or not a subject would tell a lie that would offer them a benefit. Subjects answered the question with a score from 1 to 7 (1: Disagree, 7: Agree).

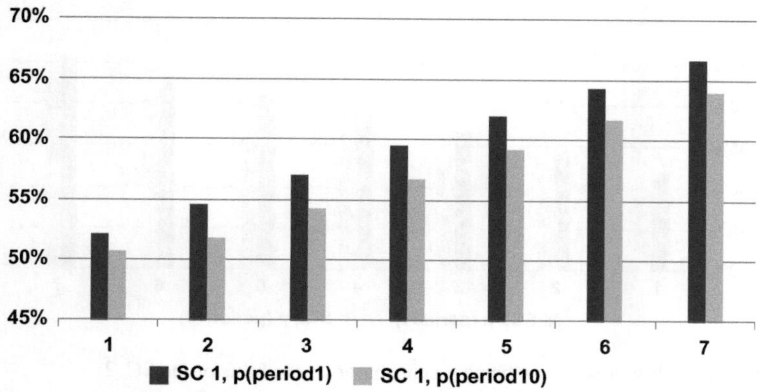

Fig. 7.7 Probability of someone being a contributor on the basis of the SC_1

(b) SC_2: Whether or not, and to what extent, do they disagree or agree with the following statement: "Some people do not cooperate because they only pursue their own personal short-term benefits. Therefore, things that could have been done well if people did cooperate, usually fail because of these people." Subjects answered the question with a score from 1 to 7 (1: Disagree, 7: Agree).
(c) SC_3: Whether subjects believe that most people will try to take advantage of them (score of 1) or will be fair and just (score of 2).
(d) SC_4: Would you say that in most instances:
  (i) People try to be helpful/useful.
  (ii) People are only interested in themselves.
  (iii) Subjects scored 1 if they answered (i) and 2 if they answered (ii).

The results of the probit analysis for the behavioral variables for social capital are shown in Table A.5 (Appendix A).

Figure 7.7 shows the probabilities of whether or not someone will be a contributor based on social capital level as expressed by SC_1 for period 1 and period 10. The probability of someone being a contributor increases because subjects consider that some people do not cooperate because they aim for personal benefit by lying. Subjects do not like this behavior and their response is the amelioration of social prosperity by attempting to contribute to this end.

Figure 7.8 shows the probabilities of whether or not someone will be a contributor based on social capital level as expressed by SC_2. We found that the probability of someone being a contributor increases because people consider that others do not cooperate as they only pursue their own short-term interests. Hence, those who agree with this statement wish to change the current situation and contribute to the good of society. In addition, the probability of someone contributing decreased by approximately 3 % from period 1 to period 10.

Figure 7.9 shows the probabilities of whether or not someone will be a contributor based on social capital level as expressed by SC_3. We found that the probability of someone being a contributor increases when they believe that others will not

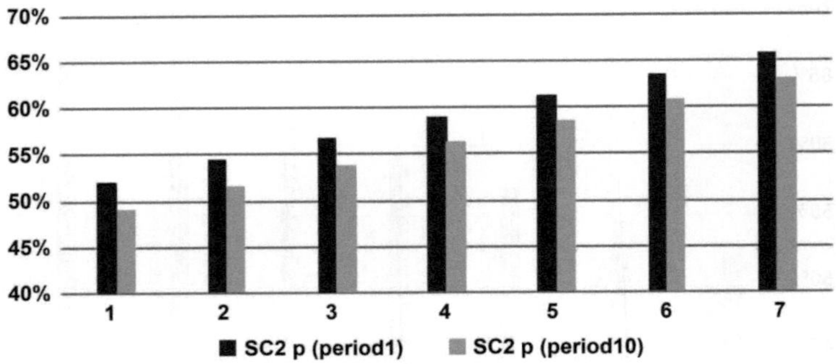

Fig. 7.8 Probability of someone being a contributor on the basis of the SC_2

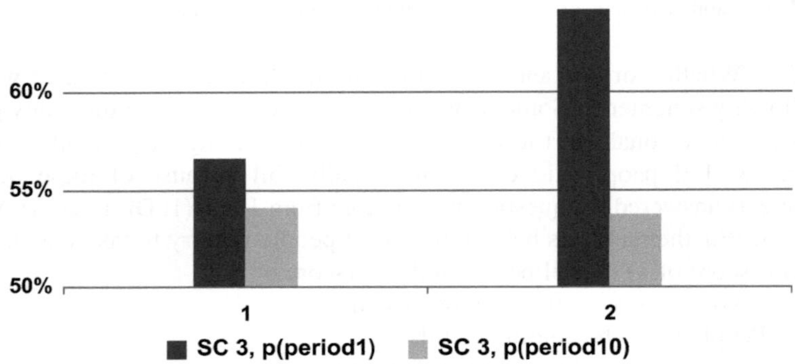

Fig. 7.9 Probability of someone being a contributor on the basis of the SC_3

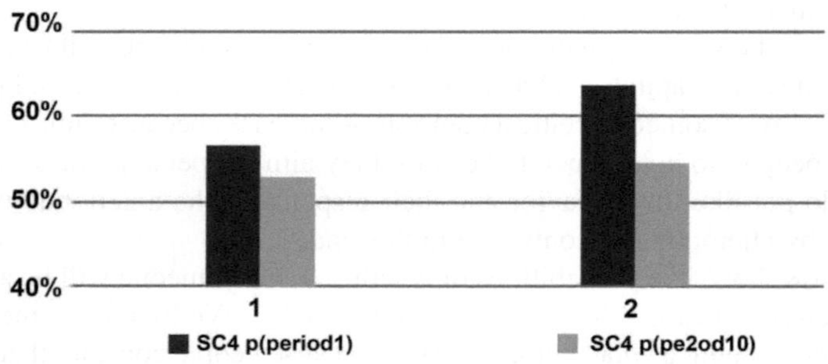

Fig. 7.10 Probability of someone being a contributor on the basis of the SC_4

try to take advantage of them and that they will be fair and just. However, as the experiment reached its end, the probability to contribute decreased by approximately 10 % (difference between period 1 and period 10).

Figure 7.10 shows the probabilities of whether or not someone will be a contributor for SC_4. We observed that during period 1, those who considered that people are helpful/useful are more likely to be contributors themselves; this probability further increased during period 10. Those who consider that people are only interested in themselves are more likely to contribute in period 10, but at a lesser extent.

An individual's expectations are not stable and change over time as new information becomes available; thus, they readjust their choices. A main finding of this experiment is that higher levels of social capital accumulation contribute to an increase in the willingness to be cooperative.

References

Barry B (1970) Sociologists, economists and democracy. Collier-MacMillan, London

Becker GS (1957) [1971 2nd ed.] The economics of discrimination. University of Chicago Press, Chicago

Collard D (1978) Altruism and economy: a study in non-selfish economics. Oxford University Press, New York

Fischbacher U (2007) Z-tree: Zurich toolbox for ready-made economic experiments. Exp Econ 10 (2):171–178

Fudenberg D, Maskin E (1986) The folk theorem in repeated games with discounting or with incomplete information. Econometrica 54(3):533–554

Gintis H, Bowles S, Boyd R, Fehr E (2006) Moral sentiments and material interests: the foundations of cooperation in economic life. MIT Press, Cambridge

Gray JA (1987) The psychology of fear and stress. Cambridge University Press, Cambridge

Harsanyi J (1969) Rational choice models of political behavior vs. functionalist and conformist theories. World Polit 21:513–538

Henrich J, Boyd R, Bowles S, Camerer C, Fehr E, Gintis H, McElreath R (2004) Overview and synthesis. In: Henrich J, Boyd R, Bowles S, Camerer C, Fehr E, Gintis H (eds) Foundations of human sociality. Oxford University Press, Oxford, pp 8–54

Kreps DM (1990) Corporate culture and economic theory. In: Alt JE, Shepsle KA (eds) Perspectives on positive political economy. Cambridge University Press, Cambridge, pp 90–143

Lane DE (1992) Management science in the control and management of fisheries: an annotated bibliography. Am J Math Manage Sci 12(2–3):101–152

Ledyard J (1995) Public goods: a survey of experimental research. In: Kagel JH, Roth AE (eds) Handbook of experimental economics. Princeton University Press, Princeton, NJ, pp 111–194

North DC (1981) Structure and change in economic history. W.W. Norton, New York

North DC (1990) Institutions, institutional change and economic performance. Cambridge University Press, Cambridge

Phelps ES (ed) (1975) Altruism, morality, and economic theory. Basic Books, New York

Taylor M (1987) The possibility of cooperation. Cambridge University Press, Cambridge

Part II

The Cultural Dimensions and the Cultural Background Change

The second part of this book describes various cultural dimensions and changes within cultural background. This investigation offers real insight into the wider concept of cultural background with reference to societal traits and the prevailing factors of cultural change.

This part contains four chapters. Chapter 8 makes reference to commonly used cultural surveys that identify the quantitative elements used for the quantitative analysis of cultural background. In contrast, cultural dimensions are analyzed in a descriptive manner. In Chap. 9 the characteristics of the cultural dimensions of collectivism versus individualism are analyzed, and the nature of power distance, uncertainty avoidance and time are analyzed in Chap. 10. Finally, Chap. 11 presents the issue of cultural background change.

8 Cultural Surveys

Measuring cultural dimensions is in itself an extremely complex task because they are based on complex behavioral description indices; hence, their quantification is extremely difficult. Despite this, their use is necessary to show the subject matter of the survey.

This chapter is structured as follows. The issue of the measurement of cultural dimensions is presented in Sect. 8.1. Section 8.2 shows the way in which the dimensions of cultural background are presented at a global level. Section 8.3 analyzes the elements of culture and the dimensions of a society's social effectiveness using the surveys of Hofstede (1980, 1991, 2001) and GLOBE (House et al. 2004). Section 8.4 portrays cultural traits according to the World Values Survey (WVS). Finally, a comparative analysis of the cultural dimensions from a geographical perspective is conducted in Sect. 8.5.

8.1 Cultural Background, Measurements and Time

There is extensive research that attempts to determine the dimensions of cultural background in human society. These studies generally have a national background, i.e., they measure a state's demonstration of culturalism using available statistical data. As of 2009, 93 papers on cross-cultural organizational behavior have been counted (Tsui et al. 2009); these studies categorized the dimensions of cultural background as follows:

- Individualism/collectivism (inter-group behavior is included)
- Independence/interdependence
- Acceptance of inequalities
- Acceptance of hierarchical structures
- Achievement of targets (investment oriented, human oriented)
- Globalized perception, conservatism
- Time orientation (preference for the present or future)
- Masculinity (imposition or sovereignty)/femininity
- Uncertainty avoidance

P.E. Petrakis, *Culture, Growth and Economic Policy*,
DOI 10.1007/978-3-642-41440-4_8, © Springer-Verlag Berlin Heidelberg 2014

- Acceptance of change
- Materialism/spiritual view

Such approaches have two fundamental drawbacks, highlighting the issue of the measurement of cultural values. A lack of consistency and cohesion in the way cultural values are measured and the use of the concept of nation (in 60 of the 93 papers) as a measurement unit and an construal variable for cultural values raise the issue of whether those approaches can be considered as independent or dependent variables. Independence in terms of variables means exogeneity regarding their system of creation. Extraneous variables may be extrinsically formed factors, i.e., without being influenced by the "system" under consideration, for example the climate or environment. Finally, dependent variables constitute the outcome of the influence exerted by other measurable characteristics.

It is clear that all variables that suggest a cultural dimension are intrinsically formed. The question that is raised, however, is to what extent are cultural dimensions and stereotypes stable at a particular time? If they have been stable, for example, for hundreds of years, then they essentially constitute extraneous variables for the current system of decisions. Despite the fact that cultural dimensions may have intrinsic origins, time is of paramount importance because there is the possibility that over a short-term period cultural dimensions and syndromes become stable; they are unchangeable with an extraneous interpretative ability. Today's generations have observed a significant and wide-ranging change in cultural values. The value of individualism appears to be appreciated more by the young than by older people who tend to adopt collective values (Ralston et al. 2006). The same trend was also observed by Georgas (1989) in his study of Greek society.

The above suggests that it is of some value to assess the use of inter-cultural data in terms of their endogeneity or exogeneity. Hence, according to Tsui et al. (2009), the following should be fulfilled:

(a) The cultural background of the group under examination must be identified to have at least one of the following features:
   (i) Distinguishable total characteristics. Such characteristics, for example, are GDP or the number of schools per 1,000 people.
   (ii) Characteristics that are common for all members of the group.
   (iii) Distinguish differentiations in cultural background among individuals in the group.

(b) It is possible to treat cultural background as a coherent sum of interlinked and presumably interdependent characteristics of the group and not as a sum of independent characteristics (Lytle et al. 1995). By fully itemizing the approximately 70 different dimensions recorded in previous studies, Lytle et al. (1995) created six wide categories: (a) the definition of concepts, (b) orientation of incentives, (c) relationship among the members of the society, (d) communication methods, (e) time orientation and stance toward change and uncertainty, and (f) the organization of social institutions.

(c) A "polycontextual" approach should be used to describe cultural background by introducing all the concepts (e.g., extraneous factors, cultural environment, and

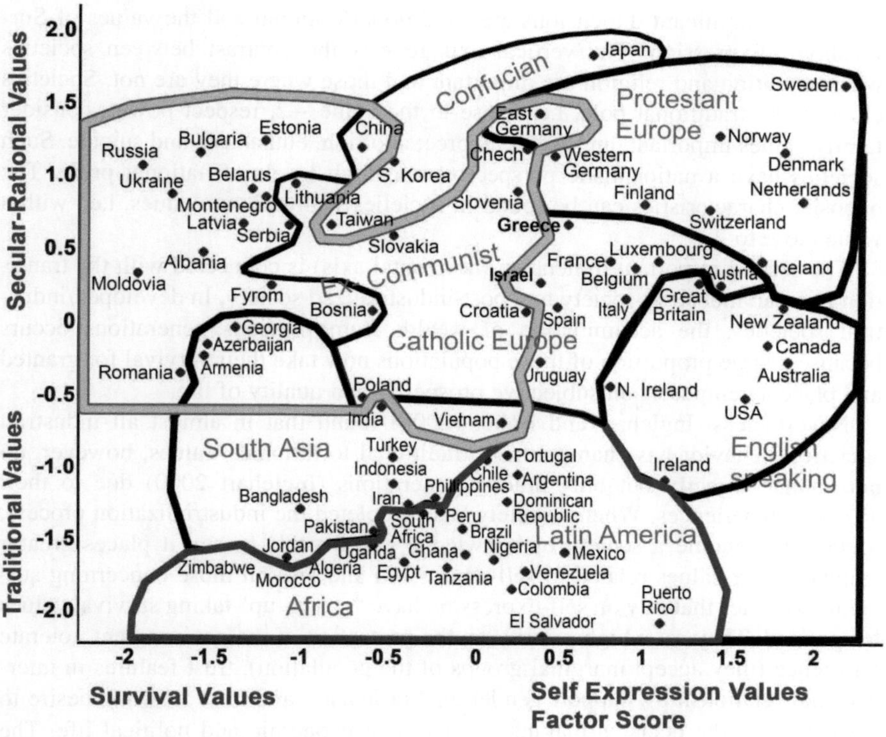

Fig. 8.1 Inglehart's map of values (2000)

social dimension) that are necessary for cultural background to be well understood.

8.2 Map of Cultural Values

Inglehart (2000), Schwartz (1994), Georgas and Berry (1995) and Georgas et al. (2004) used empirical data to design a series of variables that describe the cultural dimensions and characteristics of societies under examination. More specifically, Inglehart (2000) depicted in his map of cultural dimensions a detailed measurement of those variables relevant to human interest (religion, politics, economy and sociability).

Figure 8.1 shows that many fundamental values are connected with each other and can be depicted using just two important dimensions: degree of tradition and industrialization. It is worth noting that every country has been placed in accordance with the values of its population and not in terms of its geographical position. For instance, Australia, the United States and Great Britain are cultural neighbors because they reflect similar values, despite their actual geographical distance.

The two dominant dimensions are Traditional/Rational and the values of Survival/Self Expression. The vertical axis reflects the contrast between societies where tradition and religion are important and those where they are not. Societies close to the traditional pole, i.e., close to the value −2, respect power, consider family values important, and reject divorce, abortion, euthanasia and suicide. Such societies have a nationalistic perspective and high levels of national pride. The opposite characteristics can be found in societies with rational values, i.e., with a value close to 2.

The second important dimension (horizontal axis) is connected with the transition from an industrial society to a post-industrialized society. In developed/industrial societies, the accumulation of wealth from previous generations occurs because a large proportion of those populations now take their survival for granted and place an emphasis on subjective prosperity and quality of life.

Nevertheless, Inglehart and Baker (2000) found that in almost all industrial societies, behavior has changed from traditional to rational. Values, however, do not change directly but only among generations (Inglehart 2000) due to their different experiences. When a society has completed the industrialization process, it starts to become a society of knowledge and for this reason it places greater emphasize on values related to self-expression and less on those concerning survival. Societies that rely on self-expression have "grown-up" taking survival values for granted. They set a high priority on the protection of the environment, tolerate difference (they accept marginal groups of the population), trust features in interpersonal relationships, support gender egalitarianism, and have a strong desire to participate in the decision-making processes of economic and political life. The transition from survival values to self-expression also includes a transition from an emphasis on hard work to an emphasis on the values of imagination and tolerance in teaching and raising children. The aforementioned characteristics of societies are of vital importance in the smooth operation of democracy.

In his theory of cultural values, Schwartz (1994) sought to determine a relationship between culture and important social phenomena. He was able to identify cultural values in his attempt to compare cultures and to provide answers to various problems faced by all societies.

The first issue concerns the relationship between the individual and the group, i.e., autonomy or embeddedness. In cultures characterized by autonomy, individuals are treated as autonomous entities; they cultivate and express their own preferences, emotions, ideas and skills. There are two types of autonomy: spiritual autonomy, which includes breadth of mind and creativity, and emotional autonomy, which includes joy and diversiform life. In cultures that emphasize embeddedness, the meaning of life is derived, to a great extent, from social relationships. Individuals have common goals and a common way of life, and they avoid any activity that might harm the group's unity. The fundamental values are obedience, safety, prudence and the respect of the group's traditions.

The second social problem concerns ensuring responsible behavior to maintain the social network and the extent to which individuals behave with egalitarianism or on the basis of hierarchy in the structure of society. Society members that function on the basis of egalitarianism treat other members as equals and respect their particular characteristics. In such societies, the fundamental values are equality, social justice, responsibility and honesty. In contrast, hierarchical societies use hierarchical systems that are characterized by inequality in the allocation of power and roles. In addition, individuals are expected to comply with the obligations and rules governing their roles. Values such as social power, power, humbleness and wealth are important to societies with a hierarchical structure.

The third social problem concerns the behavior of societies toward humans and nature. Hence, there are societies that rely on harmony and those that rely on mastery. In the first case, the fundamental values are peace, a relationship with nature, respect toward the environment and its protection and respect toward foreign property. In the second, aggressive behaviors are encouraged for their members to prevail over other members and gain control. Individuals in this society attempt to change their natural and social environment to achieve personal goals. The fundamental values are ambition, daring, success, competition and egoism.

Using seven cultural variables and multi-dimensional measurements, Schwartz (1994) designed Fig. 8.2 with an axis for each variable—they point in the direction of their greatest value. This particular two-dimensional figure shows the scores of all societies with regard to the embeddedness variable. By drawing a vertical line from any society toward the embeddedness axis, the position (score) of this society is revealed in relations to other societies.

Small arrows show other cultural variables and suggest the direction of their axes. The extensions of all seven axes coincide at the center of the figure. For example, Sweden (top left) emphasizes harmony, egalitarianism and intellectual autonomy, but not affective autonomy. Furthermore, a very low emphasis is placed on embeddedness, hierarchy and mastery. The opposite applies to Zimbabwe (bottom right), where hierarchy, mastery and embeddedness are important, affective autonomy is of moderate importance, and harmony, egalitarianism and intellectual autonomy have very little cultural standing.

Schwartz (1994) also grouped the societies under consideration into eight cultural areas, as depicted below (Fig. 8.3); his groupings are very similar to those in Inglehart's (2000) map. Most of these groups reflect some geographic relation. Hence, one can see cultural groups that are related in terms of geographic proximity and, as a result, certain similarities are clear. These similarities stem from either the effusion of values, norms and practices beyond the countries" borders, or via shared religion, history and growth level.

Thus, cultural profiles for the following regions have been created using Schwartz's (1994) groupings:

1. Western Europe: This grouping shows that Western Europe favors equality, autonomy and harmony more than any other region. It has low levels of hierarchy, mastery and embeddedness. These characteristics constitute an appropriate cultural profile for a democratic society, which aims at a good life for citizens and cares about the environment (Ester et al. 1994). Nevertheless, there are significant differences among Western European countries regarding affective autonomy.

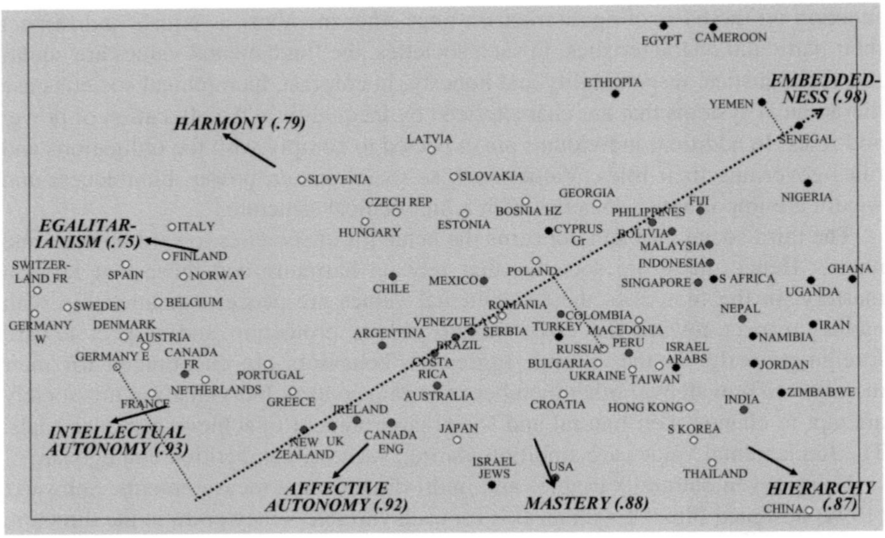

Fig. 8.2 Schwartz's (1994) map of values

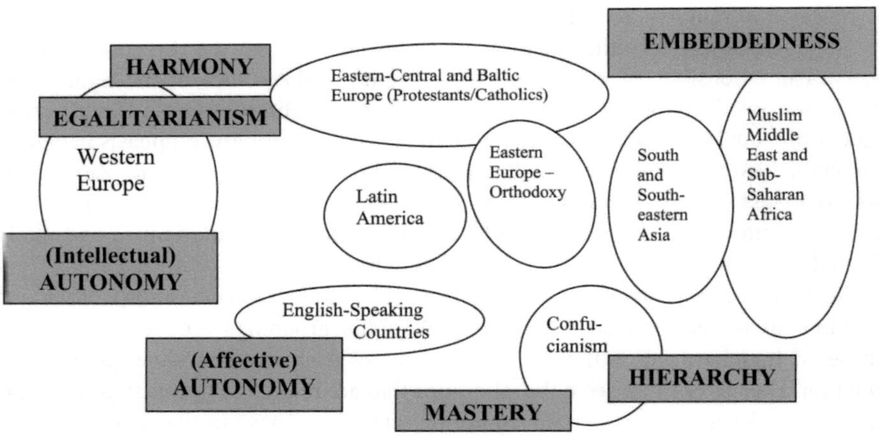

Fig. 8.3 Schwartz's (1994) grouping

2. English-Speaking Countries: The culture of the English-speaking region is particularly rich in mastery and affective autonomy. This profile encourages entrepreneurship and the exploitation of social and natural environments.
3. Confucianism (East Asia): This region stresses mastery, and is thus entrepreneurship-oriented, which is accompanied by hierarchy and the rejection of egalitarianism. This region also emphasizes embeddedness. Within this region there are differences in intellectual autonomy, especially for Japan and Singapore.

4. Muslim Middle East and Sub-Saharan Africa: This region stresses mastery rather than harmony. Changes to and the exploitation of the environment are encouraged, possibly as means to reduce poverty. Furthermore, embeddedness and group solidarity are dominant features.
5. South and Southeast Asia: Culture in this region highly values hierarchy and embeddedness, and thus the individual's obligations are fulfilled in a hierarchical system by abiding by the rules and traditions of the group.
6. Eastern Europe (Central and Baltic Orthodoxy): Harmony is stressed in this region, with no emphasis on mastery. Culture reflects the consequences of adaptations in life, within the framework of communist regimes (Schwartz and Bardi 1996; Schwartz and Bardi 1997; Schwartz et al. 2000). An emphasis is placed on harmony, as opposed to mastery, which is the result of the awareness that many problems are avoided in this manner.
7. Latin America: This region appears to be in all three dimensions. The greatest differences within the region can be seen in mastery and harmony. The culture of Latin America has been described as a culture of collectivists and collectivism prevails (Triandis 1995). This true compared with Western Europe (it has higher hierarchy and embeddedness compared with Western Europe) but not when compared with North Asia or Africa.

According to Schwartz's (1994) research, economic growth promotes autonomy and egalitarianism and restrains hierarchy and embeddedness. Furthermore, he determined the manner in which culture influences economic growth. Hierarchy and embeddedness stifle incentives and the creativity of individuals, thus restraining society's potential for further growth. Furthermore, the role of culture is important given that it also leads to ideology, which is chosen whether or not the economic system is competitive. As far as the relationship between culture and the dominant political system is concerned, autonomy and egalitarianism are positively associated with democracy, contrary to embeddedness and hierarchy. Moreover, culture influences and is influenced by family size. Autonomy and egalitarianism are supported by smaller families as each family member is more able to develop their own skills and interests, and women are encouraged to undertake greater constructive roles. Schwartz (1994) also found that societies with low-scoring embeddedness and egalitarianism variables were more likely to have investments at an international level. Finally, the analysis showed that harmony encourages foreign investments.

In his research, Hofstede (1980, 1991, 2001) suggested four cultural dimensions, stating that these describe the fundamental problems of humanity. The four dimensions (explained in more detail below) are as follows: power distance (i.e., the acceptance of inequalities), uncertainty avoidance, individualism/collectivism and masculinity/femininity.

Georgas and Berry (1995) attempted to identify similarities and differences in data concerning psychology and relating to the ecological and social characteristics of particular population groups, as well as the entire population. The results of that study have significant value in that they:

(a) Offer assistance toward the more cautious categorization of nations, based on their cultural characteristics.
(b) Assist in the comparison of economic and sociological variables with cultural psychology variables.
(c) Lead toward the measurement and forecast of the impact of psychology on various civilizations.

Georgas et al. (2004) later expanded the aforementioned study by including psychology variables. Their aim was to study the relationship among categorized countries based on ecological, sociopolitical and psychological variables.

The studies described above show that the combined influence of wealth and religion predict psychological variables at a cross-cultural level. Nevertheless, contrary to the results of the study by Inglehart and Baker (2000), religion was found to be more powerful than wealth. It is possible for the two dimensions to have opposite results. For instance, as far as most religions are concerned, the greater the number of followers a religion has, the greater the emphasis on interpersonal relationships, such as power distance, uncertainty avoidance and hierarchy. In contrast, the more wealth that is created, the greater the emphasis on personal values, such as individualism and the continuous improvement of the quality of life.

8.3 Elements of Culturalism According to Hofstede and GLOBE

Cultural dimensions concern the fundamental problems of humanity faced by every society (Hofstede 1980). Hence, "the different performance each country has in every dimension proves that different societies confront such problems in a different manner" (Hofstede 1980). In his research, Hofstede (1980, 1991, 2001) filled an important gap in the field of comparative transnational research on values by presenting the characteristics of values that could be used to measure a society's cultural background.

Hofstede (1980) initially suggested four cultural dimensions (Table 8.1) based on two studies conducted in the 1970s. These studies were carried out among employees of the US multinational company IBM and its branches around the world. The research involved the gathering of 116,000 questionnaires spanning 50 different professions and 66 different nationalities between 1970 and 1973. It is worth mentioning that despite the homogeneity due to the corporate culture of a multinational company, there were significant differences in the values of employees from different countries. Furthermore, what was surprising was that the IBM subsidiaries had not adapted to the values and culture of the parent company but instead continued to reproduce local values.

Hofstede later added a fifth dimension of culture "Confucian dynamism (long-term versus short-term orientation)" (Hofstede 1991) (Table 8.1), based on research by Michael Bond who carried out international research on students, and Chinese employees and administrative staff in 23 countries. In 2010 Hofstede presented a

Table 8.1 The dimensions of social culturalism according to Hofstede

1. Power distance (acceptance of inequalities)
2. Uncertainty avoidance
3. Individualism/collectivism
4. Masculinity/femininity
5. Long-term orientation
6. Indulgence/restraint

sixth dimension "indulgence/restraint" (Hofstede et al. 2010) based on an analysis by Michael Minkov using the WVS applied in 93 countries.

Hofstede's (1980) Power Distance Index measures the degree to which less powerful members in a society accept the unequal distribution of power among society members. Inequality can exist in relation to wealth, social status, laws and principles, abilities (spiritual and physical) or prestige. Such inequality is reflected in both the values of the less powerful members of society and in the values of the more powerful ones. It is cultivated through fundamental relationships of early socialization, such as those of parent/child or teacher/pupil. Certain national cultures are characterized by great inequality, greater tolerance of the accumulation of power in the hands of a small and permanent elite, centralized organizations with high hierarchical pyramids and limited communication from the bottom to the top. In contrast, other cultures are characterized by less inequality, greater social mobility, less accumulation of power in the hands of a few, decentralized organizations with flatter hierarchies and relatively free upwards communication.

The Uncertainty Avoidance Index (UAI) constitutes the second dimension of cultural background. Uncertainty constitutes a significant factor in people's lives. Since ancient times, individuals have faced a multitude of unexpected situations, which they could not predict (e.g., forces of nature, the economy, political instability and death and disease). In their attempt to shelter against uncertainty, individuals have developed technology and laws, and at the same time they have followed religion. Technology protects us against uncertainties stemming from nature, legislation against uncertainties due to human behavior and religion attempts to interpret anything that cannot be understood by the human mind.

The "uncertainty avoidance" dimension refers to the lack of tolerance shown by society toward uncertainty and doubt. This lack is expressed by means of high levels of concern regarding the future and the release of higher amounts of energy, a greater need for formal rules and absolute truth and less tolerance toward people or groups with ideas and behaviors that deviate from the norm. More active cultures tend to apply greater specialization, formalism and standardization and assign a greater value to uniformity than to divergent ideas. They are characterized by bureaucracy and moderate resistance to change. Furthermore, they avoid high-risk decisions. In contrast, less active cultures assign less importance to formal rules and specialization, are not interested in uniformity and are tolerant toward a wider range of ideas and behaviors. A lack of formalism allows for a quick response and adaptation to change. Finally, such societies assume the risk of temporary decisions with greater ease.

The classification of countries as having a high or low UAI depends to a great extent on the structure of society and whether or not its members are willing to live with uncertainty. Hence, this is how cultural background emerges to shape the aforementioned behaviors. Societies with a low aversion to uncertainty are dominated by feelings of happiness, have low stress levels, students are taught about the significance of personal achievements, there is professional stability, and there is an assumption of initiatives and entrepreneurial plans. In contrast, a high aversion to uncertainty is accompanied by high labor stress, a lack of joy and professional insecurity and contrariety against anything new and different. Finally, in low UAI societies the existence of incentives for success, in conjunction with entrepreneurship, lead to economic growth; this does not appear to happen in high UAI societies.

The "individualism/collectivism" dimension describes the relationship between the individual and the group or society as a whole. It shows the degree to which individuals within a country learn to act more as individuals rather than as members of a group. In countries where collectivism prevails, a greater emphasis is placed on social, friendship or kinship ties. People have a group mindset and look after the benefit of the group, many times suppressing their personal achievements for the interests of the group. Group members show elements of interdependence and believe that maintaining the group's prosperity is the best guarantee for their personal prosperity. In contrast, in individualistic societies, ties among members are loose and people are mainly interested in their own private interests. Personal achievements and freedom are of utmost importance. People are self-sufficient and do not feel the need to rely on others. They consider their personality as a separate entity and give priority to the fulfillment of their own personal goals instead of the goals of the group.

Special reference should be made to the institution of family with regard to the individualism/collectivism dimension. Family constitutes the first group to which individuals are integrated in from the moment of their birth. It is the source of the first elements that shape their cultural background. The institution of family constitutes a factor of paramount importance in shaping teamwork in a society. There are families whose members have strong ties with one another, function like a group and are not comprised merely of parents and children, but also include members of the wider family group, such as uncles, aunts, grandmothers, grandfathers, cousins and even neighbors. In this situation, children learn to think and function in terms of "we", as a group, in all aspects of their lives. In contrast, there are societies in which individualism prevails over the interests of the family and, in general, the group in which the individual belongs.

The difference between "masculinity/femininity" mainly concerns the degree to which masculine values, such as good performance, success and competition prevail over feminine values, such as the quality of life, maintaining close personal relationships, service, taking care of the vulnerable and solidarity. A further characteristic of this particular dimension is whether or not there are inequalities between the two genders and elements of imposition of the strong over the weak.

Family in a masculine society drives children toward ambition and competition by imposing different roles to men and women. The role of the father is visibly distinguishable and constitutes a model for children. There are deviations between boys and girls even in education. Performance and good grades are ends in themselves. A possible failure is considered a disaster, and society rewards high-achieving pupils. Society is interested in results and rewards according to performance. Employment plays a dominant role in an individual's life and therefore is characterized by higher labor stress.

In contrast, feminine societies emphasize social relationships and mutual help, stances that may be reflected in governmental policies that favor income redistribution and a high level of social expenditure. At the center of attention are people, by giving priority to the establishment of strong foundations for cooperation. In addition, it is difficult to identify differences in the values men and women believe in, and teamwork in decision-making constitutes their fundamental characteristic. With regard to the education system, schooling is a springboard for the socialization of children, supplying them with values and knowledge. Tutors do not discriminate between good and bad pupils, boys and girls, but treat them all in the same manner. Finally, compared with masculine societies, feminine societies tend to spend more resources on the protection of the environment and make use of new technologies that are environmentally friendly.

In their research, Hofstede (1980) determined a fifth dimension while attempting to explain differences in thinking between societies in the West and East, which they named "Confucian Dynamism" or subsequently "Time Orientation". This dimension distinguishes short-term oriented cultures from long-term oriented ones.

A long-term orientation (LTO) entails persistence, the classification of relationships according to social status and compliance with such order, financial saving and the feeling of shame. More specifically, emphasis is given to the proper education of children by their family. From an early age, children learn not to be extravagant and to be patient with regard to their wants. Austerity leads to an increase in saving and the availability of capital for investments. Entrepreneurship is oriented toward the establishment of businesses in the market. Hence, businesses do not expect immediate results but are patient in their planning. A short-term orientation (STO) relates to personal stability, the protection of pride, respect for tradition and the exchange of greetings, grace (favor) and gifts.

In contrast with LTO, STO cultures are dominated by a lack of patience, seek quick profits and make myopic decisions. Nepotism is often seen in management. Children learn to be loyal to tradition, follow social trends and to enjoy spare time. Finally, a fundamental characteristic is also a reluctance to save, which is connected to low growth rates.

In their attempt to describe the concept of cultural background more effectively, Hofstede et al. (2010) included a new dimension in their latest study, i.e., "indulgence/restraint". Indulgence mirrors societies that are flexible in terms of the individual's freedom and allow for the fulfillment of human needs by means of enjoying life and having fun. In contrast, societies that restrain human expression limit the individual's expression through strict social rules.

The fundamental characteristics of societies with high indulgence scores are individuals' happiness, the value of spare time, high degree of positive feelings, extroversion and ambitiousness, and low rates of cardiovascular disease. In contrast, societies with high restraint scores have low degrees of happiness, do not value spare time, have moral barriers, are distant, dominated by pessimism and cynicism and have high rates of cardiovascular disease.

A more recent and equally important study is GLOBE (Global Leadership and Organizational Effectiveness), which is complementary to the cultural dimensions of Hofstede. The research titled "Culture, Leadership and Organization—The GLOBE study of 62 societies" was published based on the results of approximately 17,300 middle managers from 951 organizations in the food, financial, telecommunication and industrial sectors. GLOBE examined interactions among societal culture, organizational culture and organizational leadership. The theoretical basis of GLOBE is the integration of presumptive organizational leadership (Lord and Maher 1991), the theory of cultural values (Hofstede 1980) and the theory of incentives (McClelland 1985).

This research defined nine dimensions (Table 8.2) of culture, which reflect both the perceptions of the middle managers on the current situation of society and their preferences regarding the desired situation. In this manner, similarities or differences in standards, values, beliefs and practices among societies were identified. On this basis, nine dimensions emerged: power distance, uncertainty avoidance, institutional collectivism (collectivism I), in-group collectivism (collectivism II), gender egalitarianism, assertiveness, future orientation, performance orientation, humane orientation.

The surveys conducted by Hofstede and GLOBE share some cultural dimensions. For this reason, we only present those identified by GLOBE.

Institutional collectivism reflects the degree to which the business practices of organizations or societies encourage and reward collective action and the collective distribution of the resources of their members. This dimension is particularly high in Asian cultures that practice Confucianism and in societies whose members enjoy a high degree of unification.

In-Group collectivism reflects the degree to which the members of a society express loyalty and belief in the institution of family or in the organization to which they belong. This relates to low divorce rates because the concept of family is important.

Gender egalitarianism is the degree to which an organization or society minimizes gender-related discriminations by promoting equality. An example of calculating such a variable is the number of females with income and access to various resources. "Societies, which are far from discriminating men and women, are less compared to those which do so, but societies in favor of egalitarianism existed in every region of the world" (Coltrane 1992). A common reason for differentiation among societies is the extent to which they assign different roles to men and women (Hofstede 1980).

Assertiveness is one of the most important factors of a society's culture; however, few researchers have addressed how it differentiates various cultures. Many

Table 8.2 The cultural dimensions identified by GLOBE

1. Power distance
2. Uncertainty avoidance
3. Institutional collectivism (Collectivism I)
4. In-group collectivism (collectivism II)
5. Gender egalitarianism
6. Assertiveness
7. Future orientation
8. Performance orientation
9. Humane orientation

studies compare of the concept of dynamism with aggressive and assertion, whereas GLOBE (2004) also compared it with the masculinity/femininity variable used by Hofstede (1980). The comparison showed that the two variables significantly differ.

Performance orientation constitutes a very important dimension shaping the cultural background of every society. It is the degree to which a society encourages and rewards its members to improve their performance and supremacy. Its importance can be seen in the way in which society handles the challenges that stem from the external environment.

Humane orientation refers to the degree to which individuals of a society encourage and reward other individuals for their fairness, veraciousness, friendliness, generosity, care and politeness. Behaviors that are of a high level of humane orientation include care, respect and assistance toward others. Low humane orientation behaviors are characterized by a lack of respect and the promotion of self-interest.

8.4 Cultural Traits According to the World Values Survey

The WVS offers a series of variables that can be used to identify cross-cultural differences among societies. For this purpose and on the basis of the last measurements of the WVS (4th wave, 2005–2008), we created three cultural dimensions, which reflect the fundamental aspects of cultural background.

Based on Lane and Ersson (2005), we used the following three values in our analysis:

(a) Individualism: An individualistic attitude may be defined as the difference between the variables "people should take more responsibility" and the sum of "competition is harmful" and "hard work does not generally bring success". Higher percentages suggest greater individualism.
(b) Postmaterialism: Postmaterialism orientation is based on Inglehart's post-materialist four-item index.
(c) Interpersonal Trust: Interpersonal trust is measured as the percentage of people who positively answered the question "Generally speaking, would you say that most people can be trusted or that you cannot be too careful when dealing with

people?" The greater the number of positive answers, the higher the level of generalized trust toward society.

The postmaterialism theory is based on a set of assumptions with regard to changing values in advanced societies. The first assumption, the scarcity hypothesis, states that people move to new concerns once the previous ones have been resolved. The second assumption, the socialization hypothesis, concerns an individual's socialization and the change in the hierarchization of values when an individual enters adolescence (Inglehart 1990). Finally, the third assumption, the silent revolution assumption, states that after World War II a change occurred between the hierarchization of values of older and younger generations. In many of his surveys, Inglehart (1977, 1990, 1997) attempted to define a postmaterialism dimension. The following values (from the WVS) can be used to define postmaterialism: more say at jobs, more human society, more say in government, ideas count more than money, protecting freedom of speech, making cities more beautiful, strong defence forces, fighting rising process, fighting against crime, high level of economic growth, maintaining order in the nation, a stable economy.

Apart from the fundamental value shaping human relationships, the contribution of trust in every society also presents crucial social and economic aspects (Tocqueville 1990; Almond and Verba 1965, 1989). Interpersonal trust (social capital) tends to create cohesion bonds among the members of a society by stabilizing society and the democratic regime. At an economic level, trust is positively correlated with economic growth (Fukuyama 1995; Putnam 2000). High-trust nations tend to decrease transaction costs, promote economic efficiency, offer incentives for large-scale investments and, ultimately, boost economic development.

Table 8.3 presents cultural dimensions based on WVS data. As with measurements by Hofstede and GLOBE, North European countries achieve better results compared with those of other country groups regarding the issue of cultural values. High degrees of individualism in North European countries promote the achievement of the individual goals of society's members by rewarding individual initiative. It is not by chance that countries with high per capita income also have higher individualism rates. Arab counties also have high individualism rates, whereas North European countries have lower rates.

Regarding postmaterialism, developed countries have higher scores compared with other countries because these values can be found in a greater extent in societies that have higher standards of living and have resolved issues concerning basic needs.

Finally, as far as levels of trust toward society are concerned, the Arab world and Mediterranean countries have the lowest rates. Interpersonal trust among society members and trust toward institutions (government, political parties, police etc.) are particularly low. This results in the development of a suspicious and uncertain climate in society, which discourages entrepreneurial activity.

On the basis of the aforementioned analysis, it is clear that there are different cultural models in the groups of countries under examination, with a clear distinction between that of North European countries and the others. North European

Table 8.3 WVS (4th Wave, 2005–2008) weighted average results for country groups (According to Population)

	Individualism	Postmaterialism	Trust
Mediterranean countries	**69.41 %**	**15.16 %**	**16.95 %**
Italy	77.80 %	19.30 %	29.20 %
Spain	67.30 %	11.90 %	20.00 %
Turkey	63.80 %	13.80 %	4.90 %
Northern European countries	**86.58 %**	**18.57 %**	**54.27 %**
Finland	88.20 %	11.60 %	58.90 %
The Netherlands	84.80 %	17.30 %	45.00 %
Sweden	88.80 %	24.80 %	68.00 %
Southeast Europe	**56.72 %**	**4.35 %**	**24.81 %**
Hungary	60.00 %	25.80 %	28.40 %
Poland	59.20 %	7.30 %	19.00 %
Russia	55.70 %	1.90 %	26.20 %
Slovenia	66.20 %	15.20 %	18.10 %
Arab world	**72.24 %**	**6.78 %**	**11.32 %**
Iran	77.10 %	6.90 %	10.60 %
Morocco	60.90 %	6.50 %	13.00 %

Source: WVS (4th wave) and own calculations

countries are more oriented toward values that concern individuals and their personal goals, and interpersonal trust and trust toward institutions constitutes a distinctive feature of such societies. In contrast, there are clear differences observed in the other groups, where the value of individual achievements is less esteemed, and rules governing the functioning of the society are not valued.

8.5 Comparative Analysis of Cultural Dimensions

The quantification of cultural dimensions enables us to make cross-regional comparisons and form an image of the differences between not just countries but entire regions. We chose to compare the countries of Mediterranean Europe (Spain, Italy, Portugal, Greece and Turkey), Northern Europe (Denmark, the Netherlands, Sweden and Finland), Southeast Europe (Poland, Russia, Hungary and Slovenia), certain Arabian countries (Iran and Morocco) and the United States. Tables 8.4 and 8.5 show the weighted results and the ranking of the country groups by Hofstede and GLOBE, respectively, for each cultural dimension based on population.

The cultural model of the Mediterranean countries is dominated by high levels of acceptance of inequalities, with uncertainty aversion influencing their choices. With regard to individualism, Mediterranean countries tend to be characterized by moderate levels of individualistic behavior. The same applies to masculinity. Future orientation places Mediterranean countries in a middle ranking, and they show a preference for indulgence values.

Table 8.4 Hofstede weighted results and ranking for the groups of countries (according to their population)

Dimensions/Groups of Countries	Mediterranean	North-European	South-Eastern Europe	Arab	United Stated
Power distance (acceptance of inequalities)	58.5 (32–51)	32.5 (63–74)	85.7 (6–55)	58.6 (22–75)	40 (53)
Uncertainty avoidance	84.8 (1–33)	43.3 (50–74)	93.8 (7–26)	62.6 (28–50)	46 (56)
Individualism	51.6 (9–51)	74.3 (4–22)	45.2 (4–51)	43.0 (30–38)	91 (1)
Masculinity	52.0 (7–65)	30.7 (6–73)	44.1 (3–70)	45.9 (31–47)	62 (17)
Future Orientation	50.0 (28–48)	54.4 (22–57)	70.0 (10–51)	15.4 (51–85)	28 (68)
Indulgence/Restraint	41.1 (37–66)	69.2 (8–27)	22.6 (39–77)	33.7 (52–74)	68 (24)

Notes: (a) The number in parentheses corresponds to the ranking of each country among the 93 countries in the research
(b) Higher scores suggest higher variables (no variable is in descending order)

Table 8.5 GLOBE weighted average results and ranking for the groups of countries (According to Population)

Dimensions/Groups of Countries	Mediterranean	North-European	South-Eastern Europe	Arab	United States
Institutional collectivism	3.83 (43–61)	4.73 (1–23)	4.45 (17–60)	3.91 (22–50)	4.2 (34)
In-Group collectivism	5.43 (5–41)	3.72 (54–61)	5.59 (19–37)	5.91 (3–44)	4.25 (53)
Gender egalitarianism	3.10 (14–56)	3.63 (5–31)	4.06 (1–4)	2.96 (41–58)	3.34 (32)
Performance orientation	3.74 (37–61)	4.08 (19–48)	3.49 (43–59)	4.39 (7–38)	4.49 (12)
Humane orientation	3.67 (37–60)	4.02 (14–43)	3.84 (38–58)	4.21 (23–30)	4.17 (28)

Notes: (a) Numbers in parentheses correspond to the ranking of each society among the 62 societies
(b) Numbers concern practices, i.e., the score depicts the current situation of that society
(c) Higher scores suggest higher variables, with the exception of "Gender egalitarianism", which is in descending order (lower scores suggest higher dominance by males)

North European countries have an extremely different cultural background because they tend not to accept social and economic inequalities. At the same time they have low levels of risk and uncertainty aversion, accompanied by a strong level of individualism. They are also dominated by more feminine values, and future orientation has a particularly important place in their map of values. Finally, they appear to enjoy life.

Countries in the Southeast Europe group have a strong acceptance of inequalities, with uncertainty aversion dominating every aspect of their economic and political life. Individualism is particularly low, with collective action and team spirit being prevalent. Masculine values do not seem to prevail for members of those societies. Future orientation is particularly high, and they have particular restraint.

Arab countries have a high level of power distance. This is verified by the diachronic existence of inequalities in societies in the Arab world. Uncertainty avoidance is at relatively high levels, and collectivism, as a form of society organization, overrides individualism. Masculine values are dominant, with a distinctive example being the role of men in society as opposed to that of women. A lack of long-term planning is reflected in the dimension of future orientation. Finally, indulgence is outside the network of values in Arabic societies.

As a wider geographical region, the United States, just like North European countries, does not accept inequalities. Its stance toward risk and uncertainty is positive, which is mirrored in high levels of entrepreneurial endeavors. A fundamental distinctive feature of US society is the dimension of individualism, because personal success and the achievement of individual priorities have the highest ranking in the pyramid of values. Masculine values are high, compared with other developed societies, and future orientation is particularly low. Finally, the United States, like North European countries, likes to enjoy life.

According to GLOBE and regarding issues concerning the acceptance of inequalities, Mediterranean countries scored the lowest, followed by the Arab world and Southeast European countries, which are characterized by extensive social inequalities and a permanent concentration of power in the hands of just small percentage of the population (Table 8.5).

In Mediterranean countries, the value of individual achievements is low, followed by those countries in the Arab world. In contrast, the United States and North European countries place significant emphasis on individual success. At the same time, the organizational and socially established norms in all groups under examination are not widely valued, with the exception of North European countries. Nevertheless, individuals show pride, faith and cohesion with their families and any organizations in which they belong. Feminine values, such as quality of life, looking after the vulnerable and solidarity, play a small role and constitute a distinctive feature of North European countries. Hence, assertiveness and controversy are not dominant.

All country groups showed no value for future orientation, with short-term perceptions being dominant and with limited use of programming and long-term planning. The exception to this rule is once again the North European group. Furthermore, there is also low performance orientation and low humane orientation, with the exception of North European countries and the United States.

Compared with Mediterranean countries, Southeast European countries seem to have less faith in the institution of family and in the group in which they belong. In contrast, they accept the significance of gender egalitarianism to ensure the smooth operation of society. Nevertheless, feminine values, such as social allowances, protection of the environment and solidarity, play just small roles, and authoritarianism and competitiveness place Southeast Europe in first place regarding assertiveness. A lack of future orientation and decision-making that are focused on present generations and less so on future generations constitute distinctive features of both Mediterranean and Southeast European countries, with the former having a slightly better performance. Nonetheless, there are also similarities in the other two dimensions of social culturalism, where both Mediterranean and Southeast European countries have low scores for performance and humane orientation.

The value of family is at the top of the hierarchy in Arab societies, and collective action and harmonious relationships among the group are also encouraged. In addition, Arab countries are dominated by men, with women having a limited role in society. Men are the family decision makers, whereas the role of women is limited to the day-to-day needs of family life. Feminine values play a limited role in Arab societies, and its members do not have authoritarian tendencies and are not aggressive in their social relationships with other members (compared with Mediterranean countries). Finally, they encourage and reward their members, thus enabling them to improve and progress, and values of solidarity, generosity, respect toward others, hospitality and politeness are common in the Arab world.

References

Almond GA, Verba S (1965) The civic culture: political attitudes and democracy in five nations. Little, Brown and Company, Boston, MA

Almond GA, Verba S (eds) (1989) The civic culture revisited. Sage, Beverly Hills, CA

Coltrane S (1992) The micro-politics of gender in non-industrial societies. Gend Soc 6:86–107

Ester P, Halman L, Seuren B (1994) Environmental concern and offering willingness in Europe and North America. In: Ester P, Halman L, Tilburg R (eds) The individualizing society: value change in Europe and North America. Tilburg University Press, The Netherlands

Fukuyama F (1995) Trust: the social virtues and the creation of prosperity. The Free Press, New York, NY

Georgas J (1989) Changing family values in Greece: from collectivist to individualist. J Cross Cult Psychol 20:80–91

Georgas J, Berry JW (1995) An ecocultural taxonomy for cross-cultural psychology. J Cross Cult Res 29:121–157

Georgas J, Vijver FJR, Berry JW (2004) The ecocultural framework, ecosocial indices and psychological variables in cross cultural research. J Cross Cult Res 35:74–96

Hofstede G (1980) Culture's consequences: international differences in work-related values. Sage, Beverly Hills, CA

Hofstede G (1991) Cultures and organisations. Harper Collins Business, London

Hofstede G (2001) Culture's consequences – comparing values, behaviors, institutions and organisations across nations, 2nd edn. Sage, London

Hofstede G, Hofstede JG, Minkov M (2010) Cultures and organizations-intercultural cooperation and its importance for survival, 3rd edn. Mc Graw Hill, New York, NY

House RJ, Hanges PJ, Javidan M, Dorfman PW, Gupta V (2004) Culture, leadership and organisations – the GLOBE study of 62 societies. Sage, Thousand Oaks, CA

Inglehart R (1977) The silent revolution: changing values and political styles among western publics. Princeton University Press, Princeton, NJ

Inglehart R (1990) Culture shift in advanced industrial society. Princeton University Press, Princeton, NJ
Inglehart R (1997) Modernization and postmodernazation: changing values and political styles in advanced industrial society. Princeton University Press, Princeton, NJ
Inglehart R (2000) Globalization and postmodern values. Wash Q Winter:215–228, MIT Press
Inglehart R, Baker WE (2000) Modernization, cultural change and the persistence of traditional values. Am Sociol Rev 65:19–51
Lane JE, Ersson S (2005) Culture and politics, a comparative approach. Ashgate, Burlington, MA
Lord RG, Maher KJ (1991) Leadership and information processing: linking perceptions and performance. Unwin Hyman, Boston, MA
Lytle AL, Brett JE, Barsness ZI, Tinsley CH, Janssens M (1995) A paradigm for confirmatory cross-cultural research in organizational behaviour. In: Staw BM, Cummings LL (eds) Research in organizational behaviour. JAI, Greenwich, pp 167–214
McClelland DC (1985) Human motivation. Cambridge University Press, New York, NY
Minkov M, Blagoev V (2009) Cultural values predict subsequent economic growth. Int J Cross Cult Manage 9(1):5–24
Putnam RD (2000) Bowling alone: the collapse and revival of American community. Simon and Schuster, New York, NY
Ralston DA, Terpstra-Tong J, Terpstra RH, Wang X, Egri C (2006) Today's State-owned enterprises of China: are they dying dinosaurs or dynamic dynamos? Strat Manag J 27 (9):825–843
Schwartz SH (1994) Beyond individualism/collectivism: new cultural dimensions of values. In: Kim U, Triantis HC, Kagitcibasi C, Choi SC, Yoon G (eds) Individualism and collectivism. Sage, Thousand Oaks, CA
Schwartz SH, Bardi A (1996) Relations among sociopolitical values in Eastern Europe: effects of the communist experience? Polit Psychol 17:525–550
Schwartz SH, Bardi A (1997) Influences of adaptation to communist rule on value priorities in Eastern Europe. Polit Psychol 18:385–410
Schwartz SH, Bardi A, Bianchi G (2000) Value adaptation to the imposition and collapse of communist regimes in Eastern Europe. In: Renshon SA, Duckitt J (eds) Political psychology: cultural and cross cultural perspectives. Macmillan, London
Tocqueville A (1990) Democracy in America I and II. Vintage, New York, NY
Triandis HC (1995) Individualism and collectivism. Westview, Boulder, CO
Trommsdorf G (1983) Value change in Japan. Int J Intercult Relat 7:337–360
Tsui SA, Sushil SN, Amy Yi O (2009) Nagging problems and modest solutions in cross-cultural research: illustrations from organizational behaviour literature. In: Wyer RS, Chiu CY, Hong YY (eds) Understanding culture: theory, research and application. Psychology press, New York, NY, pp 163–188

9 Collectivism as an Aid or Obstacle to Economic Growth

The present chapter analyzes a cultural dimension of particular importance, which concerns the extent that individualism and collectivism characterize every society. Collectivism can primarily be defined as a social stereotype comprising strong cohesive ties among individuals that consider themselves members of one or more groups (e.g., family, race and nation). Individuals act on the basis of the group's norms and give priority to group goals over their own. Individualism, on the other hand, can be defined as a social stereotype in which individuals consider themselves as independent entities. These particular individuals act primarily on the basis of their own preferences, needs and goals, and the only incentive to enter into social relationships is for their own personal benefit.

Section 9.1 presents the concepts of individualism and collectivism in social sciences. Section 9.2 makes reference to the factors that shape individualism and collectivism. Section 9.3 refers to the characteristics of collectivism, and Sect. 9.4 describes those of individualism. Section 9.5 comments on individualism and collectivism and their relationships with growth. Finally, Sect. 9.6 introduces the concept of collectivism that can either hinder or advance economic growth.

9.1 Individualism and Collectivism in Social Sciences

The terms individualism and collectivism were used for the first time by English political philosophers in the eighteenth and nineteenth centuries. According to Triandis (1995), individualism was synonymous with liberalism and included concepts relating to an individual's freedom, equality and participation in groups, of which anybody could become a member. Authoritarianism, on the other hand, as the opposite of individualism, rejected individual freedoms and required obedience and the subjection of will in authoritarian regimes. In those times, subjection to authority was widely accepted as a means to avoid anomy and anarchy.

The dominant ideas on individualism during the American Revolution (equality and the quest for happiness) and the French Revolution (freedom and equality) caused a wave of reaction and gradually led to the use of the term collectivism. In

P.E. Petrakis, *Culture, Growth and Economic Policy*,
DOI 10.1007/978-3-642-41440-4_9, © Springer-Verlag Berlin Heidelberg 2014

his work *Social Contract* (1762), Jacques Rousseau mentioned that individuals "are free to surrender their ego in favor of the general good". The concept of "will" was touted as a core theory of collective decision making and for the protection of social interests.

In the field of economic science, the doctrine of laissez-faire, which encourages individuals to use their initiatives, was contrary to the ideas of Marx and collectivism, and in conflict with the state management of production factors. In the field of politics, one view called for limits on bureaucracy to reduce the complexity of government structures; this perspective represented a fundamental principle of capitalism. However, there were also extreme forms of governance where the wants of the leader were integrated with the wants of the entire nation. The supporters of social democracy, socialism and communism followed the middle path between sheer liberalism and fascism with increasing levels of collectivism.

There is extensive literature on individualism and collectivism because of the fact that these two concepts commonly appear in all social sciences. At the same time, they act as bridges between the sociopsychological theories of the West and the theory of social reality in Third World and Asian countries.

The sophists of Ancient Greece (fifth century BC) are considered amongst the first individualistic philosophers. Individuals can set behavioral rules on their own, without the need to follow particular norms of the group(s) to which they belong. The main concern of sophists was to teach their students how to achieve individual success by any means. Athenian democracy with its ecclesia favored the emergence of persons who would become skillful and successful rhetoricians.

During the same period, Confucius in the East greatly emphasized the value of virtue. Religions such as Hinduism, Buddhism and Taoism were embracing (directly and indirectly) the significance of virtue in the shaping of human personality.

Hofstede (1991) claimed that the dominant ideologies of the East stressed the significance of virtuous action and the need to effect rituals dictated by tradition, whereas religions in the Middle East emphasized the correct "faith". Consequently, the Western world is associated with rationality, documented thinking and theory, whereas countries in the East are considered to focus more on following tradition, moral behavior, rituals and the correct way of life, as taught by religion. Individuals in the East constitute an integral part of the chain that links past, present and future societies. In contrast, individuals in the developed West have incentives to create something from scratch, without necessarily remaining faithful to tradition, nor rejecting it.

Macfarlane (1978) attempted to depict the development of individualism in England. According to his data, a premature form of individualism first emerged as early as 1200 AD. Focusing on the institution whereby first-born sons inherited land from their parents, he identified the first elements of personal initiative. The younger sons had to work hard to find their path in life. By embracing the fundamental principles of their family, they had to work hard and undertake entrepreneurial initiatives to gain their personal income. The presence of raw materials (mainly tin) offered many opportunities for trade relationships and the provision of many goods. Hence, this abundance offered incentives to show individual initiative, with the end purpose being profit.

Mead (1967) examined the degree of cooperation and competitiveness among primitive humans from 30 tribes. Triandis (1988) used that data to conduct a series of statistical analyses. He found that societies with a high degree of individualism tend to be mainly engaged in fishing, hunting and the search for food. In contrast, collectivistic societies mainly engaged in agriculture. Individualistic societies conclude commercial relationships with other tribes and urge their children to become independent as quickly as possible. However, societies that favor team spirit have limited commercial transactions with third parties, given that they themselves produce everything they consume.

The goals set by individualistic cultures for their members include self-sufficiency, to seek personal success and social evolution. Cultures with high collectivity promote the interests of the group, and group members do not consider being different than the others as an end in itself. Finally, individualistic cultures consider that humans are in a constant struggle with the universe and God, whereas group cultures consider that if they do their share, then everything will be fine.

The main conclusion stemming from the study by Triandis (1988) is that there are no purely individualistic or collectivistic societies. Cultural standards change and adapt to every circumstance. For instance, a society may appear to be deeply individualistic in its relationships with other societies, but its members nonetheless may have strong ties of respect, solidarity and collectivism in their consociations.

Hui (1984, 1988) attempted to develop different individualism–collectivism graduations regarding various institutions including family and friendship. Triandis (1990) suggested that as far as that particular graduation was concerned, it would be better if they were based on situations that concerned society, economy, politics, truth, religion and aesthetics. Therefore, in Mao's China the state played a central role in all six situations, which made that society the most collectivistic culture for a significant period. Even today, Muslim societies impose their own standards in each of these six situations.

In highly individualistic cultures, almost none of the aforementioned situations are under state control. As far as social life is concerned, there is no particular family standard, but instead society itself is tolerant toward the existing structures. Regarding issues of economy, there is a large degree of freedom (e.g., there is generally no control over prices, only in extreme occasions when it is considered necessary). In terms of politics and religion, there are many choices, and these are constitutionally established. Finally, the same applies to the predominance of truth and freedom of the press—these are not subject to the control of interest groups.

Gross and Rayner (1985) suggested two types of cultures: those that emphasize interpersonal relationships (e.g., between employer and employee or child and parent), and those emphasizing the group (behavior is defined on the basis of the commonly accepted norms of the group). The first form of culture promotes individualism, whereas the second promotes collectivism. To categorize societies into either of the two types of cultures, Gross and Rayner (1985) suggested five indices to measure the significance of the group:

(a) the proportion of a member's time budget spent in the group,
(b) the frequency of the group's meetings,
(c) the closeness of the ties among members and the degree of engagement of different characteristics,
(d) the ratio of common ties and non-common ties, and
(e) obstacles to the accession of new members to the group.

The aforementioned criteria are different than those used by most researchers to identify collectivism. However, many scholars have used at least some of Gross and Rayner's (1985) criteria without having identified any relationship using other collectivism criteria (Kashima and Kashima 1993).

Hsu (1983) is a leading anthropologist who has contributed much to this particular research field. By conducting an in-depth comparison between the cultures of China and Japan with that of the United States, he showed that China is a model collectivistic culture. The research also found that the influence of Confucianism was obvious in all aspects of Chinese life, on the basis of what is deemed "appropriate" in society. He assigned a high level of significance to the harmonious coexistence of members within a group. He also noted low crime rates, fewer admissions to hospitals, lower rates of drug addiction, more scientific achievements, and democratic institutions. Hsu (1983) also ascribed significant importance to the relationship between individualism and competitiveness. He stated that the relationship results in the increase of creativity by any means, whether lawful or unlawful, an increase in military expenditure and the establishment of a climate of suspicion among different social groups because dominant groups use minorities for the advancement of their own interests. Nevertheless, Hsu (1983) avoided making any reference to the lack of trust that may dominate many collectivistic cultures. Individuals in this kind of cultures avoid trusting people that do not belong to the same group with them or are in their close family environment.

Bellah et al. (1988) conducted an important survey in which they expressed their concerns regarding the direction of society in the United States and the repercussions of the increasing lack of team spirit. Individualism was to the United States the means to achieve a series of personal goals such as self-reliance, competitiveness and materialistic satisfaction. The most important characteristics of US society, according to the aforementioned survey, was freedom, equality, trust, competition, transactions, independence, loose ties between adult children and their families, individual progress and the wish for distinction and recognition. A lesser emphasis on family and the church, together with changes in the way of life, led to the isolation of the individual and even to alienation. In the same survey, Bellah et al. (1988) also identified a divergence between individual goals and those of the state.

Bellah et al. (1988) identified three types of individualism in their study: religious, materialistic and expressive individualism. For instance, according to religious individualism, the individual is directly linked to God. Materialistic individualism excludes transactions that aim to make a profit, and expressive individualism emphasizes an individual's pleasure and entertainment; the "I" is all that matters. Despite these definitions, individualism, to a certain extent, helps individuals to comply with laws and unwritten rules. Members of higher social classes place significant emphasis on tradition and social rules to safeguard their positions in society, whereas the lower classes perform their duties to keep their jobs.

Hofstede (1980) found strong correlation (−0.7) between individualism and power distance. The negative correlation of these two cultural dimensions proves that the acceptance of hierarchy and power is particularly low in individualistic cultures.

By comparing traditional Greek society to that of the United States, Triandis (1995) concluded that Greece is dominated by collectivism, as opposed to individualistic Americans. The findings of Hofstede (1980) are similar to the contrarieties identified by Triandis (1995).

Many studies have focused on the creation of appropriate methods to measure the degree of individualism–collectivism at an individual level (Hui 1984, 1988; Triandis et al. 1985), and among different cultures (Triandis et al. 1988, 1990b). Triandis (1988, 1990) offered a more comprehensive presentation of the literature on methods to measure individualism–collectivism. The measurements show that individualism is inwrought with ideas such as independence and self-reliance, distance between the group and third parties and competition. In contrast, collectivism is strongly connected with interdependence, socialization and family integrity (children should live with their parents until they are married and the elderly should be taken care of by their children until they die).

9.2 Factors Shaping Individualism and Collectivism

The degree of individualism and collectivism in every culture is the outcome of various factors, including two fundamental cultural syndromes: tightness versus looseness and cultural complexity versus simplicity. The term cultural syndrome refers to a model network, which is characterized by common perceptions, behaviors, stances, roles and values in a given geographic area and historical period. Individualism in most cases is the outcome of looseness and complexity, whereas collectivism arises when tightness and cultural simplicity are dominant.

Tightness (Pelto 1968) refers to the degree to which the members of a culture (a) agree as to what is correct, (b) behave in accordance with its rules, and (c) exert severe criticism when they ascertain any deviation from the predefined rules. We can find these syndromes in conflicting cultures. For example, the United States constitutes a loose culture, whereas Japan is considered relatively tight.

Tight cultures tend to be quite homogeneous and separated from other cultures. There is often high population density, a lack of dynamism and their production base relies on agriculture. In early forms of social organization, tightness was directly connected with the central control over property and food, religious leaders and high taxation (Pelto 1968). Members of collectivistic cultures tended to be emotionless and distant. An example is Turkish immigrants from Western Europe, who came from low social classes. Their behavior is explained as an attempt to protect their culture from third parties.

In contrast, loose cultures have a multitude of rules (that are often conflicting) regarding many aspects of human existence. People that deviate from predefined standards will not necessarily be punished. Looseness can be seen in heterogeneous cultures, where the individual is rewarded for using initiative and engaging in entrepreneurial action; such cultures also have low population densities. Furthermore, cultures whose geographic boundaries lie between other larger cultures are in danger of becoming extinct (an example is Thailand, which is essentially between China and India), because people are aware of the fact that there are many ways to respond to a given circumstance. Thailand constitutes a novel form of loose culture. It is a society where minimum attention is given to labor rules and ceremonies. For example, if an employee wishes to stop working (for any reason whatsoever), then that person can leave without having to submit an official resignation (Phillips 1965). Thais also have strong elements of heterogeneity and there is not enough pressure for them to function interdependently. Moreover, there are a variety of acceptable ways to handle a given situation.

An important factor that greatly affects the sustainability of a culture is climate conditions. Cultures that develop in warmer climates can be characterized as loose cultures and colder climates shape concrete and tight cultures (Robbins et al. 1972). For example, in warmer climates, individuals do not need to exhibit "self-control" to live together with the environment, because the environment is friendly toward individuals. In contrast, in a cold environment where living conditions are particularly harsh, individuals need to act in a specific manner to safeguard their existence. In very inhospitable climates such as Antarctica, deviating behaviors can lead to death.

Finally, it should be noted that tightness and looseness do not characterize all aspects of every culture. Hence, a culture may be disciplined in terms of social and political circumstances and looser in terms of issues relating to economy and religion.

9.3 Characteristics of Collectivism

The degree of collectivism is directly linked to the moral development of the individual. Children go through six basic stages of moral development (Eckensberger 1994). At the first level, children focus on obedience and punishment. In the second stage they learn to do what is best for their own interests, thus showing the first signs of individualism. In the third stage they learn how to behave within a group by undertaking a particular role. It is during this stage that children get in touch with early forms of collective action. The fourth stage is dedicated to learning about the obligations of individuals in society by acquiring a more responsible collective position. In the next stage, emphasis is given to social contacts and individual freedoms. This is a stage with strong elements of individualism. Finally, in the sixth stage, individuals might "reach" their most individualistic aspect. During this stage, their interest is focused on universally acceptable moral principles. The laws and rules are acceptable only if they abide by such principles. Principles like justice, equality and respect toward human dignity are not negotiable.

Generally speaking, children follow the aforementioned stages of moral development. However, the first, fifth and sixth stages are rarely seen, whereas the second, third and fourth characterize most cultures. Higher moral development stages reflect the socio-economic class of the parents (a higher income entails a higher class), religion and the rural–urban background of the sample. Furthermore, the higher the educational level, the higher the stages of moral achieved. Proper edification starts with the accession of children to the notion of "group" by cultivating them with basic moral values that will be with them for life. As children grow up, they are equipped with values that focus on the individual's personal integration, learning to set goals and make their dreams come true.

The relationship between the dimension of collectivism/individualism and moral level is relatively imperfect (Triandis 1995). Lower social classes have lower levels of moral development, as do developing countries.

Triandis (1995) viewed the association between crime and individualism as a fundamental question in the debate on ethics and politics, concerning the advantages and disadvantages of individualism and collectivism. There is no doubt that the weaker the social control mechanisms, the higher the crime rate (Triandis 1995). The 1980s is a prime example of a period during which individualism and competition were strong. As a result, crime rates in industrialized countries tripled; Japan was the exception.

Policies implemented in developed economies orientate toward short-term goals (an election win) and less toward long-term goals (improvements in the economy). Even in collectivistic societies, however, it is individuals leading society and therefore long-term policies are not substantially different than those implemented in self-centered societies. At the same time, there is an aversion by citizens toward taxation, which is the same in all countries. However, the motives for this aversion differ among societies.

Societies whose members are linked with cohesive bonds of mutual trust and solidarity have low rates for homicide, drug use and suicide. By examining various religious societies in the United States and Canada, Trimble (1994) identified a very low incidence of drug use. Bacon (1973) found that cultures that do not allow their children to become independent have low drug use and alcoholism rates. Therefore, collectivistic societies acquire an advantage in this field.

By moving on to the disadvantages, it is common for children in collectivistic cultures to find it difficult to say goodbye to their families when it is time for them to leave home (e.g., study abroad or for professional reasons). At the same time, there is data showing increased rates of homelessness when a child leaves the family home (Cardem 1993). Perhaps the most negative aspect of collectivism at an individual level concerns low self-esteem and low levels of happiness and prosperity (Gallup 1976).

At a public level, extreme forms of collectivism create a negative impact on the relationship between the individual and the state. For example, Nazism and Communism established regimes that forced citizens to set aside their needs and goals for the purposes of the state. In addition, anyone who posed a threat to the regime was deported abroad. As far as the field of sciences and technology is concerned, dictatorial regimes attempt to downgrade the role of science because they do not want to confront anything that constitutes a source of "truth".

Collectivism is often linked to tradition, which results in the creation of impediments for economic growth. Decision making for the benefit of society is commonly avoided because of adherence to tradition. In addition, individuals' increased obligations within society deprive them of the necessary energy to innovate and create by setting a further obstacle to the accumulation of wealth.

9.4 Characteristics of Individualism

The importance of individualism is considered important to defend human rights and democracy, to establish multiculturalism in every society, to apply laws (and the equal treatment of all regarding such laws), to promote innovation and, more generally, creation, freedom and advancement.

High GDP per capita is associated with individualism (Hofstede 1980). The most likely scenario is that the relationship between wealth and individualism is bidirectional. Wealth leads to risky investments, whose success leads, in turn, to the further accumulation of wealth. Wealth means more choices for the individual and, hence, more autonomy and individualism. Economic growth, according to Pareek (1968), is a function of the "need for advancement" (which is usually linked to individualism and competition).

The feeling of self-esteem that dominates individualists, as well as that of having faith in their abilities, favors the undertaking of activities and, thus, advancement is associated with individualism.

The negative aspects of individualism include loneliness, alienation, deficient social support (Triandis et al. 1985), domestic disputes and divorce (Brodbar and Jay 1986). Individuals rely on their own powers as long as they feel strong, both physically and mentally. However, when they are required to confront a given situation that exceeds their abilities, they are unable to find support because of loose social relationships. Violence, crime and delinquency are associated with individualism (Macfarlane 1978; Hsu 1983; Sinha 1988). The intense competition that prevails in individualistic cultures may possibly lead to conditions of increased tension and stress. Individuals find themselves constantly seeking success, wondering whether they are good enough or whether they need to try harder. In terms of creativity and innovation, extreme competition often produces results that are the opposite of those anticipated. Helmreich et al. (1978) found that intense competition is negatively associated with scientific achievements. Instead of being fully engaged with their central work, competitors spent significant time keeping notes and writing critiques on how much better they were than the rest.

Norem-Habeisen and Johnson (1981) showed that pupils with high levels of cooperation achieve more than competitive pupils who are more prone to failure. Westcott (1988) suggested that excessive freedom leads to loneliness, alienation and merciless competition. Donohue (1990) linked excessive freedom with juvenile delinquency, drug use, teenage pregnancy, suicide, divorce and HIV/AIDS.

Finally, individualism has a significant disadvantage regarding the issue of international economic competition—as professions become more complex and demanding, they require more training. In an ideal situation, a company would be certain that an employee would be with them for a long period before they spent valuable resources on training them. Nevertheless, employees with an increased degree of individualism often change employers, and thus, training can entail risks for the employer. At the same time, when a company trains an employee, there is the risk that the employee will then move to a competitor. Aside from the issue of competition, companies operating in individualistic cultures also face the mobility of their manpower.

9.5 Individualism and Collectivism and Their Relationships with Growth

The repercussions of individualism and collectivism (Triandis 1995) can be grouped into four basic categories: repercussions against (a) the individual, (b) interpersonal relationships, (c) relationships among groups, and (d) social institutions.

One of the most important repercussions of the transition of societies to individualism is the alienation of individuals (Sinha 1988). Sinha (1988) examined the rapid changes toward individualism that occurred in India and suggested that they had a direct impact on the structure of family, damaging the mental health of individuals. For example, individuals do not wish to depend on other members of the group in which they belong and, hence, reject any help. Human relationships in this instance are not tight enough, especially between parents and children, to offer assistance to those in need.

Although collectivistic societies tend to have a smaller number of social groups, their members have nonetheless developed cohesive ties and entry to the group can be difficult. Collectivists usually have just a few relationships but they are close, whereas individualists have many relationships of limited intimacy. Wheeler et al. (1989) mentioned that because individualists have limited social relationships, they must act to preserve them. This results in the development of skills for effective social interactions.

Conflict occurs in both collectivistic and individualistic cultures, but tends to appear in different ways. A quarrel within a group in a collectivistic society may stem from the quest for improvement to the group's conditions and function. In an individualistic society, individuals usually struggle to change certain conditions relating to their own benefit, and alienation often appears to be the basis of conflict.

Triandis et al. (1990a) examined the perception of social behavior as a function of social inequalities in China and the United States. According to their conclusions, China has greater discord among the members of a group regarding third parties compared with the United States. This finding is similar to the fact that collectivistic cultures are more discriminatory compared with individualistic ones. The Chinese also show superiority to individuals who do not belong to the same group as them. Finally, compared with Americans, the Chinese show greater obedience toward other members in their group and less toward third parties.

An important theory that links individualism–collectivism with labor behavior was first expressed by Erez and Earley (1993) and Erez (1994). Erez and Earley (1993) suggested that for any administrative strategy to be effective, culture should be taken into consideration.

A further factor that affects labor environment and depends on culture is socialization. In cases where the degree of individualism is high, a lack of social relationships among employees is noted. In contrast, socialization is deemed necessary in collectivistic cultures where the group must follow a common action.

Communication is another sector that produces variations between the two kinds of cultures. In individualistic cultures, communication is generally limited to the official language of that culture and is often in written form. In collectivistic cultures, communication takes place on a face-to-face basis, without having to worry about norms. In the former, the solution lies at an individual level, whereas in the latter it concerns the entire group and the solution is adopted jointly.

Examining the goals of various collectivisms, Erez and Earley (1993) found that an individual's contribution to the goals of such groups depends on the degree of individualism–collectivism in their culture. They also identified that collectivism has many negative elements as far as issues of organization are concerned. One of these concerns the fact that in collectivistic cultures the dominant tendency is to conceal information from the entire group because the possession of information equals power. At the same time, competition is relatively strong (Espinoza and Garza 1985), which leads to the exploitation of individuals outside the group (Pandey 1986).

As far as the institution of religion is concerned, in collectivistic cultures, religion takes the form of group worshiping. In most instances personal salvation is directly connected with the actions of the group to which the individual belongs. Furthermore, it is very uncommon for members of collectivistic cultures not to adopt the same religious doctrine. Nevertheless, societies such as that of India, which is a collectivistic society with powerful religious beliefs, generally tolerates deviations from orthodoxy.

Many of the steering principles of East Asia are not rooted in religion, as happens in the West. Confucianism essentially offers a notional framework for the individual's way of life, rather than religious principles and norms. In fact, Confucius expressed appropriate ways of action for the individual and not how to worship and be faithful to God.

In contrast, individualistic cultures consider religious beliefs and worshiping as a personal matter and avoid mass ceremonies worshiping God. Furthermore, they express their faith without necessarily being in an area specifically for worshiping and in the presence of priests. Great emphasis is placed on the "personal" relationship with religion and deities. Certain doctrines, such as those of Calvinism, support the accumulation of wealth (Weber 1930) and, as such, are fully compatible with individualism. Wealth allows individuals to act as they wish and to invest and further increase their wealth. This ultimately leads to greater levels of independence. Of course, the examples mentioned above do not imply that someone who does not belong to a collectivistic culture cannot become wealthy. The Japanese are a nation with obvious collectivism characteristics but at the same time they are one of the strongest economies in the world.

The political system constitutes one of the most important institutions for the smooth operation of a law-abiding society. In collectivistic cultures, the political system is considered as the means to preserve collectivism, usually at state and political party levels. Political parties constitute groups of people that engage in verbal confrontations with opposition parties. In particular, the more their members are in favor of collectivism, the less willing they are to agree on a proposal by a political rival, even if it is clearly beneficial for the country. In the vast majority of cases, if not in all cases, political leaders act on the basis of the interests of their political party and not for social benefit.

In contrast, in individualistic societies, the planning of the political system is strongly connected with the needs of the individual. The control the state exerts over its citizens is limited. In addition, great significance is placed on the protection of human rights and the freedom of individuals. Of course, such an emphasis on civil liberties can lead to situations where general good is overlooked.

Triandis (1995) found an association between individualism and modernity. Giddens (1991) claimed that modernity creates high levels of specialization, thus differentiating manpower, excluding less competitive parties and marginalizing those who cannot adapt to new social conditions. In this way, individuals should always act to improve themselves and acquire new skills. Nevertheless, the constant quest for success and evolution can often lead to the alienation of individuals from their family, higher divorce rates and parents neglecting their children (Pilisuk and Parks 1985).

Hillhouse (1993) suggested that the transition from collectivism to individualism in Germany was due to the fall of East Germany. The participation of thousands of German citizens in social movements within the framework of the state, political parties and church played a determinative role to the fall of the Berlin Wall. The emergence of hundreds of voluntary organizations, which were based on religion, politics and music, resulted in the differentiation of the dominant political culture in East Germany. Furthermore, consumerism (via television advertisements) in conjunction with the ability to choose from a multitude of goods greatly influenced East Germans.

Hillhouse (1993) viewed increased pluralism and the ability to choose as the means for individuals to acquire their own separate identity. She stated that various studies conducted in East Germany between 1962 and 1990 showed powerful changes in the map of values of East Germans, which are associated with the transition from collectivism to individualism. Such a transition led to the democratization of Germany (Triandis 1995). Shifting toward the direction of consumerism was politically neutral, but the fact that the state continued to follow the same economic policy had significant political extensions, and at its core was the loss of support from citizens.

The case of East Germany is particularly interesting, because it is possibly the most successful state to have embraced the theories of Marx and Lenin, and then transition to a high level of consumerism and very high living standards. In her analysis, Hillhouse (1993) mentioned that while the political party itself constituted the only social group in 1950, by 1980, several hundred voluntary organizations had been established. In totalitarian regimes, such as Nazism and Communism, the state makes significant effort to restrain and efface the establishment of social groups.

9.6 Collectivism to Either Promote or Inhibit Economic Growth

To be balanced, each political system must first identify the appropriate mixture of restraints and freedoms. The point of balance should therefore be based on the formation of society regarding the degree of individualism–collectivism.

However, it is not merely the balance between collectivism and individualism that plays an important role in the organization of a society's cultural background. The separate characteristics of cultural dimensions also play important roles. As stated in the reviews in Sects. 9.4 and 9.5, it seems particularly important to differentiate collectivistic characteristics that can either promote (progressive collectivism) or hinder the process of economic growth (regressive collectivism). Hence, it appears that there is some degree of collectivity that conceptualizes the concept of collectivism as having a constant and persistent presence in all economic activity as a regulatory and responsible nature. Such a concept has an extraneous influence and usually originates from religious and historical factors. This can be seen, for example, in the functioning of institutions, the state, or trade unions.

Inclusive economic institutions are those that allow and encourage participation by the masses in economic activities, making best use of their talent and skills, and that enable individuals to make the choices they wish. This requires that such institutions feature secure private property, a fair legal system, the provision of public services, contracting procedures and low entry barriers for new business. The opposite applies to extractive economic institutions (Acemoglu and Robinson 2012). Their fundamental characteristic is the obligation of absolute faith in that institution, but not the (economic or social) responsibility for preserving them. As an institution, it has an extracting character, given that it ultimately imposes procedures for the absorption of surpluses produced for its functional survival.

Progressive collectivism is at the opposite end of the spectrum from regressive collectivism, which constitutes the evolution of the concept of social democracy and state intervention for the elimination of the market's imperfections. These traits are generally seen in the social democratic model of social organization and have an inclusive character. Because of the manner in which its activity is renewed, it does not constitute a bottleneck for individualism, despite the fact it absorbs significant resources.

References

Acemoglu D, Robinson JA (2012) Why nations fail: the origins of power, prosperity and poverty. Crown Publishers, New York, NY

Bacon MK (1973) Cross-cultural studies in drinking. In: Bourne PG, Fox R (eds) Alcoholism: progress in research and treatment. Academic, New York, NY

Bellah RN, Madsen R, Sullivan WM, Swidler A, Tipton SM (1988) Individualism and commitment in American life: readings on the themes of habits of the heart. Harper & Row, New York, NY

Brodbar N, Jay Y (1986) Divorce and group commitment: the case of the Jews. J Marriage Fam 48:329–340

Cardem A (1993) Homesickness. Seminar given at the East–west Center in Hawaii, October

Donohue WA (1990) The new freedom: individualism and collectivism in the social lives of Americans. Transaction Publishers, New Brunswick, NJ

Eckensberger LH (1994) Moral development and its measurement across cultures. In: Lonner WJ, Malpass R (eds) Psychology and culture. Allyn & Bacon, Boston, MA

Erez M (1994) Toward a model of cross-cultural industrial and organizational psychology. In: Triandis HC, Dunnette M, Hough L (eds) Handbook of industrial and organizational psychology. Palo Alto Consulting Psychologists Press, Palo Alto, CA

Erez M, Earley PC (1993) Culture, self-identity, and work. Oxford University Press, New York, NY

Espinoza JA, Garza RT (1985) Social group salience and interethnic cooperation. J Exp Soc Psychol 21:380–392

Gallup G (1976) Human needs and satisfactions: a global survey. Public Opin Q 40:459–467

Giddens A (1991) Modernity and self-identity. Stanford University Press, Stanford, CA

Gross JL, Rayner S (1985) Measuring culture. Columbia University Press, New York, NY

Helmreich RL, Beane WE, Lucker GW, Spence JT (1978) Achievement motivation and scientific attainment. Pers Soc Psychol Bull 4:222–226

Hillhouse RJ (1993) The individual revolution: the social basis of transition toward democracy? Dissertation, University of Michigan

Hofstede G (1980) Culture's consequences. Sage, Beverly Hills, CA

Hofstede G (1991) Cultures and organizations: software of the mind. McGraw-Hill, London

Hsu FLK (1983) Rugged individualism reconsidered. University of Tennessee Press, Knoxville, TN

Hui CH (1984) Individualism-collectivism: theory, measurement and its relationships to reward allocation. Dissertation, University of Illinois at Champaign-Urbana

Hui CH (1988) Measurement of individualism-collectivism. J Res Pers 22:17–36

Kashima E, Kashima Y (1993) Perceptions of general variability of social groups. Soc Cognit 11:1–21

Macfarlane A (1978) The origins of English individualism: the family, property and social transition. Cambridge University Press, New York, NY

Mead M (1967) Cooperation and competition among primitive peoples. Beacon Press, Boston, MA

Norem-Habeisen AA, Johnson DW (1981) The relationship between cooperative, and individualistic attitudes and different aspects of self-esteem. J Pers 49:415–426

Pandey J (1986) Socio-cultural perspectives on ingratiation. In: Maher BA, Maher WB (eds) Progress in experimental personality research 14. Academic, Orlando, FL

Pareek U (1968) A motivational paradigm of development. J Soc Issues 24:115–122

Pelto PJ (1968) The difference between "tight" and "loose" societies. Transaction 5:37–40
Phillips HP (1965) Thai peasant personality: the patterning of interpersonal behaviour in the village of Bang Chan. University of California Press, Berkeley, CA
Pilisuk M, Parks S (1985) The healing web. University Press of New England, Hanover
Robbins MC, de Walt BR, Pelto PJ (1972) Climate and behaviour: a biocultural study. J Cross Cult Psychol 3:331–344
Rousseaou J (1762) [2008] The social contract. Cosimo Publications, New York.
Sinha D (1988) The family scenario in a developing country and its implications for mental health: the case of India. In: Dasen P, Berry J, Sartorius N (eds) Health and cross-cultural psychology. Sage, Newbury Park, CA
Triandis HC (1988) Collectivism v. Individualism: a reconceptualization of a basic concept in cross-cultural social psychology. In: Verma GK, Bagley C (eds) Cross-cultural studies of personality, attitudes and cognition. Macmillan, London
Triandis HC, Bontempo R, Villareal MJ, Asai M, Lucca N (1988) Individualism and collectivism: cross-cultural perspectives on self-ingroup relationships. J Pers Soc Psychol 54:323–338
Triandis HC (1990) Cross-cultural studies of individualism and collectivism. In: Berman J (ed) Nebraska symposium on motivation. University of Nebraska Press, Lincoln, Lincoln
Triandis HC (1995) Individualism and collectivism. Westview, Boulder, CO
Triandis HC, Leung K, Villareal M, Clack FL (1985) Allocentric vs. idiocentric tendencies: convergent and discriminant validation. J Res Pers 19:395–415
Triandis HC, Bontempo R, Leung K, Hui CH (1990a) A method for determining cultural, demographic, and personal constructs. J Cross Cult Psychol 21:302–318
Triandis HC, McCusker C, Hui CH (1990b) Multimethod probes of individualism and collectivism. J Pers Soc Psychol 59:1006–1020
Trimble JE (1994) Cultural variations in use of alcohol and drugs. In: Lonner WJ, Malpass R (eds) Psychology and culture. Allyn & Bacon, Boston, MA
Weber M (1930) [1958] The protestant ethic and the spirit of capitalism. Scribner's, New York, NY
Westcott MR (1988) The psychology of human freedom. Springer, New York, NY
Wheeler L, Reis HT, Bond MH (1989) Collectivism-individualism in everyday social life: the Middle Kingdom and the melting pot. J Pers Soc Psychol 57:79–86

Power Distance, Uncertainty, Time and Growth

10

Power distance and uncertainty avoidance are two key cultural dimensions strongly interrelated with economic growth. The role of time has attracted interest because thinking about future actions constitutes a basic feature of human thought. From an individual's perspective, future orientation requires the development of a series of abilities. These include cognitive and mental processes (such as planning, prediction of circumstances and ways of behavior), as well as emotions and attitudes (such as optimism, pessimism and hope). Similarly, incentives, which are expressed as interests, values and goals, play a primary role in the individual's future actions. Time orientation is closely connected with individual progress. By predicting the future, people feel as though they are predicting their own development, resulting in the fact that we set the directions we wish to follow.

The present chapter is structured as follows. Section 10.1 analyzes power distance, and Sect. 10.2 discusses uncertainty avoidance. Finally, Sect. 10.3 analyzes the role of time as a source of an individual's expressions and decision making.

10.1 Power Distance

Power distance in society is linked to the degree with which its members accept the existence of inequalities (wealth, power and social status) and the way in which they understand the distribution of income. High power distance societies tend to be dominated by significant inequalities, and the distribution of power affects the distribution of wealth in a direct manner. At the same time, societies, whose members accept inequalities, develop rent-seeking behaviors aimed at economic and social growth.

The reduction of inequalities without the simultaneous reduction of prosperity is a challenge for economic policy. The elimination of inequalities is linked to the creation of additional costs, which are associated with planning and implementing government programs and policies. If redistribution costs are large enough, they can result in less national income (Okun 1975). Thus, an important issue is raised,

P.E. Petrakis, *Culture, Growth and Economic Policy*,
DOI 10.1007/978-3-642-41440-4_10, © Springer-Verlag Berlin Heidelberg 2014

which is directly linked to human behavior and the way in which decisions are made. Despite the reduction of inequalities (achieved through the implementation of redistribution policies), everyone will be worse-off given that there will be less rent-seeking behavior and lower capital productivity will result in a decrease in living standards (Stevans 2012).

A series of incidents in recent decades have raised many questions regarding the direction of the relationship between growth and inequalities. The exponential economic growth of the United States in the 1990s, in conjunction with a simultaneous increase in income inequalities, and low levels of inequality in East Asian economies before World War II, signaled the need for a series of relevant empirical studies.

The relationship between economic development and level of income inequalities sparked the interest of researchers, starting with Kuznets (1955). His pioneering work examined economic growth and income inequalities. The empirical literature follows Kuznets's analysis by focusing on whether or not inequalities enhance growth rates. A negative relationship between growth and income inequalities has been found in many studies (Alesina and Rodrik 1994; Persson and Tabellini 1992, 1994; Perotti 1996). The justification behind the aforementioned findings is based mainly on the political economic consequences of inequality, the unequal distribution of natural resources and a lack of equal opportunities in education. In contrast, other studies have identified a positive relationship (Li and Zou 1998; Forbes 2000). Barro (2000) found a negative association between economic inequality and growth for poorer countries and the opposite for richer nations.

The theoretical background, on which the aforementioned approaches are based, stems from the perception that higher inequality either stimulates or discourages "productive investments", which, consequently, influence the products produced (Stevans 2012).

A further approach that examines the efficiency in income inequalities and economic growth is the equity–efficiency approach. This approach provides a positive relationship between inequality and capital accumulation due to incentives. The existence of power distance in a society encourages human behavior aimed at gaining profits to make use of existing opportunities. We can imagine an economy as a zero-sum game, where each player wishes to maximize their profit to the detriment of their "opponent".

The existence of a progressive taxation system can reduce income inequalities. At the same time, however, it also has a negative influence on the shaping of incentives, thus discouraging entrepreneurial initiative. Higher income inequality leads to higher taxation, thus reducing capital yield after taxes, and thereby reducing investments and economic progress (Bertola 1991).

Confronting inequalities requires the coalescence of the power of the ruling class and efficiency costs emerging from such processes. Rent-seeking societies (Krueger 1974) are characterized by economic institutions shaped by unequal political and social processes (Bourguignon et al. 2007). The term rent-seeking applies to the entire process through which political institutions help high-income classes to take risks. Hence, in many cases income inequalities are the result of rent-seeking behavior. The differences among the members of society, as a result of profit seeking, may have a positive influence on economic growth through the activation of incentives and goals. In summary, power distance, as a fundamental cultural trait of every society, may contribute to economic growth via human incentives.

10.2 Uncertainty Avoidance

The way in which individuals understand risk is directly linked to decision making. Risk constitutes an integral part of social and economic life. The outcome of human choices involves an element of uncertainty. The decision to take risks differs among individuals, who are influenced by socioeconomic characteristics and psychological traits. Deciding to undertake a risk-taking activity depends on the expected output. The bigger the yield, the greater the effort made by individuals to achieve their goals. However, beyond a certain point, the reduction of the marginal benefit of any additional risk unit acts to discourage the individual from assuming greater risks (Markowitz 1952).

Many studies have attempted to identify whether risk aversion constitutes a personal trait or a characteristic extending to the context of entrepreneurial decisions. Ray (1994) considered that an individual's attitude toward risk is not stable but depends on specific situations that they are called to confront. McCarthy (2000) similarly argued that risk aversion is not a static personality trait but reflects the knowledge and experience gained by an individual in a business context.

The perception of risk is important for two reasons (Palsson 1996). First, at an aggregate economic level, the opportunities for attracting high-risk capital are directly linked to the attitude of investors toward risk-taking. Risk aversion behaviors tend to increase the price of risk capital, thus restraining investments in high-risk projects and resulting in holding back economic growth.

Second, at a micro level, risk attitudes affect household welfare. Higher yields are followed by higher levels of risk. Households not willing to undertake high-risk investments cannot expect to increase their wealth to a level above the society average. In contrast, households willing to include risky assets in their investment portfolio will achieve a higher rate of return.

Uncertainty plays an important role in holding liquidity (Keynes 1936). The tradeoff between deposits and liquidity defines the investment pattern of the economy. Uncertainty, as Keynes understood it, differs from risk because risk can involve possibilities for something to happen in the future whereas in the case of fundamental uncertainty, which emerges from underlying structures and economic relationships, one cannot predict the possibilities. Fundamental uncertainty generally emerges because of the uniqueness of the facts because a lack of past experiences cannot be used as a given fact for future events. Novel economic activities, new technology regimes and a lack of knowledge in existing economic relationships can result in an increase in fundamental uncertainty. A new investment project is a unique procedure that includes new elements and, consequently, there is limited accumulated knowledge regarding future expectations.

Knight (1921) approached fundamental uncertainty from the perspective that the agent doubts the assessment of the possibilities of something happening because their estimations are based on vague and subjective knowledge. Fundamental uncertainty constitutes an integral part of our non-ergodic world as economic processes evolve over time (Davidson 1987; de Carvalho 1988).

Uncertainty in human expectations drives macroeconomic outcomes. High uncertainty levels tend to hinder the growth course of economies. Many scholars have identified a causal link between high uncertainty and weak recovery (Bloom 2011). Economic uncertainty refers to an environment in which little or nothing is known about the future state of the economy (Kose and Terrones 2012). Changes in economic institutions and economic policies, dispersion in future economic development and geostrategic and political disturbances can be seen as sources of economic uncertainty (Bloom 2009). Periods of economic recession intensify economic uncertainty by creating a vicious cycle from which it is difficult for economies to escape. At the same time, it is observed that in periods of strong economic growth, uncertainty is lower than during periods of recession.

The negative influence of uncertainty on economic outcomes can be approached from two sides: the demand side and the supply side. Regarding the demand-side, uncertainty in terms of the future discourages businesses from undertaking investment projects (or makes them delay their realization) until better information regarding the future is obtained. In relation to the supply-side, in their attempt to cut wage costs because of uncertainty, businesses do not readily employ new personnel.

Policy uncertainty is another type of uncertainty, and refers to the influences exerted on the undertaking of new initiatives because of government instability, social unrest, an unstable incentives framework, complicated legal framework and the degree of protection afforded to property rights. Barro (1991) concluded that the differences in levels of investment among countries stemmed from government instability and political violence. Knack and Keefer (1995) showed that uncertainty regarding property rights enforcement is negatively associated with investment rates. Corruption, as an indicator of institutional uncertainty, is negatively associated with investments according to Mauro (1995). Studying a large sample of entrepreneurs, Brunetti et al. (1997) concluded that perceived government instability, corruption and reliability of the judiciary influence the undertaking of investment initiative throughout the economy.

Thus, the existence of uncertainty, as well as the way in which society understands it, plays a determinative role in the course of economic growth. Risk aversion could be characterized as a deal breaker for economic growth. Societies where there is risk aversion tend to show smaller growth perspectives because investment initiatives are restrained. At the same time, a low-quality institutional framework because of political uncertainties act as an obstacle to the activation of human incentives, limiting the exploitation of opportunities.

10.3 Time Orientation

Hall (1983) considered the concept of time to be at the center of culture's organization and operation: "given that time constitutes the core of the system of each culture, and given that it plays such an important role in understanding culture as a cultural system, it is almost impossible to separate time from culture at certain levels". Many surveys have been carried out, both at empirical and theoretical levels, seeking the origin, structure and repercussions of time (Zimbardo and Boyd 1999). Culture functions at a collective level, just as personality functions at an individual level (Strathman and Joireman 2005).

One dimension of Hofstede's (2001) cultural background is Confucian dynamism (or time orientation). High scores in this area are linked to future planning, whereas low scores characterize societies that place a strong emphasis on the present and past. Regarding this dimension, there are two points that require explaining. First, Confucian dynamism should not be viewed as the future vs. the past but as a middle ground that every society should achieve. In other words, neither a completely present or completely future orientation is desirable. Second, both extremes are positively associated with economic change because they are measured through GDP changes.

A fundamental feature of each society, which differentiates it from the rest, is the way in which the concept of time is approached. Such differentiation lies with the fact that certain cultures are future oriented, whereas others tend to prefer the present. Nevertheless, there are also cultures and societies that do not acknowledge the existence of the future and only that of the present and past. In African cultures, the future constitutes a "hypothetical structure" and does not have a tangible place in human behavior. Ancestors play an important role in shaping and promoting culture because their life and spirit are responsible for the present. The chain of life is a circular process, directed from the present to the past with merely an evanescent moment with which the short-term future can offer a blurred perspective (Strathman and Joireman 2005).

Time is at the core of the concept of cultural background and is responsible for shaping behaviors and perspectives. Hofstede (2001) considered future orientation as a value, and a value is born from faith in possible changes in the current condition and future results (Jones 1988). More particularly, believing that a given action in the present can increase the possibility of achieving future goals gives value and creates the necessary conditions to control their behaviors.

The time perspective, according to social psychology, is treated as a wider concept and refers to the complex cognitive structures that characterize the way in which an individual plans, is granted access, evaluates and organizes facts taking place in different periods of time. Time orientation represents a more delimited notion in relation to the time perspective and includes behavior which is influenced by thoughts, emotions and incentives in a discrete "area" of time (Strathman and Joireman 2005).

Time orientation constitutes a separate variable for each individual, which predicts and affects various aspects of their social behavior. A time perspective generally refers to the procedures used regarding the handling and evaluation of time information, whereas time orientation constitutes the products of thinking and syllogistic procedure, which creates a discrete model of attitudes and perceptions toward facts and situations that involve a given period of time.

The relationship between time and the individual's social and psychological processes has long concerned social scientists. Nonetheless, only recently have researchers provided a cohesive framework that integrates all definitions of time experience in a survey (Gjesme 1983). Despite the fact that many scholars have brought the two concepts (time perspective and time orientation) together, some fine distinctions can be drawn between the two.

The multidimensional view of time perspective and its concurrent association with time orientation have been studied by many researchers. Any research that focuses on time should take care to ensure that all the dimensions of time have been included; if not, the study will be of limited interpretative power. Many recent research programs have attempted to combine the multitude of works on time and extract a consolidated theory (Jones 1993; Zimbardo and Boyd 1999).

Kastenbaum (1961) supported the misguided tendency of researchers to alternatively use the terms of time orientation, time perspective and time perception. Kastenbaum (1961) listed the following dimensions of future-oriented time: expansion (how far in time one can see oneself), density (degree of cohesiveness of an individual's views on the future), consistency (the degree with which one sees one's future) and direction (the degree to which one sees that they will progresses in the future). These dimensions fully take into account an individual's perceptions regarding their future orientation.

The significance attributed to time orientation by individuals varies throughout their lifetime and during various stages. For instance, an individual's cognitive abilities in early childhood are limited and do not allow the individual to plan and schedule for long periods of time in the future. In addition, children do not have the autonomy that enables them to make long-term decisions regarding how they want their lives to be in the future. As an individual passes into adolescence, future orientation becomes more prominent in their way of thinking. This largely occurs because of the development of cognitive abilities, increased autonomy from parents and social pressures pushing them to determine their role in society. Thoughts of the future continue to be significant in early adulthood when the individual faces many changes. Time orientation remains significant for adults and in advanced years, and is triggered by external stimuli (significant life decisions, crises, big changes).

To describe how people think and act in relation to the future, researchers have created various notional approaches. The most common approach is that of "future orientation" (Trommsdorff et al. 1982). It is a relatively wide concept that embraces the expectations, hopes and fears of individuals, how far in the future such expectations and hopes are predicted, how humans think about facts that will affect their future, how they feel about the future, and the abilities and means they have acquired to fulfill their goals (Nurmi 1991). To examine future orientation, participants are usually given questionnaires with questions regarding their goals, hopes and fears, feelings, views and plans.

In addition to future orientation, there are other concepts associated with the ways in which people consider the future. Examples of such concepts are found in surveys that examine anticipated facts (Crockett and Bingham 2000), personal goals (Little 1983), ways of solving problems (Strough et al. 1996), the identification of the personal identity of the individual and obligations (Bosma 1985).

10.3.1 Future Orientation Model

Future orientation is a complex phenomenon that includes a multitude of cognitive and emotional processes and incentives (Nurmi 1991; Trommsdorff et al. 1982). The cognitive process includes the acquisition of knowledge regarding time and future, the prediction of possible future facts, the planning and making of decisions based on the future and the identification of future opportunities. Incentives include future goals, interests, values and obligations on the one hand, and worries, fears and doubts on the other. The emotional view of time orientation includes many emotions that are used to evaluate individuals such as optimism, pessimism and despair.

According to Nurmi (1989a, 1991), an individual's predictions about the future are based on the knowledge, perceptions and beliefs the individual acquires throughout life, and from participation in social groups. The comparison between knowledge and individual incentives and the values stemming from the individual's past determine the foundations for the delimitation of future-oriented goals (Strathman and Joireman 2005). By comparing an individual's incentives with their cognitive abilities regarding future opportunities, the individual is helped to define their life's course, which will satisfy their personal needs. An example of this particular process is choosing a career path. The values and interests of young people constitute the driving forces when choosing their professional career. Hence, certain values lead youngsters to choose a profession that will offer them a high income and material prosperity, whereas other kinds of values emphasize interpersonal relationships and team spirit.

By having determined future goals, the individual must find ways to make them come true. This requires a search for future opportunities and conceiving further goals, which will lead to the materialization of basic goals, establish necessary strategies and regulate behavior (Nurmi 1989b, 1991). As is the case with the delimitation of goals, knowledge of future opportunities also plays an important role toward effective planning and appropriate decision making. The individual abilities of cognitive perception and their distance in time provide the basis for future orientation. By developing these kinds of abilities, the individual can improve planning for the future by using information regarding the course of society and the many opportunities that are suitable for their own future development. The source of such information for teenagers comes from their parents, peers, school and the mass media.

Finally, the individual develops a variety of assessment tools to process information concerning the future and any possible challenges (Nurmi 1989a, 1993). At the same time, the individual also considers that they will be able to largely control factors affecting their future life. In turn, such mechanisms influence the individual's predictions about the future and, ultimately, future goals. These mechanisms can also be used to improve people's optimism toward the future. For example, a typical way to encourage an unemployed person to search harder for employment is to give them the opportunity to believe in their abilities and skills.

Future orientation can be integrated with human life development stages in two important ways. First, according to Nurmi (2004), a given stage in life that concerns a sum of challenges and opportunities defines the way in which the individual thinks and acts in the future. Many aspects of human life are characterized by different sociocultural structures in terms of age, which establish predictable and socially recognizable "road maps" (Hagestadt and Neugarten 1985). Such structures may be described as developmental processes (Havighurst 1948), a change of roles (Elder 1985) and as attempts at pursuing a professional career (Mayer 1986), all of which affect the individual's future planning in various ways. These factors create a sum of opportunities in a given period of life, which in turn offers the basis for setting long-term goals. In addition, knowledge exerts influence over plans and strategies. Successful planning requires accurate knowledge regarding future choices. Furthermore, the individual's predictions provide a basis to assess the future. Cross-cultural and historical differences, which mirror the individual's thoughts and actions regarding the future, are noted in all stages of human life. For example, 200 years ago, young people from agricultural societies saw their future in a totally different light than they do today; today they are offered a multitude of opportunities and possibilities.

Second, future actions and how people act work to establish foundations as to how humans will direct their development and choose a specific life course (Nurmi 1993). For example, the hierarchism of alternative goals leads to the choice of a specific perspective regarding the future and the elimination of other choices. Similarly, correct scheduling in terms of the future, together with the intellectual abilities of the individual, form the means for adaptation to future transitional periods.

10.3.2 Time Orientation and Decision Making

The role of time enters into many, if not all, of the decisions we make on a daily basis regarding all aspects of our lives. People are required to balance benefits gained (and the possible consequences of all their actions) with regard to the present and future. Regarding prosperity today and in the future, an individual should be able to evaluate all circumstances on the basis of the expected result. Hence, some people place a greater emphasis on the present and prefer to have a good time today, even though they are aware that they may be deprived of future resources and will not be able to maintain the same level of prosperity. Preferences and choices in time can explain why some people make rational decisions whereas others behave spontaneously and in an imprudent manner.

To understand how economic theory and the basic framework of rational expectations can prove useful in analyzing the role of time, it is important to note how economists define rationality and how they use it to predict and explain human behavior. Modern economic thinking focuses on making decisions that are effected on the basis of increasing prosperity and human happiness, and are not exclusively limited to the maximization of wealth.

To economists, all behaviors, even those that seem unreasonable (such as drug use or suicide) are seen to maximize prosperity and, as such, reflect the individual's choices. For example, drug addicts have different preferences to others. Depressed people may possibly assess their future prosperity in a significantly different way than those who are not depressed. Given that all people are assumed to make choices for personal advancement, if seen through the eyes of the one making the decisions, then all actions are rational. Economics does not make a judgment on what creates incentives—the individual's references are judged to the extent they affect decisions concerning economic theory.

As a means of transactions, money constitutes a useful tool through which the value of goods and services is quantified and compared; at the same time it also constitutes a useful tool for economics. Modern economic thought is focused not on money but on benefit and usefulness (the relevant satisfaction the individual takes from an action). Economists consider that the individual makes decisions aimed at maximizing benefit, and rejected choices offer less benefit; access to resources leads to greater levels of usefulness for the individual.

Economics can be characterized as the science of "compromises" (Strathman and Joireman 2005). Many compromises and exchanges include a combination of a series of resources, including time. Time increases the degree of complexity in economic analysis because there is no concurrent exchange of resources. Hence, economists attempt to compare today's value with future value and then decide which one maximizes benefit.

The renewal of economists' interest in the time orientation has led to the rebirth of the theory of diachronic preferences. The acknowledgment and measurement of individual time orientation or preferences over time has evolved through economic theory over the last 30 years, by means of a series of empirical surveys that include a multitude of behaviors and actions (Frederick et al. 2002). Although simple in its conception, the theory of time preferences can provide explanations and predict behaviors.

If all individuals are rational, then any exchange of benefit from one time period (today) to another (in the future) should lead to the maximization of benefit. Such an exchange should be based on the individual's improvement, given the individual's temperament. The individual's willingness to exchange a future and current benefit can be expressed with a factor that can be measured and be systematically applied to all benefit exchanges diachronically. This time preference factor is known as the discount factor (r) and differs among individuals; it constitutes a significant element of the rational expectations theory (Samuelson 1937).

When the individual faces a multitude of choices, they take their diachronic consequences into account and make their choice with the aim of maximizing their utility. Economists suggest that utility is a function of consumption and that higher consumption leads to higher utility. Let current consumption be C_t and consumption for future periods of time until period T be $C_2, C_3, \ldots, C_T$. The utility function can take the form $U_t (C_t, \ldots, C_T)$. If the individual is rational, then their decisions will be aimed at maximizing their utility by examining the impact that any of their choices will have on future consumption.

Balancing preferences involving future consequences includes a comparison of changes in the near future, as well as those in more distant time periods. The process becomes quite complex because of the individual's tendency to attribute lower value to future utility compared with current utility. Such a natural and rational tendency (to assign less value to future changes) can be explained as an attempt to gain protection against future uncertainty. Instead of the simple addition of the positive and negative consequences of every preference regarding all future periods, changes in future utility can be discounted by means of *r*.

In every diachronic decision, the individual steadily applies their own discount factor. The higher *r* is, the less important is a possible positive or negative change in future utility. Furthermore, *r* is used to discount any change in future utility. As far as the maximization of total utility is concerned, the individual examines the present condition (t), as well as the future ones until the last condition (T) and combines the preferences that ensure the maximum possible discounted utility from consumption.

To make a rational choice, the individual should balance the present discounted value of the utility of a preference against an alternative one. Utility in distant time periods is discounted more than utility in the near future. Individuals face a multitude of choices everyday that involve future consequences. Approaching such consequences rationally requires that future discounts will be consistently applied to all available choices. Individuals with a lower *r* are more willing to make decisions that reflect a less myopic (or spontaneous) time orientation (for example, they prefer to save and spend less today to have resources when they retire) compared with individuals with a higher discount factor.

References

Alesina A, Rodrik D (1994) Distributive politics and economic growth. Quart J Econ 109:465–490

Barro R (1991) Economic growth in a cross section of countries. Quart J Econ 106:407–443

Barro R (2000) Inequality and growth in a panel of countries. J Econ Growth 5:5–32

Bertola G (1991) Market structure and income distribution in endogenous growth models. NBER working paper no 3851. National Bureau of Economic Research, Cambridge

Bloom N (2009) The impact of uncertainty shocks. Econometrica 77(3):623–685

Bloom N (2011) The uncertainty shock from the debt disaster will cause a double-dip recession. VoxEU.org, http://www.voxeu.org/article/uncertainty-shock-will-cause-recession-evidence-16-previous-episodes

Bosma HA (1985) Identity development in adolescence. Coping with commitments. Rijksuniversiteit Te Groningen, Groningen

Bourguignon F, Ferreira F, Walton M (2007) Equity, efficiency and inequality traps: a research agenda. J Econ Inequal 5:235–256. doi:10.1007/s10888-006-9042-8

Brunetti A, Kisunko G, Weder B (1997) Credibility of rules and economic growth: evidence from a Worldwide Survey of the Private Sector. World Bank Policy research working paper no 1760. The World Bank, Washington, DC

Crockett LJ, Bingham CR (2000) Anticipating adulthood: expected timing of work and family transitions among rural youth. J Res Adolesc 10:151–172

Davidson P (1987) Sensible expectations and the long-run non-neutrality of money. J Post Keynesian Econ 10(1):146–153

de Carvalho FJC (1988) Keynes on probability, uncertainty, and decision making. J Post Keynesian Econ 11(1):66–99

Elder GH Jr (1985) Perspectives on the life course. In: Elder GH Jr (ed) Life course dynamics. Cornell University Press, Ithaka

Forbes K (2000) A reassessment of the relationship between inequality and growth. Am Econ Rev 90:869–887

Frederick S, Loewenstein G, O'Donaghue T (2002) Time discounting and time preference: a critical review. J Econ Lit 40:351–401

Gjesme T (1983) On the concept of future time orientation: considerations of some functions' and measurements' implications. Int J Psychol 14:443–461

Hagestadt GO, Neugarten BL (1985) Age and the life course. In: Binstock RH, Shanas E (eds) Handbook of aging and the social sciences. Van Nostrand Reinhold, New York, NY

Hall ET (1983) The dance of life: the other dimension of time. Anchor Press/Doubleday, Garden City

Havighurst RJ (1948) Developmental tasks and education. McKay, New York, NY

Hofstede G (2001) Culture's consequences. Sage, Newbury Park, CA

Jones JM (1988) Cultural differences in temporal perspectives: instrumental and expressive behaviours in time. In: McGrath E (ed) The social psychology of time: new perspectives. Sage, Newbury Park, CA

Jones JM (1993) An exploration of temporality in human behaviour. In: Schank R, Langer E (eds) Beliefs, reasoning, and decision making: psycho-logic in Honour of Bob Abelson. Lawrence Erlbaum Associates, Hillsdale, MI

Kastenbaum R (1961) The dimensions of future time perspective, an experimental analysis. J Gen Psychol 65:203–218

Keynes JM (1936) The general theory of employment, interest and money. MacMillan, London

Knack S, Keefer P (1995) Institutions and economic performance: cross-country tests using alternative institutional measures. Econ Polit 7:207–227

Knight FH (1921) Uncertainty and profit. University of Chicago Press

Kose MA, Terrones MA (2012) Uncertainty weighing on the global recovery. VoxEU.org. http://www.voxeu.org/article/uncertainty-weighing-global-recovery

Krueger AO (1974) The political economy of the rent-seeking society. Am Econ Rev 64(3):291–303

Kuznets S (1955) Economic growth and income inequality. Am Econ Rev 45:1–28

Li HY, Zou HF (1998) Income inequality is not harmful to growth: theory and evidence. Rev Dev Econ 2:318–334

Little BR (1983) Personal projects: a rationale and method for investigation. Environ Behav 15:273–309

Markowitz H (1952) The utility of wealth. J Polit Econ 60(2):151–158

Mauro P (1995) Corruption and growth. Q J Econ 110:681–712

Mayer KU (1986) Structural constraints on the life course. Hum Dev 29:163–170

McCarthy B (2000) The cult of risk taking and social learning: a study of Irish entrepreneurs. Manag Decis 38(8):563–575

Nurmi JE (1989a) Adolescents' orientation to the future: development of interests and plans, and relates attributions and affects, in the life-span context. Commentationes Scientiarum Socialium 39 Helsinki: The Finnish Society for Sciences and Letters

Nurmi JE (1989b) Development of orientation to the future during early adolescence: a four-year longitudinal study and two cross-sectional comparisons. Int J Psychol 24:195–214

Nurmi JE (1991) How do adolescents see their future? A review of the development of future orientation and planning. Dev Rev 11:1–59

Nurmi JE (1993) Adolescent development in an age-graded context: the role of personal beliefs, goals, and strategies in the tackling of developmental tasks and standards. Int J Behav Develop 16:169–189

Nurmi JE (2004) Socialization and self-development: Channeling, selection, adjustment, and reflection. In: Lerner R, Steinberg L (eds) Handbook of adolescent psychology. Wiley, Hoboken, NJ

Okun AM (1975) Equality and efficiency: the big tradeoff. The Brookings Institution, Washington, DC

Palsson AM (1996) Does the degree of relative risk aversion vary with household characteristics? J Econ Psychol 17:771–787

Perotti R (1996) Growth, income distribution, and democracy: what the data say. J Econ Growth 1:149–187

Persson T, Tabellini G (1992) Growth, distribution and politics. Eur Econ Rev 36:593–602

Persson T, Tabellini G (1994) Is inequality harmful for growth? Am Econ Rev 84:600–621

Ray DM (1994) The role of risk taking in Singapore. J Bus Ventur 9:157–157

Samuelson P (1937) A note on measurement of utility. Rev Econ Stud 4:155–161

Stevans L (2012) Income inequality and economic incentives: is there an equity-efficiency tradeoff? Res Econ 66:149–160

Strathman A, Joireman J (2005) Understanding behaviour in the context of time: theory, research, and application. Lawrence Erlbaum, Mahwah, NJ

Strough J, Berg CA, Sansone C (1996) Goals for solving everyday problems across the life span: age and gender differences in the salience of interpersonal concerns. Develop Psychol 18:415–427

Trommsdorff G, Burger C, Fuchsle T (1982) Social and psychological aspects of future orientation. In: Irle M (ed) Studies in decision making. de Gruyter, Berlin

Zimbardo PG, Boyd JN (1999) Putting time in perspective: a valid, reliable individual – differences metric. J Pers Soc Psychol 77:1271–88

The Cultural Background Change 11

The present chapter deals with a fundamental question concerning possible changes in values and cultural background over time. Examining the dynamic nature of cultural background may help to explain possible economic failures due to economic systems' inability to adapt to social conditions. The proper analysis of the prevailing conditions in each society is essential to setting appropriate economic growth policies. If values remain steady over time, then economic policy should adapt to the prevailing values. When social development is in line with changes in economic conditions, the result is an improvement in living standards and increased prosperity.

The structure of the chapter is as follows. Section 11.1 analyzes the role of globalization in the convergence and divergence of cultural background, and reference is also made to the modernization theory and the endurance of traditional values in modern societies. Section 11.2 examines the relationship between economic growth and a change in values. Section 11.3 presents the diachronic development of culture, and Sect. 11.4 touches on the evolution of values from generation to generation. Finally, the role of religious beliefs over the years is discussed in Sect. 11.5.

11.1 Convergence and Divergence of Cultural Background

Globalization is a process in which different cultural backgrounds affect each other through various processes such as the realization of commercial transactions, immigration and the exchange of information. Therefore, the importance of globalization in human activity has been of key interest in social science fields (Hermans and Kempen 1998). Globalization became more understandable through colonization, and its spread in recent years has been assisted by the exponential evolution of telecommunications, the movement of goods globally and the flow of capital in international markets (Arnett 2002; Hermans and Kempen 1998).

The fact that both the developed and developing countries cannot "escape" the course of globalization has raised questions for researchers as to how local cultures,

P.E. Petrakis, *Culture, Growth and Economic Policy*,
DOI 10.1007/978-3-642-41440-4_11, © Springer-Verlag Berlin Heidelberg 2014

as well as individuals, react to such change. Recently, research on socioeconomic changes has led to the creation of two conflicting schools of thought. The first emphasizes the convergence of values as a result of the modernization theory, according to which economic and political forces lead to a change in culture. The supporters of this school of thought predict the diminishment of traditional values and their substitution by "modern" values (Inglehart and Baker 2000).

Globalization leads to the convergence of cultural backgrounds and their practices, and that of the psychological mood of society's members who participate in the changing institutional framework. Because of globalization, people around the world now have the ability to use identical goods and follow a common way of living. Values that are prevalent in the Western world, such as privacy and consumerism, have spread to other parts of the world and play an important role in the process of cultural restructuring (Lam et al. 1999). Inkeles (1998) stated, "the transforming power of modern organizations is so big, that people's response would be the same, irrespective of the cultural background or the socioeconomic framework, to which they belong". He has also proposed two forms of convergence: one that concerns institutional standards and one that accepts a common global culture.

The second school of thought underlines the stability and endurance of traditional values despite the economic and political changes experienced in the globalized environment. A fundamental hypothesis of this particular school of thought is that values are relatively independent from economic change (DiMaggio 1994). As such, it foresees that convergence around a set of "modern" values is improbable and that traditional values will continue to exert influence over cultural change that stems from economic change. During the process of globalization, local and global culture interact, leading to a cultural transformation and high cohesion among cultural backgrounds (Hermans and Kempen 1998).

A version of the modernization theory emerged in post-war United States, which linked underdevelopment to the particular characteristics of each society: traditional economies, traditional psychological and cultural traits and traditional institutions (Lerner 1958; Weiner 1966). From this perspective, traditional values should not only be mutable, but also offer their place to modern values by assisting societies to follow the path of economic growth (Inglehart and Baker 2000). Wealthy and developed economies act to stimulate the modernization of underdeveloped nations through economic, cultural and military assistance.

The key argument of the modernization theory is based on economic growth, which is linked to coherent and, to a certain extent, predictable changes in social structures, political life and cultural background. Evidence from all over the world suggests that economic growth tends to propel societies toward an almost predictable path: industrialization leads to occupational specialization, rising education and income levels, and a series of unpredictable changes such as changes in the roles of gender, change in attitudes toward authority, a decline in the fertility rate and greater civic participation.

Nevertheless, a change in culture does not follow the simple linear trajectory envisioned by Marx (1976), that is, that the working class will continue to grow until the outbreak of a proletarian revolution that will signal the end of the process.

In 1956, the majority of the US workforce was employed in the service sector. Bell (1973) stated that in the decades that followed, almost all of the OECD member states followed the same course by acquiring traits of a "post-modernized" society. The changes that occurred in the employment sector had a significant impact on politics and culture (Bell 1973). Both increased materialism, which was linked to the industrial revolution, and unprecedented existential security have led to an intergenerational shift in values, placing a greater emphasis on "feminine values". While industrialization is directly linked to economic growth without examining the cost and consequences, whatever they may be, wealthy societies stress quality of life, environmental protection and self-expression. Bell (1973) and Inglehart (1977, 1990, 1997) saw changes in culture as representing a new direction, with the former emphasizing changes in employment and the latter endorsing the consequences of economic security.

The shift from a preindustrial to a postindustrial society was forged by extensive changes in peoples' everyday habits and dominant worldviews (Bell 1973; Inglehart 1997; Spier 1996). Life before industrialization, according to Bell (1976), constituted a "game against nature", which involved attempts to survive and cope in a hostile environment. However, as societies developed and the degree of industrialization grew, people became less dependent on and vulnerable to the forces of nature. Human life then becomes a "game against fabricated nature" (Bell 1973), in a world dominated by elements of rationalism, red tape and fabricated means to achieve absolute dominance over the environment. Furthermore, the greater an individuals' control over their external environment, the less their faith in God and religion.

The emergence of the postindustrial society is now moving toward the further stimulation and development of the dominant worldview, albeit in a different direction. Life in post-industrialized societies is focused on the provision of services and, as such, life becomes a "game between persons" (Inglehart and Baker 2000), in which people are alienated from nature. At the same time, individuals turn their interest and energy toward communication with others and the acquisition of information, and their attempts to produce material goods is limited. In the work environment, employees participate in groups to which certain specific goals have been assigned. Innovation and freedom of expression are features of modern businesses. An individual's self-expression is at the center of this process. The increase of wealth for the majority of the population has meant that survival is now taken for granted and is considered guaranteed. The change in values, which takes the form of a shift from an overwhelming emphasis on economic and physical safety to the search for prosperity and quality of life, constitutes a distinctive feature of modern societies. Hence, while cultural change cannot be linear, the emergence of a post-industrialized society pushes it in a new direction.

Nevertheless, different societies follow different trajectories, even if they are subject to the same forces of economic growth. This occurs because there are certain factors in each case, such as cultural heritage, which shape the way in which a society develops. Weber (1958) [1904] claimed that traditional religious values have an enduring influence on the institutions of each society. Similarly, Huntington (1993, 1996) claimed that the world can be divided into eight basic civilizations or "cultural zones" (Western world, Orthodox world, Islamic world, Confucianism, Hinduism, Africa, Japan and the Latin American zone) on the basis of cultural differences that have survived for centuries. These zones were shaped by the dominant religious traditions of the past, which are still powerful today despite the forces of modernization and globalization.

Scholars from various scientific fields have observed that the distinctive traits of each culture endure over long periods of time and continue to shape their social, economic and political structures. For example, Putnam (1993) showed that the regions of Italy, in which democratic institutions are successfully functioning today, are the same regions in which organized societies existed in the nineteenth century. Hamilton (1994) argued that apart from being an economic system, capitalism has also established a universal way of life. Nevertheless, civilizational factors continue to contribute toward the shaping of the structure of economy, institutions and society: "What we witness with the development of a global economy is not increasing uniformity, in the form of a universalization of Western culture, but rather the continuation of civilizational diversity through the active reinvention and reincorporation of non-Western civilizational patterns". In other words, a change in values is based on particular factors, resulting in the fact that the differences between cultural backgrounds endure over time. Thus, it makes sense for there to be striking cultural variations in organizations, institutions and organizational practices (DiMaggio 1994).

In conclusion, as far as the short-term horizon is concerned, we should accept cultural background as stable, whereas the long-term horizon is changing. In other words, the cultural characteristics of societies reflect psychological social stereotypes, which have been created in the long run and are human constructions prior to the current conditions of transactions and institutions. Cultural values present stability through time. In general, cultural stereotypes present great resistance towards change and to their own redefinition (Johnston 1996).

11.2 Economic Development and Changes in Values

A key focus of social sciences lies in the fundamental question that concerns the relationship between social development and a change in values. Studies that examine the existence of this relationship, as well as its direction, can be divided into three basic categories.

Political determinism claims that basic cultural values are responsible for the invigoration of economic growth (Weber 1958 [1904]; McClelland 1961; Franke et al. 1991; Sowell 1994; Harrison and Huntington 2001; Barro 2004). Protestant ethics influence economic growth in Western countries in a positive manner by cultivating the individual's need for distinction and progress and, consequently, aids entrepreneurship and individual initiative (Weber 1958 [1904]; McClelland 1961). Subsequent studies concerning the relationship between the need for achievements and economic growth have been less supportive of this idea (Tekiner 1980; Frey 1984). Nevertheless, cultural determinism has reappeared in other forms such as Confucian dynamism, which influenced the development of East Asia after World War II (Franke et al. 1991). Furthermore, elements of Protestantism, in conjunction with other religious beliefs, foresaw the economic growth of various nations after 1960 (Barro 2004).

Contrary to cultural determinism, economic determinism suggests that economic change also changes values and culture. Indicatively, Marx (1976) stated that technological progress and the forces of the productive process act to preserve the socioeconomic system, which, in turn, influences socioeconomic elements and cultural values. Bell (1973) identified the catalyst in changing values as the workforce, stating that the agricultural sector is a force against nature, industry controls nature with machines and services constitute strategic information structures among people. As the workforce shifts from agriculture to industry and then to services, the individual's view of nature, social roles and the wider cultural values also becomes different.

Certain theorists have identified the golden mean between cultural and economic determinism, stating that economic growth and a change in values are interrelated, given that certain values are linked with specific stages of economic growth. This particular approach makes reference to the existence of a causal nexus between culture and economy, which leads to an association between changes in values and economic growth.

Despite their differences, all three approaches mentioned above have one thing in common: they all suggest that a change in culture and economic growth are undeniably interconnected. Their differences lie with the direction of such a relationship, i.e., whether or not economic growth causes the change in values or the other way around. Some theorists (i.e., those who claim that there is a weak relationship between growth and a change in values or those that focus on the appropriateness of the methodology and conceptual framework used) strongly oppose the aforementioned ideas (Smith and Bond 1998). Yeh and Lawrence (1995) claimed that certain studies not only suffer from conceptual restrictions (for example, they arbitrarily use some variables as independent facts), but also overestimate the role of culture by excluding variables concerning political stability and economic policies. Finally, by summarizing the literature that links individualism to economic progress, Smith and Bond (1998) stated that "the force of the relationship between wealth and various indices of individualism is different from survey to survey and in certain cases . . . it is weak".

11.3 Culture, Values and Their Diachronic Development

The following questions are essential to identify differences and to conduct a comparison. First, does cultural background constitute a dynamic figure and, second, does economic growth lead to a change in values and the amelioration of an individual's prosperity?

There are a limited number of studies to date on the diachronic changes in values, institutions and culture; thus, this field is open to further thorough research. De Jong (2009) considered that culture (values) remains stable provided the conditions shaping it also remain relatively stable. The structure of a society's values is open to diversities, by rapidly responding to significant economic, technological and political changes (Schwartz 1992). Using interviews with IBM personnel, Hofstede (1980) was able to identify various dimensions of cultural background. These interviews occurred during two periods of time: 1967–1969 and 1971–1973. Regarding the countries included in both measurements, Hofstede (2001) examined the differences in the results and found a clear increase in "individualism" in the 4 years between the start of each period (Table 11.1). This increase is positively associated with increases in income, which determines the direction of the relationship from wealth toward individualism. In his own words, "poverty makes people depend on the support of their in-groups, but when a country's wealth increases, its citizens get access to resources that allow them to do their own thing". Regarding "power distance" and "uncertainty avoidance" indices, no changes were detected in the attitudes of those questioned as time went by and, hence, such indices cannot be used to examine the diachronic change of cultural background (Hofstede 2001). Regarding "masculinity", the long-term influence was weak. Nevertheless, the 4-year period between measurements is quite short to allow for robust conclusions. To ensure more credible conclusions, observations should cover a longer period of time.

One of the surveys that dominates the literature in this specific research field is that of Ng et al. (1982), which was repeated in 2002. Their aim was to examine the extent to which the map of values of eight nations in East Asia and the Pacific has changed over a period of 20 years and, if the answer to that is positive, whether or not such changes are linked to economic growth. Ng et al. (1982) carried out a survey among the different cultural backgrounds of Bangladesh, Australia, Japan, Malaysia, New Guinea, India, Taiwan, New Zealand and Hong Kong (given that it was a separate sovereign state when the survey was conducted). Choosing students from each nationality, they created a broader version of the Values Survey by Rokeach (1973), which comprised values weighted in accordance with the importance attributed to them by respondents.

In their analysis, Ng et al. (1982) grouped the values based on the answers they received: submission versus Dionysian values and inner strength versus materialistic values. Therefore, they classified societies in accordance with their value orientations, by underlining hierarchy and obedience (i.e., submission, politeness and national security) on the one hand and values oriented toward the individual with a strong hedonistic or "Dionysian" tendency (i.e., indulgence and mutual love) on the other. In general, poorer countries such as Malaysia, India and Bangladesh seemed to adopt submission. In contrast, richer countries such as Australia, New Zealand and Japan were oriented toward Dionysian values. Hong Kong and Taiwan were somewhere in the middle or slightly closer to submission.

Using the results of Ng et al. (1982) as their point of reference, Allen et al. (2007) assessed any shifts in values in the nine societies between 1982 and 2002. As

Table 11.1 Average changes in answers for 1967–1969 and 1971–1973: Hofstede's Surveys

Code	Question	1967–1969 Average[a]	1971–1973 Average[a]	Respective variance of the Index[b]	Number of countries that participated in both measurements	Variance towards the same direction
Questions for the determination of the "Power Distance" dimension						
B46	Employees being afraid to express disagreement	3.09	2.93	+	26	18*
A55	Perceived manager	47.9	45.4	–	29	22**
A54	Preferred management method	27.1	22.9	–	29	22**
B55	Lack of employees' respect	4.02	4.10	–	20	15**
A52	Manager helps ahead	2.34	2.52	+	29	23***
A13	Importance of freedom	529	544	–	19	16***
B52	Corporation's responsibility	1.74	1.72	0	22	11
B53	Interesting work important	1.78	1.84	–	23	16*
Questions for the determination of the "Uncertainty Avoidance" dimension						
B60	Rules should not be broken	2.80	2.87	0 (–)	20	12
A43	Employment stability	20.0	20.7	0 (–)	28	12
A37	Stress	3.19	3.10	+	29	24***
B9	Preference for specialist career	3.09	3.23	–	13	11*
B44	Preference of manager of own nationality	1.73	1.68	+	21	14*
B54	Competition harmful	3.02	2.84	+	21	17**
B57	Individual decisions better	3.53	3.64	+	17	13*
B61	Most employees avoid responsibility	3.36	3.38	0	20	11
A10	Importance of benefits	376	392	+	19	14*
A15	Importance of advancement	546	510	+	19	17***
A58	Overall satisfaction	2.79	3.14	–	28	27***
A2	Seniority in a company	3.10	3.27	+	29	22**
A57	Age	3.87	4.03	+	29	24***

(continued)

Table 11.1 (continued)

Code	Question	1967–1969 Average[a]	1971–1973 Average[a]	Respective variance of the Index[b]	Number of countries that participated in both measurements	Variance towards the same direction
Questions for the determination of the "Individualism" dimension						
A18	Importance of free time	438	484	+	19	19***
A9	Importance of training	578	526	+	19	18***
A12	Importance of physical condition	363	348	0 (+)	19	13
A17	Importance of use of skills	555	530	+	19	17***
B24	Preference of foreign company	1.79	1.88	+	22	15*
B25	Exercise of another profession	1.85	1.87	0	25	15
B59	Staying with one company desirable	3.19	3.06	–	21	16**
IMP	The importance of goals	197.2	199.7	0	19	13
Questions for the determination of the "Masculinity" dimension						
A7	Importance of profit	501	525	+	19	14*
A16	Importance of the manager's role	566	531	+	19	16***
A8	Importance of cooperation	554	542	0 (+)	19	11
A11	Importance of recognition	480	486	+	19	14*
A6	Importance of desirable areas	433	468	–	19	14*
A5	Importance of challenges	587	619	+	19	17***
A14	Importance of employment security	496	495	0	19	11
A1	Gender (% of women)	7.0	7.3	0	26	16

Source: Hofstede (2001)

Note: The asterisks indicate levels of statistical significance: *$p = 0.05$, **$p = 0.01$, ***$p = 0.001$

[a]Expressed in percentages for questions A1, A43, A54 and A55, in standardized scoring for questions A5–A18 and in scores from 3-, 4-, 5-, 6-, 7-point scales for the remaining questions

[b]Change sign multiplied by correlation sign between question and factor

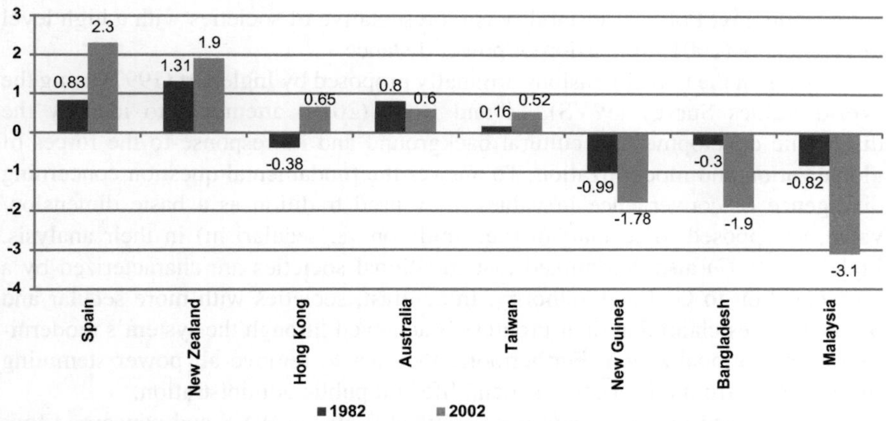

Fig. 11.1 National averages for submission and Dionysian values in 1982 and 2002. *Source*: Allen et al. (2007)

depicted in Fig. 11.1, the nations in the 2002 measurement showed change regarding the dominant values in 1982 (with certain exceptions of course). More specifically, the nations that supported Dionysian values in 1982, such as Japan and New Zealand, increased their emphasis on such values in 2002. In the 2002 measurement, Bangladesh, New Guinea and Malaysia scored higher for submission than in the 1982 measurement.

The findings of this survey indicate that changes occurred in the cultural values of the surveyed counties between 1982 and 2002; nonetheless, it should be stressed that such change concerns the extent to which societies adopt such values and not their perceptions, beliefs and institutions. In addition, the 20 years that lapsed between the two measurements constitutes a reasonable length of time with which to observe any deviations in scores. Hence, based on that study, it is not unreasonable to claim that values and culture remain relatively stable in time or undergo changes following long-term processes.

The results of the survey also support the view of economic determinism, i.e., that economic growth leads to a change in values. If one attempts to identify the deeper cause behind this, then one might consider technological development and innovation as the primary determinative factors of the course of modern societies. In turn, such development and innovation requires the existence of a labor force equipped with high education levels. Education and social mobility can act to reduce social inequality. An increased emphasis on the upward social mobility of the lower and middle classes signals the emergence of values oriented toward individualism (Allen et al. 2007). At the same time, when the upper classes oppose the implementation of social justice, this results in dissention in the middle and lower classes—political instability does not favor social mobility. Thus, economic growth in a significant part of the economy is restrained and, ultimately, affects the entire economy. Political instability is representative of societies with a high level of Hofstede's (2001) dimension of power distance.

Relying on the two dimensions originally proposed by Inglehart (1997) using the World Values Survey (WVS), Li and Bond (2010) attempted to identify the diachronic development of cultural background and its response to the forces of globalization and modernization. To answer the fundamental question concerning divergence or convergence in values, they used tradition as a basic dimension/value, as opposed to secularism (i.e., tradition vs. secularism) in their analysis. Inglehart (1997) also determined that traditional societies are characterized by a high devotion to God and authority. In contrast, societies with more secular and rational values claim that their progress is achieved through the system's modernization and rationalization. Furthermore, they act to remove all power stemming from religion from all aspects of social life and public administration.

The data used in that survey were sourced from the WVS and concerned four measurements (1981–1984, 1989–1993, 1994–1999 and 1999–2004) in 72 countries. To examine whether values change through the process of globalization, they used five elements stemming from each WVS measurement as a measure for the tradition/secularism dimension: the autonomy index, "Is it more important for a child to learn to be obedient and have faith in religion than to be determinative and independent", "God is important in the life of the person questioned", "The person questioned shows respect towards the authorities", "The person questioned has a developed sense of national pride" and "The person questioned gives priority to individual expression and quality of life through economic and physical security". The human development index of the United Nations Development Programme was also used as a measure of social development to examine whether national progress is responsible for the secularization of values.

To examine whether values converge under the influence of globalization, the typical divergence of the tradition/secularism score was used from measurement to measurement. Any differences in the typical divergence from measurement to measurement, whether positive or negative, suggest a divergence or convergence of the values, respectively. Nevertheless, the typical divergences for each pair of measurements were not significantly different; thus, there is no evidence over the 20-year period of either convergence or divergence of the cultural dimensions under examination.

Through their findings, Li and Bond (2010) rejected the basic assumption connected with globalization and the convergence or divergence of values. Over a period of 20 years, the values remained steady and resistant to change in different countries. The influence of the West was not strong enough to turn the local cultures of developing countries in the direction of secularism. The conclusions of Esmer's (2007) survey follow the same path. Using data from the WVS, he found just a small change in values and no evidence to establish even a slight convergence of values and institutions (e.g., marriage and family) between 1980 and 2000 in 20 countries.

Inglehart and Baker (2000) examined the theory that economic growth is linked to systematic changes in the basic values of every society. Using data from three

WVS measurements, they identified evidence certifying a change in values, as well as the endurance of traditional values.

Inglehart and Baker (2000) considered economic growth to have a powerful influence on cultural values. The system of values of wealthier countries is significantly different from that of poorer nations. At the same time, economic growth drives societies toward a common direction, irrespective of their cultural heritage. The change from agricultural to industrial production, appears to coincide with a shift from traditional values to secular-rational values. Despite this, two centuries after the start of the industrial revolution there are still discrete "cultural borders" among societies because of the cultural heritage that follows them.

Former communist societies did not follow a common path. Some successfully transitioned to a market economy, whereas some others faced social and economic collapse. Those in the latter group also experienced a shift back to survival values, whereas those who enjoyed economic growth moved in the opposite direction. The combination of economic, political and social collapse, from which Soviet countries suffered during the 1980s and 1990s, gave rise to misery, xenophobia, lack of trust and totalitarian nationalism.

11.4 Differences in Values from Generation to Generation

In their study to determine the duration and requirements for a change in values and cultural background, Inglehart and Baker (2000) assumed that an analysis of the differences in values among generations might provide a clearer image as to how values behave over a longer period of time. The survey clearly showed that the basic values acquired during childhood remain steady until adolescence (Inglehart 1977, 1997; Baker et al. 1981). Schuman and Scott (1989) claimed that every generation portrays memories of childhood and early adolescence, which affect an individual's way of thinking throughout their life. Hence, it is quite possible that there are essential differences between younger and older members of society, which may be attributed to the different environments and prevalent circumstances of their childhoods. An increased feeling of security constitutes an important factor pointing toward this direction (Inglehart 1997).

The experiences that shaped the character and personality of young people in industrialized societies during the twentieth century are significantly different from those of their elders, because their basic needs for survival were safeguarded and living conditions improved. Using WVS data from 1907 to 1976, Inglehart and Baker (2000) grouped countries into four categories on the basis of their income and economic history in the twentieth century: developed countries, former communist countries, emerging economies and low-income societies. They then divided the study period (1907–1976) into 7 birth-year classes to identify how values change from generation to generation.

Their results showed that younger generations after 1950 in industrialized and former communist countries placed a greater emphasis on secular-rational values to the detriment of traditional values; it was during this period that significant economic growth was observed. A change of economic conditions seems to play a significant role in the differences among generations. Older people in former communist countries scored higher for secular-rational values compared with people of the same age in other societies; during their childhood, former communist countries experienced rapid economic growth and prevailed over capitalism. At the same time, the restraint of religion and traditional values contributed to the establishment of the secular-rational values.

As far as survival/self-expression values are concerned, the most rapid changes among generations were identified in developed and former communist societies. The changes in developing economies were relatively small, and no significant differences were observed between the values of young and old people in low-income societies. Former communist countries were ranked quite low compared with other societies in terms of cultural syndromes such as trust, patience, prosperity, civic participation and individual expression. This fact partly mirrors the prevalent conditions in such societies. After the fall of communism and the Soviet Union, life for people in these countries became insecure and unpredictable, and life expectancy dropped dramatically. Finally, little difference among generations in low-income societies indicates the majority of the population continues to place an emphasis on the survival values. In contrast, one decade after the fall of the Soviet Union, levels of economic security in former communist countries were particularly high and then dramatically dropped in the years that followed.

11.5 The Preservation of Religious Beliefs Over Time

As societies evolved from traditional agricultural production to mainly industrial production, their system of values was also influenced. The production of necessary goods for the survival of the population, technological progress and improvements in living standards has guaranteed survival for many populations. Nevertheless, the gap among religious beliefs around the world remains and acts to create a divergence between culture and the values of societies.

Hence, questions are raised: why has religion not been effaced or at the very least why has its role not been reduced in modern societies? The answers to these questions vary. The critical point to understand this particular situation lies with the uncertainty and insecurity experienced by the majority of society and, more particularly, by the lower social classes. Despite the increased physical and economic security enjoyed by modern societies, and the fact that religious faith may not be a dominant force in society, it nevertheless influences the way decisions are made. Communism was associated with secular-rational values and with a limited role for religion and traditional values. However, its fall and the upheaval that followed gave rise to insecurity and a return to religious faith.

Two conflicting theories regarding religion and economic development (Inglehart and Baker 2000): on the one hand, a decrease in religious proceedings in industrially developed countries and on the other, the survival of religious and spiritual beliefs. Table 11.2 shows that participation in religious ceremonies

Table 11.2 Participation (at least monthly) percentages in religious ceremonies per country and year

Country	1981	1990–1991	1995–1998	Net change
Developed industrial republics[a]				
Australia	40	–	25	−15
Belgium	38	35	–	−3
Canada	45	40	–	−5
Finland	13	13	11	−2
France	17	17	–	0
E. Germany	–	20	9	−11
W. Germany	35	33	25	−10
G. Britain	23	25	–	+2
Iceland	10	9	–	−1
Ireland	88	88	–	0
N. Ireland	67	69	–	+2
S. Korea	29	60	27	−2
Italy	48	47	–	−1
Japan	12	14	11	−1
The Netherlands	40	31	–	−9
Norway	14	13	13	−1
Spain	53	40	38	−15
Sweden	14	10	11	−3
Switzerland	–	43	25	−18
USA	60	59	55	−5
Former communist societies[b]				
Belarus	–	6	14	+8
Bulgaria	–	9	15	+6
Hungary	16	34	–	+18
Latvia	–	9	16	+7
Poland	–	85	74	−11
Russia	–	6	8	+2
Slovenia	–	35	33	−2
Developing and low-income societies[c]				
Argentina	56	55	41	−15
Brazil	–	50	54	+4
Chile	–	47	44	−3
India	–	71	54	−17
Mexico	74	63	65	−9
Nigeria	–	88	87	−1
S. Africa	61	–	70	+9
Turkey	–	38	44	+6

Source: Inglehart and Baker (2000)

Notes:

[a]16 out of 20 developed countries show a decrease, average variance = −5

[b]5 out of 7 former communist countries show an increase, average variance = +4

[c]5 out of 8 developing and low-income societies show a decrease, average variance = −4

decreased in 16 of the 20 listed developed industrial countries; only two experienced an increase in participation. Furthermore, General Social Survey results from 1989 to 1998 also recorded a drop in church attendance in the United States (Smith 1999). The pattern differs among former communist societies. The majority of these societies (5 of 7) show an increase in religious attendance. The results for emerging economies are mixed: approximately half experienced an increase in religious activities and half recorded a decrease.

The decrease in the prevalence of traditional and religious values characterizes the stage of industrialization, but not necessarily that of post-industrialization (Inglehart and Baker 2000). As mentioned above, people's faith in divine elements is linked to the insecurity they feel in terms of safeguarding their survival. Since ancient times, people's thoughts have been dominated by questions regarding their existence, purpose and origins. The fact that individuals placed their hope in divine elements, and the need to answer such questions, placed religion at the center of society. Although the transition to modern social structures, in conjunction with technological progress, has changed how people view the world, spiritual concerns may well exist for eternity. In addition, a scientific approach to theology and other similar scientific fields has emerged to fill the gap in the existential problems of human nature (Baker WE (1999) North star falling: the American crisis of values at the new millennium. school of business, University of Michigan, Ann Arbor, MI, Unpublished manuscript). With the emergence of post-industrialized societies, submission to religious institutions continued to decline but this was not the case with spiritual concerns. We continue to devote time to seek a deeper meaning and purpose of life.

The subjective importance of religious beliefs has changed slightly in developed industrial nations. Although the WVS showed that approximately half of the surveyed countries assigned a limited emphasis on the significance of God, faith in God remains high in the other half. Furthermore, religious following has increased in former communist countries.

References

Allen MW, Ng SH, Ikeda K, Jawan JA, Sufi AH, Wilson M, Yang K-S (2007) Two decades of change in cultural values and economic development in eight East Asian and Pacific Island Nations. J Cross-Cult Psychol 38:247

Arnett JJ (2002) The psychology of globalization. Am Psychol 57:774–783

Baker WE, Kendall RD, Hildebrandt K (1981) Germany transformed. Harvard University Press, Cambridge

Barro RJ (2004) Spirit of capitalism. Harv Int Rev 25(4):64–68

Bell D (1973) The coming of post-industrial society. Basic Books, New York, NY

Bell D (1976) The cultural contradictions of capitalism. Basic Books, New York, NY

De Jong E (2009) Culture and economics: on values. Economics and International Business, Routledge, NY

DiMaggio P (1994) Culture and economy. In: Smelser NJ, Swedberg R (eds) The handbook of economic sociology. Princeton University Press, Princeton, NJ

Esmer Y (2007) Globalization, "McDonaldization" and values: Quo Vadis? In: Esmer Y, Pattesson T (eds) Measuring and mapping cultures: 25 years of comparative value surveys. Brill, Leiden, pp 79–98

Franke RH, Hofstede G, Bond MH (1991) Cultural roots of economic performance: a research note. Strateg Manag J 12:165–173

Frey RS (1984) Does n-achievement cause economic development? A cross-lagged panel analysis of the McClelland thesis. J Soc Psychol 122:67–70

Hamilton GG (1994) Civilizations and organization in economies. In: Smelser NJ, Swedberg R (eds) The handbook of economic sociology. Princeton University Press, Princeton, NJ

Harrison LE, Huntington SP (2001) Culture matters: how values shape human progress. Basic Books, New York, NY

Hermans HJM, Kempen HJG (1998) Moving cultures the perilous problems of cultural dichotomies in a globalizing society. Am Psychol 53:1111–1120

Hofstede G (1980) Culture's consequences. Sage, Beverly Hills, CA

Hofstede G (2001) Culture's consequences: comparing values, behaviors, institutions and organizations across nations, 2nd edn. Sage, Beverly Hills, CA

Huntington S (1993) The clash of civilizations? Foreign Affair 72(3):22–49

Huntington S (1996) The clash of civilizations and the remaking of world order. Simon and Schuster, New York, NY

Inglehart R (1977) The silent revolution: changing values and political style in advanced industrial society. Princeton University Press, Princeton, NJ

Inglehart R (1990) Cultural shift in advanced industrial society. Princeton University Press, Princeton, NJ

Inglehart R (1997) Modernization and postmodernization: cultural, economic, and political change in 43 societies. Princeton University Press, Princeton, NJ

Inglehart R, Baker WE (2000) Modernization, culture change, and the persistence of traditional values. Am Sociol Rev 65:19–51

Inkeles A (1998) One world emerging? convergence and divergence in industrial societies. Westview Press, Boulder, CO

Johnston L (1996) Resisting change: information-seeking and stereotype change. Eur J Soc Psychol 26:799–825

Lam S, Lau I, Chiu C-Y, Hong Y-Y, Peng S (1999) Differential emphases on modernity and traditional values in social categorization. Int J Intercult Relat 23:237–256

Lerner D (1958) The passing of traditional society: modernizing the middle east. Free Press, New York, NY

Li LMW, Bond MH (2010) Analyzing national change in citizen secularism across four time periods in the World Values Survey. World Value Res 3(2):19–22

Marx K (1976) [1867] Capital. Penguin, Harmondsworth

McClelland DC (1961) The achieving society. Free Press, New York, NY

Ng SH, Hossain A, Ball P, Bond MH, Hayaski K, Lim SP, O' Driscoll MP, Sinha D, Yang KS (1982) Human values in nine countries. In: Rath R, Asthana HS, Sinha D, Sinha JBP (eds) Diversity and unity in cross cultural psychology. Swets and Zeitlinger, Lisse

Putnam R (1993) Making democracy work: civil traditions in modern Italy. Princeton University Press, Princeton, NJ

Rokeach M (1973) The nature of human values. Free Press, New York, NY

Schuman SH, Scott J (1989) Generations and collective memories. Am Sociol Rev 54:359–381

Schwartz SH (1992) Universals in the content and structure of values: theoritical advances and empirical tests in 20 countries. Adv Exp Soc Psychol 25(1):1–65

Smith T (1999) Church attendance declining in the U.S. National Opinion Center Press Release, June 8

Smith P, Bond MH (1998) Social psychology across cultures. Prentice Hall, London

Sowell T (1994) Race and culture: world view. Basic Books, New York, NY

Spier F (1996) The structure of big history: from the big bang until today. Amsterdam University Press, Amsterdam
Tekiner A (1980) Need achievement and international differences in income growth: 1950-1960. Econ Dev Cult Chang 28:293–320
Weber M (1904) The protestant ethic and the spirit of capitalism. English edition: Parsons T (1958). Reprint, Charles Scribner's Sons, New York
Weiner M (1966) Modernization: the dynamics of growth. Basic, New York, NY
Yeh R, Lawrence JJ (1995) Individualism and confucian dynamism: a note on Hofstede's cultural root to economic growth. J Int Bus Stud 26:665–669

Part III

Cultural Background, Growth and Policy

Part III outlines the basic elements of cultural background at a macro level. One reason why it is so very difficult to corroborate the relationship between cultural background and basic concepts lies with the problem of their functioning together within a multitude of complex concepts and relationships. Furthermore, there is also the problem of the inter-influence of a dual direction. Hence, if we wish to examine and establish a causal relationship between cultural background and growth, then we need to use a growth model that includes the main growth factors (e.g., capital, labor). Furthermore, if one were to attempt to examine the relationship between cultural background and entrepreneurship, then one could not ignore the influence of the institutional framework and transactions that influence and are influenced by cultural background. The second focus of this part is to determine the issues concerning economic policy and growth policies in relation to cultural background.

This part contains five chapters. Chapter 12 analyzes the relationships among economic growth, cultural background and cultural change. Chapter 13 examines the relationship between cultural background and transaction costs. Chapter 14 analyzes the effects of culture, transactions and institutions on opportunity entrepreneurship. Chapter 15 examines the effects of cultural background, knowledge creation and the impact on self-employment and entry density rates. The importance of cultural background in shaping the middle-income growth trap as well as the relationship between cultural background and economic policy are analyzed in Chap. 16.

12 Economic Growth and Cultural Background

The present chapter[1] aims to contribute to the interpretation of the annual growth rates of GDP with specific reference to fundamental growth factors (i.e., capital, labor and human capital) and cultural background. The focus here is on cultural background as an influential element of growth. Whether directly or indirectly, culture influences the outcome of the economic process. The importance of culture, its quantification and formal analysis can prove challenging. Acemoglu (2009) looked to the work of Montesquieu (1989), Machiavelli (1987) and Marshall (1997) for references regarding the general features of the environment that may impact on attitudes and human conventions. The role of religion has been underlined by Weber (1958) and more recently by Harrison and Huntington (2000), and Putnam (1993) broadened the meaning of cultural factors and trust as they relate to the concept of social capital.

The role of culture in growth has been carefully examined in previous chapters (see Part II). Hence, the present chapter is limited to the quantitative examination of the relationship. The chapter is structured as follows. Section 12.1 presents the data and Sect. 12.2 describes the methodology, empirical model and measurements. Section 12.3 presents the empirical work and a discussion of the results.

12.1 Data

In collecting relevant data, we treated the world as a typical country, assuming that the production process is homogenous around the world because we did not allow for heterogeneous growth experiences (Bos et al. 2010). Our limited degrees of freedom (i.e., the small sample is constrained by the limited number of observations

[1] This chapter is a summary of a scientific paper by Petrakis P.E. and Kostis P.C. (2013) "Economic Growth and Cultural Change" published in the Journal of Socioeconomics, Issue C, Vol. 47, pp. 147–157.

P.E. Petrakis, *Culture, Growth and Economic Policy*,
DOI 10.1007/978-3-642-41440-4_12,

Table 12.1 Description, sources and periods of reference of the variables used

		Variables	Description	Reference period	Source of elements
Cultural background	Efficiency orientation	Performance orientation	The degree to which a society encourages and rewards its members for performance improvement and excellence	1995–1997	House et al. (2004)
		Future orientation	The extent to which individuals engage in future-oriented behaviors, such as delaying gratification, planning and investing in the future		
		Assertiveness	The degree to which individuals are assertive, confrontational and aggressive in their relationships with others.		
		Power distance	The degree to which members of a society expect power to be distributed equally		
		Uncertainty avoidance	The extent to which members of an organization or society strive to avoid uncertainty by reliance on social norms, rituals, and bureaucratic practices to alleviate the unpredictability of future events		
	Social orientation	Gender egalitarianism	The degree to which a society minimizes gender inequality		
		Institutional collectivism	The degree to which organizational and societal practices encourage and reward collective distribution of resources and collective action		
		In-group collectivism	The degree to which individuals express pride, loyalty and cohesiveness in their organizations or families		

(continued)

Table 12.1 (continued)

	Variables	Description	Reference period	Source of elements
	Humane orientation	The degree to which a society encourages and rewards individuals for being fair, altruistic, generous, caring and kind to others		
Capital	Investment rates (percent of GDP)	Expressed as a ratio of total investment in current local currency and GDP in current local currency	Mean of the period 1998-2003	World Economic Outlook Database, http://www.imf.org
Human capital	Average years of schooling	It is the number of years of schooling achieved by the average person at various levels and at all levels of schooling combined	2000	Barro and Lee Database, v. 1.2, http://www.barrolee.com
Labor	Working population (age 25+) growth	Annual growth of working population aged 25 and over	Mean of the period 2000–2005	
Target variable	GDP annual growth rate (constant prices)	Annual percentages of constant price GDP are year-on-year changes; the base year is country-specific	Mean of the period 2001–2006	World Economic Outlook Database, http://www.imf.org

Note: The 41 countries in the sample represent 90.44 % of world GDP in 2007 (IMF database). These countries are Argentina, Australia, Austria, Brazil, Canada, China, Colombia, Denmark, Ecuador, Finland, France, Germany, Greece, Hong Kong, Hungary, India, Indonesia, Ireland, Israel, Italy, Japan, Malaysia, Mexico, Netherlands, New Zealand, Philippines, Poland, Portugal, Russian Federation, Singapore, Slovenia, South Africa, South Korea, Spain, Sweden, Switzerland, Thailand, Turkey, United Kingdom, United States and Venezuela

for entrepreneurial variables) did not allow us to deepen our analysis in this respect. The variables are precisely defined in Table 12.1.

The data for the dependent variable (GDP) concern the average annual GDP growth rates during the period 2001–2006. To measure capital, we used investment rates as a percentage of GDP during the period 1998–2003, leaving a time margin of 3 years for return on investment. Capital is measured by the total value of the gross fixed capital formation and changes in inventories and acquisitions less disposals of valuables for a unit or sector, and is calculated annually by the International Monetary Fund. Regarding human capital, we used the average years of schooling for people aged over 25 years. It is calculated as the distribution of educational attainment among the population, combined with information for each country on the duration of school at each level. The number of years of schooling has long been considered a good proxy for human capital (Hall and Jones 1999; Cohen and Soto 2007). Regarding labor, we used the mean annual growth rate of the working population (aged 25–64) during the period 2000–2005 (Owen et al. 2009). Average years of schooling and working population (aged 25+) growth are calculated every 5 years by the Barro and Lee database.

As far as the variables capturing cultural background are concerned, we used the nine cultural dimensions of the GLOBE study (House et al. 2004). GLOBE is the most comprehensive study to date to empirically research the relationship between culture and behavior in so many societies, with so many different quantitative and qualitative measures. It is based on results from 17,300 middle managers from 951 organizations in the food, financial services, and telecommunications service industries, in 62 societies around the world. The cultural dimensions were derived using questionnaires based on a 7-point scale. Although the data refer to the period 1997–1998, the social stereotypes forming cultural background may be characterized as long lasting, and cultural values present stability through time. Therefore, regarding the periods analyzed, the variables related to cultural background may be considered as constants. The descriptive statistics of the variables are given in Table B.1 (Appendix B).

12.2 Methodology Employed and Empirical Results

Following Owen et al. (2009), our estimated empirical model included regressors that capture the proximate determinants of economic growth. Investments in economy, education and population growth in the labor force are considered as direct measures of the growth of productive factors. Furthermore, the growth factors of the basic model are those of the augmented neoclassical model introduced by Mankiw et al. (1992), as well as the robust determinants of economic growth identified by Levine and Renelt (1992). The standard growth equation used in this model is as follows:

$$GDP_i = \beta_1 * CAP_i + \beta_2 * L_i + \beta_3 * HC_i + \beta_4 * C_i + \varepsilon_i, \tag{12.1}$$

where the dependent variable (GDP) is the average annual GDP growth rate in constant prices; CAP (capital) is defined by the average investment rate (percentage of GDP); L (labor) is the sum of "$n+g+\delta$", where n is the average population growth of the working population aged between 25 and 64 years, g is the growth rate of technology and δ the depreciation rate; HC (human capital) is defined as the average number of years of schooling in the initial period; and C is the principal component (PC) that arises from the variables capturing cultural background. Based on Mankiw et al. (1992), we assumed that the annual rates of technological growth (g) and depreciation ($\imath$) are constant and sum to 0.05. Subscripts i refer to the countries used in the model.

To abstract from the complexity of the explanatory variables, we use the principal component analysis (PCA). PCA enabled us to reduce the number of variables representing cultural background, while detecting the structure in the relationships among these variables. Smith (2002) commented that PCA is a way of identifying patterns in data and expressing the data to highlight their similarities and differences. More specifically, PCA is a factor-extraction method used to form uncorrelated linear combinations of observed variables, which are then used to obtain the initial factor solution when a correlation matrix is singular. The first principal component (PC) has a maximum variance. Successive components explain progressively smaller portions of the variance and all are uncorrelated with each other.

We applied PCA to the group of variables capturing cultural background. The effects of PCs on GDP were examined through a linear regression using the ordinary least squares (OLS) method, as in the model presented above. In our linear regression, we used PCs with the greatest variances (initial eigenvalues >0.91).

To check for endogeneity among the variables used, we used a version of the Hausman test (Hausman 1978) proposed by Davidson and MacKinnon (1989, 1993), which employs a test statistic for exogeneity by running an auxiliary regression. The null hypothesis stated that the model yields consistent estimates and the reported p-values stated the probability that the test statistic is zero, which would imply the acceptance of the null hypothesis. In this test, we used a set of instrumental variables that correlated with the "suspect" variable but not with the error term of the regression that applies GDP as a dependent variable. The OLS estimates will only be consistent and unbiased if there is no endogeneity. In addition, the partial instrumental variables R^2 are reported to describe how much of the squared residuals can be explained by the instrumental variables. The partial p-value, which is the probability that the F-value for each instrumental variable is zero, is also reported. Both tests describe how effective the instrumental variables are in explaining annual GDP growth rates.

Furthermore, we also conducted a sensitivity analysis of this basic scenario. The scope of this experiment was to evaluate the effect of culture on annual GDP growth rates under changing societal circumstances. We created eight combinations of cultural background in societies by increasing or decreasing the values of some cultural variables and maintaining the effect of the basic growth factors in all cases. We divided the cultural background variables in two main groups (see Table 12.1). The first group covers variables that represent the "efficiency orientation" of the societies: performance orientation, future orientation, assertiveness, power distance and uncertainty avoidance. The second covers the variables that represent the "social orientation" of societies, i.e., the attitudes and lifestyles of their members. These variables include gender egalitarianism, institutional collectivism, in-group collectivism and humane orientation. Our sensitivity analysis examined all possible scenarios where the values of the variables of each group are improved, weakened or remain unchanged. To improve/weaken the value, a variable was increased/decreased by 30 % for countries scoring below/above the average score of the sample. Regarding power distance and uncertainty avoidance, which are reverse-scored,

(1) -30% on Efficiency Orientation Cultural Background -30% on Behavioral Attitudes of Cultural Background	(2) 0% on Efficiency Orientation Cultural Background -30% on Behavioral Attitudes of Cultural Background	(3) +30% on Efficiency Orientation Cultural Background -30% on Behavioral Attitudes of Cultural Background
(4) -30% on Efficiency Orientation Cultural Background 0% on Behavioral Attitudes of Cultural Background	(5) **Basic Model**	(6) +30% on Efficiency Orientation Cultural Background 0% on Behavioral Attitudes of Cultural Background
(7) -30% on Efficiency Orientation Cultural Background +30% on Behavioral Attitudes of Cultural Background	(8) 0% on Efficiency Orientation Cultural Background +30% on Behavioral Attitudes of Cultural Background	(3) +30% on Efficiency Orientation Cultural Background +30% on Behavioral Attitudes of Cultural Background

Fig. 12.1 Sensitivity analysis

their values were decreased by 30 % for countries scoring above the average score of the sample (and vice versa).

Tables B.2 and B.3 (Appendix B) present the descriptive statistics after the sensitivity analysis. Figure 12.1 represents the sensitivity analysis plan.

After the sensitivity analysis, we ran a new PCA with PCs shaped by new forces for each case. Subsequently, we evaluated the effect of the new PCs on the variable GDP growth rates for each case, in combination with the basic growth factors.

To reach these goals (apart from the description of the new findings), a structural change check was performed, relating the alternative circumstances to the basic scenario. In other words, we wanted to assess the statistical significance of the structural change from the basic model (Regression 1) in the model formulated under the new forces arising from each case of the sensitivity analysis. For each case in the sensitivity analysis, we constructed two groups of 41 observations. These two groups created a new variable for each variable. The first (Group 1) concerned the variable's values in the basic scenario and the second (Group 2) concerned the variable's prices for each case in the sensitivity analysis. Subsequently, a dummy variable was created with a value of 0 for Group 1 and 1 for Group 2. The estimates concerning the statistical importance of newly created factors produced some interesting conclusions regarding the new configuration and conditions of annual GDP growth rates.

12.3 Empirical Work and Discussion

Our empirical work and a discussion of the results are presented in the following two sections; the first refers to the basic model and the second to the sensitivity analysis.

12.3.1 The Basic Model

In terms of cultural background, four PCs were determined (PEOC, PSOC1, PSOC2 and MESOC in Table B.4, Appendix B), which explain 37.86 %, 20.24 %, 14.86 % and 10.11 % of the total variance and present initial eigenvalues 3.41, 1.82, 1.33 and 0.91, respectively. The pro-efficiency oriented component (PEOC) is determined by the positive effects of performance orientation, future orientation, institutional collectivism, humane orientation, and uncertainty avoidance and the negative effects of assertiveness and power distance. It is a PC that is shaped by the cultural characteristics that promote efficiency and growth.

The pro-social oriented component 1 (PSOC1) is positively shaped by gender egalitarianism, institutional collectivism, in-group collectivism and humane orientation, while assertiveness has a negative effect. The pro-social oriented component 2 (PSOC2) is characterized by the positive influences of gender egalitarianism and institutional collectivism and the negative effects of in-group collectivism and power distance. Finally, the mixed pro-efficiency and social oriented component (MESOC) is positively shaped by performance orientation and institutional collectivism and negatively by gender egalitarianism.

Table B.4 (Appendix B) presents the contents of the PCs, i.e., the variables that affect PC configuration and have partial correlation values greater than 0.3 in terms of absolute values.

Table B.5 (Appendix B) presents the empirical results of the estimated regressions. The first column (Regression 1) shows the estimated basic model and presents the effect of the basic growth factors and the cultural background on annual GDP growth rates. The basic growth factors HC, PEOC, PSOC2 and MESOC are not statistically significant in Regression 1. This may be due to endogeneity between the dependent and independent variables. Table B.6 (Appendix B) presents the correlations between the variables used. By observing the correlation matrix, GDP may be endogenously determined by CAP, L, HC or PSOC2.

Because of endogeneity concerns, we used a version of the Davidson and MacKinnon (1989, 1993) test described above for all independent variables separately. To test the hypothesis, we used an instrumental variable that correlated with the suspect variable but not with the error term of the GDP equation. We sought to determine whether the instrumental variables were weak or not as robust as in the exogeneity test. Choosing the appropriate instrument is a crucial step. We checked the instruments using the correlation matrix, partial R^2 and partial F-statistic. All the variables used as instruments were assessed as strong instrumental variables and were considered exogenous with respect to GDP, as they presented a strong correlation with each independent variable but not with GDP. The instruments yielded a sufficient partial R^2 and a partial F-statistic larger than 10 when regressed on each independent variable (but not when regressed on GDP). The results of the exogeneity tests did not reveal the existence of endogeneity, as the first stage residuals were not significantly different from zero. Therefore, the evaluations we received from Regression 1 were consistent and unbiased.

The estimation of the basic model (Table B.5, Appendix B) shows that an increase of CAP, L or PSOC1 would positively affect annual GDP growth, as they present positive and statistically significant estimates. The R^2 of the regression equaled 86.7 %, and the regression is statistically strong according to the F-statistic.

12.3.2 Sensitivity Analysis

We then caused a shock in the economies by increasing or decreasing (by 30 %) the values of the variables capturing cultural background or by leaving them unchanged; thus, achieving all possible combinations. In other words, we ran a new PCA for the "new" cultural background for each scenario in Fig. 12.1. For each case, we created the new variables PEOC′, PSOC1′, PSOC2′ and MESOC′. To check for a structural change between the basic model and each case of the sensitivity analysis, we created the variables PEOC″, PSOC1″, PSOC2″ and MESOC″ (i.e., the difference of the basic scenario from that in the sensitivity analysis), which arise as values of PEOC, PSOC1, PSOC2 and MESOC for Group 1 and PEOC′, PSOC1′, PSOC2′ and MESOC′ for Group 2. The dependent variable GDP is now called GDP″, and its values for Group 1 were repeated for Group 2. The same procedure was also implemented for the basic growth factors (CAP, L, HC), whose values did not differ between the basic scenario and that in the sensitivity analysis. Table B.7 (Appendix B) presents the variables dum × PEOC″, dum × PSOC1″, dum × PSOC2″ and dum × MESOC″, which are the products of the created dummy variable and the variables PEOC″, PSOC1″, PSOC2″ and MESOC″, respectively, for each case of the sensitivity analysis.

The shock in the economies produced some statistically significant structural differences. Table B.7 (Appendix B) presents the cases where we observed statistically significant structural changes from the eight different cases of Fig. 12.1. Regarding Cases 6–8, no statistically significant structural change occurred, and they are not presented in Table B.7 (Appendix B). The same table also presents the regressions of the sensitivity analysis shock.

In Case 1, the values of all variables representing cultural background were undervalued by 30 %. More specifically, the values of performance orientation, future orientation, assertiveness, gender egalitarianism, in-group collectivism, institutional collectivism and humane orientation were reduced by 30 % and the values for power distance and uncertainty avoidance, which were reversed-scored, were increased by 30 %. The new conditions led to two statistically significant structural changes for the second and fourth cultural background PCs (see

Table B.7, Appendix B). The second cultural background PC (PSOC1′) continues to be statistically significant and is determined by the positive effects of performance orientation, future orientation, uncertainty avoidance, gender egalitarianism and institutional collectivism and the negative effect of the humane orientation variable. Furthermore, MESOC′ is statistically significant at the 5 % level and is determined by the positive effects of uncertainty avoidance, in-group collectivism and humane orientation. The adjusted R^2 of the sensitivity analysis equals 87 %, while the F–statistic shows that the regression is statistically strong. In conclusion, after the sensitivity analysis for this case, the second PC shows cultural background has a negative effect on GDP; the influence of the cultural environment is strengthened by MESOC′, which impedes annual GDP growth rates.

In Case 2, the values of all variables representing "social orientation" were undervalued by 30 %, while "efficiency orientation" cultural background variables remained unchanged. The sensitivity analysis revealed two statistically significant structural changes for the second and fourth cultural background PCs (see Table B.7, Appendix B). The influence of PSOC1′ is lost, and is replaced by MESOC′, which is determined by the positive effects of assertiveness, gender egalitarianism and institutional collectivism and is statistically significant at the 10 % level. The adjusted R^2 of the sensitivity analysis equals 86.9 %, while the F-statistic shows that the regression is statistically strong. After the sensitivity analysis for this case, the effect of PSOC1 on GDP is lost, and this structural change is statistically significant. The effect of cultural background in shaping annual GDP growth rates is negative and is shaped by MESOC′.

In Case 3, the values of all variables representing "social orientation" were undervalued by 30 %, while "efficiency orientation" cultural background variables were increased by 30 %. These new conditions led to two statistically significant structural changes for PSOC1 and MESOC (see Table B.7, Appendix B). PSOC1′ is statistically significant at the 5 % level and is determined by the positive effects of performance orientation, uncertainty avoidance, gender egalitarianism and institutional collectivism and the negative effect of humane orientation. MESOC′ is statistically significant at the 10 % level and is determined by the positive effects of uncertainty avoidance, in-group collectivism and humane orientation and the negative effect of future orientation and power distance. The adjusted R^2 of the sensitivity analysis equals 87.7 % and according to the F-statistic, the regression is statistically strong. In this case, the effect of PSOC1 on GDP becomes a negative effect (PSOC1′). The effect of cultural background is strengthened by a further PC (MESOC′) that impedes annual GDP growth rates.

In Case 4, the values of all variables representing "social orientation" remained unchanged, while the "efficiency orientation" variables were undervalued by 30 %. The sensitivity analysis in this case shows only one statistically significant structural change for MESOC (see Table B.7, Appendix B). Under the new conditions, MESOC′ is determined by the positive effects of performance orientation, future orientation, uncertainty avoidance and in-group collectivism, and is statistically significant at a 10 % level of significance. The adjusted R^2 of the sensitivity analysis equals 86.8 % and the F-statistic supports a statistically strong regression. The positive effect of PSOC1 on GDP is lost following this sensitivity analysis. The effect of cultural background on annual GDP growth rates is negative and determined by MESOC′.

12.3.3 The Effects of Culture on Growth and Cultural Change

Our empirical results confirm the effect of basic growth factors on annual GDP growth rates. Regarding the effects between culture and economic growth, a one-way relationship accrues as our suspicions regarding endogeneity problems were not confirmed. The "social orientation" cultural background of societies positively affects annual GDP growth rates. The effects of "social orientation" variables are not captured by any other explanatory variables (capital, labor, human capital). In contrast, the effect of "efficiency orientation" variables may be included in the effect of the rest of the research variables. Thus, "social orientation" cultural background in societies may be a reinforcing element for long-term economic growth, and "social orientation" factors can certainly be promoted by policy interventions. However, the issue is quite complex and has not been fully examined to date.

Furthermore, the sensitivity analysis examining all possibilities established the positive influence of special circumstances, which benefit societies as far as promoting and interceptive factors are concerned. This analysis shows that statistically significant structural changes are noted only in those cases where the "social orientation" cultural background is reduced (Cases 1–3) and in Case 4, where it remains stable, regardless of what happens to the values capturing "efficiency orientation" cultural background. The reduction of "social orientation" cultural background negatively affects annual GDP growth rates. At the same time, when "social orientation" factors remain stable, the statistically significant structural change of the model concerns the entry of new variables expressing cultural background (MESOC′), regardless of the changes to "efficiency orientation" factors.

References

Acemoglu D (2009) Introduction to modern economic growth. Massachusetts Institute of Technology, Department of Economics, London

Bos J, Economidou C, Koetter M, Kolari J (2010) Do all countries grow alike? Dev Econ 91:113–127

Cohen D, Soto M (2007) Growth and human capital: good data, good results. J Econ Growth 12:51–76

Davidson R, MacKinnon GJ (1989) Testing for consistency using artificial regres-sions. Econometr Theor 5:363–384

Davidson R, MacKinnon GJ (1993) Estimation and inference in econometrics. Oxford University Press, New York

Hall R, Jones C (1999) Why do some countries produce so much more output per worker than others? Q J Econ 114:83–116

Hausman AJ (1978) Specification tests in econometrics. Economics 46:1251–1271
House RJ, Hanges PJ, Javidan M, Dorfman PW, Gupta V (2004) Culture, leadership and organisations—the GLOBE study of 62 societies. Sage, Thousand Oaks, CA
Levine R, Renelt D (1992) A sensitivity analysis of cross-country growth regres-sions. Am Econ Rev 82(4):942–963
Machiavelli N (1987) [1519] Discourses on Livy. Oxford University Press, New York, NY
Mankiw G, Romer D, Weil D (1992) A contribution to the empirics of economic growth. Q J Econ 107:407–437
Marshall A (1997) Principles of economics. Prometheus Books, New York
Montesquieu C (1989) [1748] The spirit of the laws. Cambridge University Press, New York, NY
Owen AL, Videras J, Davis L (2009) Do all countries follow the same growth process? J Econ Growth 14(4):265–286
Petrakis PE, Kostis PC (2013) Economic growth and cultural change. J Socio-Econ. doi:http://dx.doi.org/10.1016/j.socec.2013.02.011DOI:10.1016/j.socec.2013.02.011#doilink
Putnam DR (1993) The prosperous community: social capital and public life. Am Prospect 4 (13):11–18
Smith IL (2002) A tutorial on principal components analyzing. http://www.cs.otago.ac.nz/cosc453/student_tutorials/principal_components.pdf. Accessed 27 Jul 2013
Weber M (1958) [1904] The protestant ethic and the spirit of capitalism. Scribner, New York, NY

Cultural Background, Transaction Costs and Economic Institutions

13

The main purpose of this chapter[1] is to identify the extent to which cultural background affects transaction costs and economic institutions. The role of cultural background has preoccupied researchers in their efforts to explain the differences among the economic performances of various countries. The relationship between the results of those studies and developmental growth indices demonstrates that culture can be particularly valuable (Minkov and Blagoev 2009). In addition, the institutions of a society form the "rules of the game" (North 1990) and affect the efficiency of the market. The reduction of transaction costs frees up resources. Existing literature (Acemoglu et al. 2004; Chang 2006, 2011; Easterly et al. 2006; Hofstede 1991) supports the notion that cultural background can affect economic output via institutions; i.e., culture is directly linked to the formation of institutions. The establishment of distinguishable frameworks of action for economic actors can reduce transaction costs by offering incentives for undertaking entrepreneurial activities.

This chapter is organized as follows. Section 13.1 presents theoretical studies on transaction costs economics (TCE), while Sect. 13.2 describes the variables used in our research. Section 13.3 describes the methodology employed, i.e., the empirical model and measurements, while Sect. 13.4 presents the empirical work and comments on the results. Finally, Sect. 13.5 presents the effects of culture in shaping transactions and economic institutions.

13.1 The Role of Transaction Costs

The theory of transaction cost economics (TCE) was first introduced by Coase (1937), and later presented to the general public by Williamson (1975, 1985). A key issue of interest for economists within new institutional economics is the study of

[1] This chapter is a summary of a scientific paper by Petrakis P.E. and Valsamis D.G. (2013) "Entrepreneurship, Transaction Costs and Cultural Background" published in the International Business Research, Vol. 6, No. 5.

P.E. Petrakis, *Culture, Growth and Economic Policy*,
DOI 10.1007/978-3-642-41440-4_13, © Springer-Verlag Berlin Heidelberg 2014

transaction costs. According to Arrow (1969), transaction costs are similar to the "operation" costs of a financial system. The concept of transaction costs has led to a variety of different ways of thinking regarding the design and organization of production, as well as the creation and evolution of institutions. The focus is primarily on how transaction costs are measured. TCE provides a theory to explain the choice for efficient governance structures (Spithoven 2012).

The 1930s saw the formulation of the theory of transaction costs, in particular, through the contributions of Commons (1934) and Coase (1937). Commons (1934) was the first to consider that transaction costs are central to economic analysis. However, the core of the theory was later developed by Coase (1937) in his article "The Nature of the Firm". According to Coase, transaction costs are solely the cost that accompanies the exchange of goods. The role of transaction costs is important for the interpretation of the structure of the market (Coase 1937, 1960).

Behavioral characteristics, on which theory of transaction costs is supported can be summed up as bounded rationalism and opportunity exploitation (Williamson 1981), characteristics that affect and are affected by a society's cultural background. According to Williamson (1981), bounded rationalism does not entail a lack of logic or irrational thought. On the contrary, it involves a limited capacity for the resolution of difficult and complex problems of data analysis and information processing, as well as a lack of specialization. Furthermore, individuals engage in transactions and make contracts when their goals are met, according to opportunistic behavior (Williamson 1985; Conner and Prahalad 1996).

The fundamental features of transactions are uncertainty, frequency and asset specificity (Williamson 1981) and appear in markets and public governance (Williamson et al. 2007). These components are shaped according to a society's cultural background and its overall organization. In general, as the degree of uncertainty concerning a transaction increases, there is a burden on transaction costs because of the unpredictable result of the transaction. Transaction uncertainty ultimately places an uncertainty premium on transaction costs.

Institutions set the "rules of the game" in a society (North 1990). They are defined as society's collective choices, and usually express conflicts of interest and develop under the influence of history and cultural background. Generally, favorable economic institutions (with respect to growth) are those that offer secure property rights across a wide range of society's functions (Acemoglu et al. 2004; Chang 2006; Dutt 2011). This chapter does not extend its analysis to political institutions; instead, we only focus on economic institutions that shape incentives in society, including incentives regarding physical capital, human capital, technology and the organization of production (Economides and Ehlig-Economides 2009). Primary expressions of economic institutions include property rights, contractual conditions and, ultimately, the magnitude of the effect of those conditions on economic transactions.

The various social and political processes that shape each society's cultural background guide human behavior and the characteristics of the entities involved. For instance, Greif (1994) concluded that the effect of culture is significant in (a) shaping the institutional structure, (b) planning for the future and its co-dependence with institutions and (c) preventing the acceptance institutions belonging to a foreign culture.

13.2 The Variables Used

In this chapter, the selection of variables is aimed at creating principal components (PCs) via the principal component analysis (PCA) method for two groups of variables (1) cultural background, and (2) transaction costs and economic institutions.

The selection of variables that represent cultural dimensions and transaction costs as well as specify variable characteristics that capture economic institutions is rather difficult because specific variables are (a) very difficult to quantify, and (b) even if they are quantified, it is not certain that they are collected and registered in a satisfactory manner at a societal level.

The cultural background measurements used in our model originate from House et al. (2004) and are more recent (1995–1997) than Hofstede's (1980). However, in discussing the way in which cultural variables affect real ones (in the case of entrepreneurship), Freytag and Thurik (2007, 2010) concluded that country-specific cultural variables seem to explain social preferences but not actual activity; i.e., what we observe is mainly the result of actual economic conditions and not reflections of cultural background. However, ignoring the influence of cultural background on actual activity is not intuitively correct because certain cultural traits (i.e., uncertainty avoidance or collectivism) have prevailed for long periods, and their presence is repeatedly detected through numerous social expressions. Thus, a compromise is to rely on cultural values reflecting practices adopted (as they are) and not beliefs and values (what should be); we do so in this chapter.

Cultural background is expressed in the variables developed by GLOBE (House et al. 2004): performance orientation, future orientation, gender egalitarianism, assertiveness, institutional collectivism, in-group collectivism, power distance, human orientation and uncertainty avoidance. A detailed presentation of the variables of cultural background under examination and the period of time they cover is provided in Chap. 12 (see Table 12.1).

It can be challenging to quantify transaction costs. It is impossible to identify variables that can adequately present the objective characteristics of frequency and asset specificity. One process that has been adequately quantified is the number of transactions in an economy. An economic system showing transactions pertaining to its operational processes (and not the economic result of its production system) displays unique characteristics in comparison with other systems where transactions exhibit a strong productive orientation (e.g., with no bureaucracy and corruption). We used variable starting business, which measures the time (calendar days) required for a company to commence operation, as a sign of its transaction development, with the production (developmental) orientation of its transaction organization as a point of reference. Furthermore, the risk that prevails in an economy can be adequately described by using composite risk as a proxy.

Table 13.1 Sources and periods of reference in the variables sources

	Variables	Definition	Source of data
Transaction characteristics	Composite risk	This is the weighted average of individual risk indicators (political, financial and economic risk). The larger the value, the lower the level of risk for the country. It is the mean for the period of 2001–2006	PRS Group (ICRG database), http://www.prsgroup.com
	Starting a business	Time is recorded in calendar days. This measure captures the median duration that incorporation lawyers indicate is necessary to complete a procedure with a minimum follow-up with government agencies and no extra payments. It is the mean for the period of 2004–2006	Doing business reports, The World Bank Groups
	Corruption perceptions index	Is a snapshot of perceptions of public sector corruption. It uses the counter-variable, so the prices it can assume are between 0 (highly clean) and 10 (highly corrupt). It is the mean for the period of 2001–2006	Transparency International
Economic institutions	Property rights	An assessment of the ability of individuals to accumulate private property, secured by clear laws that are fully enforced by the state. It is the mean for the period of 2001–2005	The Heritage Foundation, Index of Economic Freedom (HER), http://www.heritage.org/index/
	Rule of law	Measures the extent to which stakeholders have confidence in and abide by the rules of society. In particular, it focuses on the quality of contract enforcement, the police and the courts, as well as the likelihood of crime and violence. It is the mean for the period of 2002–2006	Business Environment Risk Intelligence (BRI), http://www.beri.com

For the expression of economic institutions, we used the following variables: property rights and rule of law. Note that it should not be taken for granted that the relationship between cultural background and economic institutions (De Jong 2011) is a positive one, as it has been demonstrated that the opposite relationship may also apply (Ahlerup et al. 2009). Table 13.1 presents a detailed presentation of the variables expressing transaction characteristics and economic institutions.

It is clear from the way the data[2] were collected that we have treated the world as a typical country, as we have not allowed for heterogeneous growth experiences. Thus, we have assumed that the production process is homogenous around the world (Bos et al. 2010). This assumption is used because the limited degrees of freedom, due to the small sample of observations (i.e., the limited number of observations for cultural variables), do not permit a deepening of the relevant analysis.

13.3 The Methodology Employed

The basic model examined is as follows:

$$TI_i = \beta_0 + \beta_i * \text{CULTURAL BACKGROUND}_i + \varepsilon_i, \quad (13.1)$$

where the dependent variable (TI_i) expresses transaction costs and economic institutions, and the independent variable CULTURAL BACKGROUND_i represents the cultural backgrounds of the 41 countries in the sample. Subscript i refers to the countries used in the model.

To represent the complexity of the model's variables, we employed the principal component analysis (PCA) method (see Chap. 12). We applied PCA to two groups of variables. One group contains variables expressing transaction costs and institutions and the other group contains variables expressing cultural background. The effect of culture on transaction costs and economic institutions is expressed through a linear regression analysis using the ordinary least squares (OLS) method, as in the model presented above. In our linear regression, we used PCs with the greatest variances (initial eigenvalues >1).

13.4 Empirical Work and Discussion

The various variables expressing transaction costs and economic institutions produced a PC that captures 82.34 % of the total variance with an initial eigenvalue of 4.117. As seen in Table C.1 (see Appendix C), the PC of transaction costs and economic institutions (TI) is negatively shaped by starting-up a business and positively shaped by corruption, composite risk, property rights and rule of law. Overall, this PC demonstrates the characteristics of TI. Increasing values of TI

[2] The 41 countries that constitute the sample represent 90.44 % of World GDP for 2007 (IMF Database). The countries are as follows: Argentina, Australia, Austria, Brazil, Canada, China, Colombia, Denmark, Ecuador, Finland, France, Germany, Greece, Hong Kong, Hungary, India, Indonesia, Ireland, Israel, Italy, Japan, Malaysia, Mexico, The Netherlands, New Zealand, Philippines, Poland, Portugal, Russian Federation, Singapore, Slovenia, South Africa, South Korea, Spain, Sweden, Switzerland, Thailand, Turkey, United Kingdom, United States and Venezuela.

indicates decreasing transaction costs and an improvement in economic institutions in the economy.

Regarding cultural background, we extracted two PCs (see Appendix C, Table C.2) that explain 61.03 % of the total variance and present initial eigenvalues of 3.795 (42.16 %) and 1.698 (18.87 %). The first PC for cultural background (C_1), which exhibits a pro-growth orientation, is determined by the positive effect of performance orientation, future orientation, institutional collectivism, human orientation and uncertainty avoidance and the negative effect of assertiveness. An increase in the value of pro-growth orientation means an improvement in the cultural background of a society. The second PC for cultural background (C_2), described as a pro-social orientation, is determined by the positive effect of gender egalitarianism and assertiveness and the negative effects of institutional collectivism, in group-collectivism, power distance and human orientation. An increase in the value of pro-social orientation leads to an aggravation of the elements of cultural background relating to the qualitative features of a society. Tables C.1 and C.2 (Appendix C) present the contents of TI, C_1 and C_2, i.e., the variables that affect the PC configuration, but only for values of partial correlations greater than 0.3.

Table C.3 (Appendix C) presents the correlations among the variables used in the basic model. By observing the correlation matrix, we believe that TI may be endogenously determined by C_1 or C_2. For this reason, we saw the need to check for the possible existence of endogeneity between TI and C_1 or C_2, by means of using the exogeneity test developed by Davidson and MacKinnon (1989, 1993). The selection of the appropriate instrumental variable was a demanding and time-consuming process; we had to locate a variable that would present a high correlation, satisfactory R^2 and an F-statistic >10 with respect to C_1 or C_2, while presenting a low correlation, low R^2 and an F-statistic <10 with TI. The "trust in justice and police" variable is considered a strong instrumental variable, as it is estimated to have a partial F-statistic of 10.46, the partial R^2 shows that 22.51 % of the squared residuals can be explained by the instrumental variable. In addition, "trust in justice and police" appears to be correlated with C_1 (0.47), constituting an additional indication of the existence of endogeneity. We should also note that based on a regression of "trust in justice and police" on TI, the partial F-statistic is estimated to be 3.93 (F-stat $<$ 10) and the partial R^2 is only 9.84 %. Thus, "trust in justice and police" can be regarded as exogenous with respect to TI. By repeating the above process to find the instrumental variable for C_2, we found that the "GDP growth" variable is a strong instrumental variable, because it is estimated to have a partial F-statistic of 20.26 and an R^2 of 34.19 %. Regressing "GDP growth" on TI, the partial F-statistic is estimated to be 6.96 and the partial R^2 equals 15.14 %. Thus, "GDP growth" can be regarded as an exogenous variable in relation to TI.

To apply the exogeneity test, we ran two OLS regressions. In the first regression, we regressed C_1 on C_2 and the "trust in justice and police" instrumental variable to retrieve the residuals. In the second regression, we re-estimated the basic model including the residuals from the first regression as additional regressors. We found that the first stage residuals were not significantly different from zero and there is no endogeneity problem between TI and C_1. Similarly, regressing C_2 on C_1 and the "GDP growth" instrumental variable, we took the residuals and re-estimated the basic model including the residuals from the first regression. Again in this case, the residuals were not significantly different from zero, and thus, the model is not affected by an endogeneity relationship and provides consistent and unbiased estimates.

Table C.4 (see Appendix C) presents the empirical results of the estimated regression. The basic model estimates the effect of a pro-growth orientation (C_1) and a pro-social orientation (C_2) on TI. An increase in C_1 would positively affect TI, as they present positive and statistically significant estimates. In contrast, C_2 presents a negative relationship with TI. The adjusted R^2 of the regression equals 64.5 %, and the F-statistic shows that the regression is statistically strong.

The results show that the improvement of pro-growth orientation tends to reduce transaction costs and enhance economic institutions because societies are future-oriented, focus on performance, prefer the future over the present, accept the risk of undertaking long-term initiatives and display reduced collectivism, because they are oriented toward individual action.

In contrast, the increase of pro-social orientation contributes to increased transaction costs and inefficient economic institutions. Societies' characterized by authoritarianism and aggression, low levels of gender equality, orientation toward the individual and a limited commitment to institutions decrease confidence and increase uncertainty.

13.5 The Effects of Culture in Shaping Transactions and Economic Institutions

Our empirical results are quite encouraging. The regression model shows that PCs describing cultural background significantly affect transaction costs and economic institutions. More specifically, according to the pro-growth orientation measure, societies oriented toward rewarding the performance of their members in designing, planning and investing in the future and that are risk-averse tend to reduce transaction costs and promote the orderly functioning of economic institutions. The existence of a strong regulatory framework that protects property rights leads to a reduction in the cost of transactions. The confidence of a society in its laws and compliance with its institutions creates coherent links by simplifying the transaction process and the number of contracts. The second PC of culture, pro-social orientation (which focuses on the factors that promote the improvement of societies) shows that the elimination of long-term structures and stereotypes is essential to reduce transactions. The reduction of inequalities, an orientation toward more "feminine" values and respect for institutions and rules can lead to reduced transaction costs, thus encouraging long-term economic growth.

Improving the cultural background of a society, especially certain aspects of it, may contribute to reducing transaction costs. Furthermore, by reducing transaction costs and strengthening the efficiency of economic institutions, the appropriate prerequisites for enhancing entrepreneurship are created.

It must be noted though that cultural change is a long-term process. Policymakers need to make significant efforts to improve various fundamental aspects of a society's cultural traits. However, the improvement of economic and political institutions may help this process. Policymakers should also understand the significance of institutions as a source of productive entrepreneurial activity and implement policies that will focus in that direction. The key purpose of economic policy should be the creation of an institutional framework that will emphasize new growth initiatives.

References

Acemoglu D, Johnson S, Robinson JA (2004) Institutions as the fundamental cause of long-run growth. CEPR Discussion Papers 4458

Ahlerup P, Olsson O, Yanagizawa D (2009) Social capital vs. institutions in the growth process. Eur J Polit Econ 25(1):1–14

Arrow KJ (1969) The organization of economic activity: issues pertinent to the choice of market versus nonmarket allocation. In: The analysis and evaluation of public expenditures: the PBB System, Joint Economic Committee, 91st congress, 1st session, vol 1. Washington U.S. Government Print Office, pp 47–64

Bos JWB, Economidou C, Koetter M, Kolari JW (2010) Do all countries grow alike? J Dev Econ 91(1):113–127

Chang HJ (2006) Understanding the relationship between institutions and economic development: some key theoretical issues. World Institute for Development Economic Research (UNU-WIDER), Working Papers DP2006/05

Chang HJ (2011) Institutions and economic development: theory, policy and history. J Inst Econ 7 (4):473–498, doi:http://dx/doi.org/10.1017/S1744137410000378

Coase RH (1937) The nature of the firm. Economica 16(4):386–405

Coase RH (1960) The problem of social cost. J Law Econ 3:1–44

Commons JR (1990) [1934] Institutional economics. Its place in political economy. The Mac Millan Company: Transaction Publishers, New York

Conner KR, Prahalad CK (1996) A resource-based theory of the firm: knowledge versus opportunism. Organ Sci 7:477–501

Davidson R, MacKinnon JG (1989) Testing for consistency using artificial regressions. Econom Theor 5:363–384

Davidson R, MacKinnon JG (1993) Estimation and inference in econometrics. Oxford University Press, New York

De Jong E (2011) Culture, institutions and economic growth. J Inst Econ 7(4):523–527, doi:http://dx/doi.org/10.1017/S1744137411000117

Dutt AK (2011) Institutional change and economic development: concepts, theory and political economy. J Inst Econ 7(4):529–534, doi:http://dx/doi.org\10.1017/S1744137411000075

Easterly W, Ritzen J, Woolcock M (2006) Social cohesion, institutions and growth. Econ Polit 18 (2):103–120

Economides MJ, Ehlig-Economides CA (2009) Sequestering carbon dioxide in a closed underground volume. In: Paper presented at Society of Petroleum Engineers annual technical conference and exhibition, New Orleans, LA, 4–7 Oct 2009

Freytag A, Thurik R (2007) Entrepreneurship and its determinants in a cross country setting. J Evol Econ 17:117–131

Freytag A, Thurik R (2010) Entrepreneurship and culture. Springer, Heidelberg

Greif A (1994) Cultural beliefs and the organization of society: a historical and theoretical reflection on collectivist and individualist societies. Polit Econ 102:912–950
Hofstede G (1980) Culture's consequences: international differences in work-related values. Sage, Beverly Hills, CA
Hofstede G (1991) Cultures and organisations. Harper Collins Business, London
House RJ, Hanges PJ, Javidan M, Dorfman PW, Gupta V (2004) Culture, leadership and organisations—the GLOBE study of 62 societies. Sage, Thousand Oaks, CA
Minkov M, Blagoev V (2009) Cultural values predict subsequent economic growth. Int J Cross-Cult Manag 9(1):5–24
North DC (1990) Institutions, institutional change and economic performance. Cambridge University Press, Cambridge
Spithoven A (2012) Public governance of healthcare in the United States: a transaction cost economics (TCE) analysis of the 2010 reform. J Inst Econ 8(4):429–457, doi:http://dx/doi.org/10.1017/S1744137412000082
Williamson O (1975) Markets and hierarchies: analysis and antitrust implications. Free Press, New York
Williamson O (1981) The economics of organization: the transaction cost approach. Am J Sociol 87:548–577
Williamson O (1985) The economic institutions of capitalism: firms, markets, relational contracting. Free Press, New York
Williamson O, Hodgson GM, Gindis D (2007) An interview with Oliver Williamson. J Inst Econ 3:373–386

14 The Effects of Culture, Transactions and Institutions on Opportunity Entrepreneurship

The concept of opportunity entrepreneurship has been of interest to researchers for many years. Early contributions on the subject include those of Schumpeter (1934) and Knight (1971) and, building on those, Shane and Venkataraman (2000) and Audretsch (2007). The aim of this chapter is to analyze opportunity entrepreneurship by considering some factors that influence entrepreneurial capital, originating from three fields: cultural background, transaction characteristics and economic institutions. These factors are not separate or isolated in their structural effects on opportunity entrepreneurship. Therefore, this chapter identifies the opportunity entrepreneurship determination framework, allowing for endogenous phenomena. This chapter also identifies ways of creating a different world, more oriented toward opportunity entrepreneurship, by postulating changed human behaviors and then analyzing the effects observed.

The order of the chapter is as follows. Section 14.1 presents the theoretical background and the variables used. Section 14.2 describes the issues around interrelationships between the variables, called the endogeneity question, and Sect. 14.3 presents the three hypotheses tested in the chapter. Section 14.4 describes the data used, while Sect. 14.5 describes the methodology. Lastly, Sect. 14.6 presents the empirical work and the discussion of the results, and Sect. 14.7 presents the overall relationships identified through the analysis.

14.1 The Theoretical Background and the Variables Used

Cultural and institutional factors may explain cross-national differences in entrepreneurial activity levels (Wennekers et al. 2002; Wennekers 2006). Thomas and Meller (2000) found that differences in cultural orientation between countries affect the personality characteristics commonly associated with motivation toward entrepreneurship. Baum et al. (1993) concluded that countries with a high societal

This chapter presents a working paper by Petrakis P.E. and Kostis P.C. (2013).

P.E. Petrakis, *Culture, Growth and Economic Policy*,
DOI 10.1007/978-3-642-41440-4_14, © Springer-Verlag Berlin Heidelberg 2014

tolerance for uncertainty are associated with higher self-employment rates, explaining that the cultural determinants of entrepreneurship act as the "push explanation for entrepreneurship". Wennekers et al. (2008) examined the influence of cultural attitudes toward uncertainty avoidance on the levels of business ownership. They identified a strong, positive effect, concluding that high uncertainty avoidance levels push people into employment (in line with Baum's hypothesis).

Furthermore, transaction cost economics seems to shed light on the economic organization of entrepreneurship (Stiglitz and Foss 2009). Entrepreneurial decision-making, according to this perspective, is aimed at managing the problems of transaction cost economics (Leiblein and Macher 2009).

In recent years, the role of institutions has re-emerged as a dominant explanation of long-term economic performance and thus entrepreneurship. According to Petrakis (2011), the relationship between institutions and entrepreneurship stems from three different sources: (a) their contribution to coordination and governance, (b) their influence on the process of knowledge development and (c) their effect on income distribution and the development of social coherence (Easterly et al. 2006).

14.2 The Endogenous Problem

If we accept that entrepreneurship requires suitable institutions and a specific environmental background, we are faced with the question of why so many national administrations fail to establish such institutions or improve existing ones (Fukuyama 2001). Perhaps there is a two-way effect between entrepreneurship and institutions. According to Spulber (2003), the economic equilibrium, including the structure of transactions, prices and allocation of goods, depends on the actions of entrepreneurs. Entrepreneurs will be successful in establishing firms only if doing so provides transaction benefits that cannot be achieved by consumer organizations. Similarly, societies with well-developed levels of entrepreneurship may shape the cultural background of their members, for example, by emphasizing the importance of assertiveness and performance-oriented characteristics. Thus, is it cultural background, transaction characteristics and economic institutions that influence entrepreneurship, or vice versa? This question of the inter-relationship between variables is referred to as the endogeneity problem.

14.3 Hypotheses Testing

Table 14.1 indicates the overall relationships expected between the independent variables (cultural background, transaction characteristics and economic institutions) and the dependent variable (opportunity entrepreneurship), based on various studies in the literature and the definitions of the variables.

The following three hypotheses were examined:

Table 14.1 Relationship of variables to the dependent variable

	Opportunity entrepreneurship
Performance orientation	+
Future orientation	+
Gender egalitarianism	+
Assertiveness	+
Institutional collectivism	+
In-group collectivism	–
Power distance	–
Human orientation	+
Uncertainty avoidance	–
Composite risk	+
Starting a business	–
Corruption perception index	–
Literacy rate	+
Property rights	+
Rule of law	+

H1: All cultural background dimensions of societies positively affect opportunity entrepreneurship levels, except for in-group collectivism, power distance and uncertainty avoidance, which have a negative effect.

H2: Higher levels of transaction costs, as expressed through high composite risk, long time taken to start up a business, high levels of corruption and low levels of literacy rates inhibit opportunity entrepreneurship levels.

H3: Well-organized economic institutions, as expressed through high property rights protection and high sentiment of rule of law in societies, enhance opportunity entrepreneurship levels.

14.4 The Data

The data for the dependent variable (OPP) concern the mean performance of each country for the time period 2001–2006. The time period for cultural background variables is 1995–1997, as there has not been a more recent organized effort to measure cultural background in enough countries. Moreover, the social stereotypes forming cultural background may be characterized as long-lasting. A more detailed explanation of the cultural background variables and the period of time is set out in Chap. 12 (see Table 12.1). Where possible, the data include a mean value for the decade 1995–2005 and 1996–2006. Where this was not possible, the variables cover at least 2 years between 2001 and 2006. The birth rate is taken from 2009, but tends not to change very much over short periods of time. The number of patents is from 2008. The precise definition of each variable is given in Table 14.2. Sample statistics are given in Table D.1 (Appendix D).

Table 14.2 Definition of variables and data sources

	Variables	Definition	Source of elements
OPP	Opportunity Entrepreneurship	It is the dependent variable. The percentage of 18–64 year-olds who are either nascent entrepreneurs or owner-managers of new businesses, who (1) claim to be driven by opportunity rather than necessity and (2) indicate that the main driver for their involvement is independence or increasing, rather than maintaining, their income. Mean for the period 2001–2006	Global Entrepreneurship Monitor (GEM)
TI	Composite Risk	This is the weighted average of individual risk indicators (political, financial and economic risk). The larger the value, the lower the level of risk for the country. It is the mean for the period 1995–2005	PRS Group (ICRG database)
	Starting up a Business	Time is recorded in calendar days. This measure captures the median duration that incorporation lawyers indicate is necessary to complete a procedure with a minimum follow-up with government agencies and no extra payments. It is the mean for the period 2004–2005	Doing business Reports, The World Bank Groups
	Corruption Perceptions Index	It is a snapshot of perceptions of public sector corruption. It uses the counter-variable, so the values it can assume are between 0 (highly clean) and 10 (highly corrupt). It is the mean for the period 2001–2005	Transparency International
	Literacy Rate	The ability to read and write as a percentage of total population (data period 1995–2005)	UNESCO Institute for Statistics http://www.uis.unesco.org
	Property Rights	An assessment of the ability of individuals to accumulate private property, secured by clear laws that are fully enforced by the state. It is the mean for the period 1996–2005	The Heritage Foundation, Index of Economic Freedom (HER)
	Rule of Law	Measures the extent to which stakeholders have confidence in and abide by the rules of society. In particular, it focuses on the quality of contract enforcement, the police and the courts, as well as the likelihood of crime and violence. It is the mean for the period 1996–2005	Business Environment Risk Intelligence (BRI), http://www.beri.com
BIRTH	Birth Rate	The number of childbirths per 1,000 people per year (2009 data)	CIA World Factbook

(continued)

Table 14.2 (continued)

	Variables	Definition	Source of elements
PAT	Patents	Total number of patents applied by a country in a year (2008 data)	Global Innovation Index 2009–2010

Note: (1) The 42 countries in the sample constituted 90.44 % of global GDP in 2007 (IMF Database). The countries are: Argentina, Australia, Austria, Brazil, Canada, China, Colombia, Denmark, Ecuador, Finland, France, Germany, Greece, Hong Kong, Hungary, India, Indonesia, Ireland, Israel, Italy, Japan, Malaysia, Mexico, the Netherlands, New Zealand, Philippines, Poland, Portugal, the Russian Federation, Singapore, Slovenia, South Africa, South Korea, Spain, Sweden, Switzerland, Taiwan, Thailand, Turkey, the United Kingdom, the United States, and Venezuela. (2) The variables representing cultural background were described in Chap. 12

14.5 The Methodology Employed

The basic model to be examined to test the hypotheses was as follows:

$$\mathrm{OPP_i} = \beta_0 + \beta_1 * \mathrm{C_i} + \beta_2 * TI_\mathrm{i} + \varepsilon_\mathrm{i},$$

where the dependent variable is opportunity entrepreneurship, C_i represents the variables expressing cultural background and TI_i represents the variables expressing transaction characteristics and economic institutions. The subscripts i refer to the countries used.

To abstract from the complexity of the explanatory variables, we used Principal Component Analysis (PCA), as set out in Chap. 12. There were two groups of variables to which PCA was applied. The first was the variables expressing cultural background, and the other was those expressing transaction characteristics and economic institutions. The effect of the principal components (PCs) on opportunity entrepreneurship was examined by using a linear regression created by the ordinary least squares method (OLS), using the principal components with the greatest variances (initial eigenvalues > 1).

To check for endogeneity between the variables used, we used the version of the Hausman test (Hausman 1978) proposed by Davidson and MacKinnon (1989, 1993), as set out in Chap. 12.

We also carried out a sensitivity analysis on this basic scenario. We tried to create a more opportunity entrepreneurship-oriented world by increasing or decreasing the values of some variables expressing cultural background. This results in the population being more performance- and future-oriented, and more competitive, with greater institutional collectivism and better prepared to implement riskier practices. The goal was to observe the impact of cultural background, transaction characteristics and economic institutions on opportunity entrepreneurship under these changing circumstances in societies. The selection of the variables for this sensitivity analysis was based on how important these were in the formation of PCs (see Table D.2). The values of performance orientation, future orientation, assertiveness, and institutional collectivism variables were therefore increased by

30 %, and the values of uncertainty avoidance were decreased by 30 % for countries scoring below average in each variable.

We also performed a structural change check comparing the alternative world to the basic scenario. In effect, we constructed two groups of 42 observations, as set out in Chap. 12. The estimates concerning the statistical importance of new factors led us to some conclusions regarding the new configuration conditions for opportunity entrepreneurship.

14.6 Empirical Results and Discussion

Three cultural background PCs were identified (C_1, C_2 and C_3 in Table D.2—Appendix D) that explain 37.86 %, 20.24 % and 14.86 % of the total variance, and present initial eigenvalues of 3.41, 1.82 and 1.33, respectively. C_1 is determined by the positive effects of performance orientation, future orientation, institutional collectivism, human orientation, and uncertainty avoidance and the negative effects of assertiveness, in-group collectivism and power distance. It is a PC that is shaped by the cultural characteristics that promote entrepreneurship. C_2 is positively shaped by performance orientation, institutional collectivism, in-group collectivism, power distance and human orientation, whereas gender egalitarianism and assertiveness have a negative effect. It can be characterized as the human-oriented cultural characteristic. The positive effect of performance orientation, future orientation and assertiveness and the negative effects of gender egalitarianism and human orientation determine C_3. It expresses the cultural characteristics of achieving efficiency.

Table D.2 (Appendix D) presents the contents of the PCs, i.e., the variables that affect the PC configuration, which have partial correlation values that are greater than 0.3. Among the variables indicating transaction characteristics and economic institutions, one PC emerged (TI) that explains 58.86 % of the total variance and presents an initial eigenvalue of 3.53. Composite risk, literacy rate, property rights and the rule of law shape the promoting effect of TI on opportunity entrepreneurship. On the other hand, the time taken to start up a business and the corruption perception index have a negative effect, as was expected.

Table D.3 (Appendix D) shows the correlations between the variables used in the basic model. Having seen the correlation matrix below, as well as in Figs. 14.1 and 14.2, we were concerned that opportunity entrepreneurship may be endogenously determined, either by transaction characteristics and economic institutions (TI) or by the components of cultural background that promote entrepreneurship (C_1). The correlation between the dependent variable and the human-oriented cultural background component (C_2) and the achieving efficiency cultural background component (C_3) are quite low, so there were no concerns about endogeneity with these.

Table D.4 (Appendix D) includes the empirical results of the estimated regressions. The first column shows the estimated basic model (Regression 1). It presents the effect of cultural background, transaction characteristics, and economic institutions on opportunity entrepreneurship. Figures 14.1 and 14.2 show

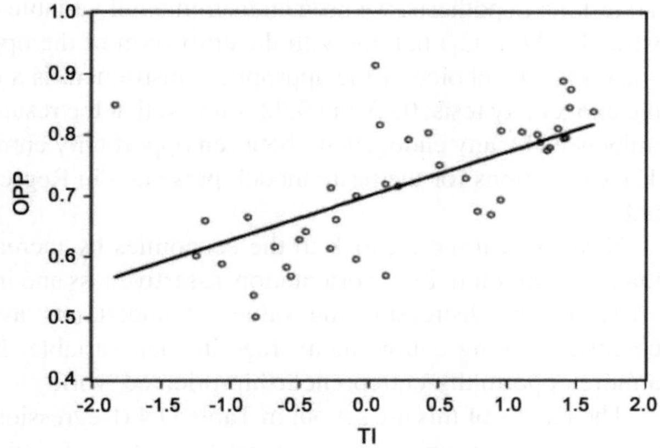

Fig. 14.1 Correlation between Opportunity Entrepreneurship (OPP) and the Transaction Characteristics and Economic Institutions component (TI). *Note*: OPP is measured in percentage points. TI is a principal component and its values are over and below zero

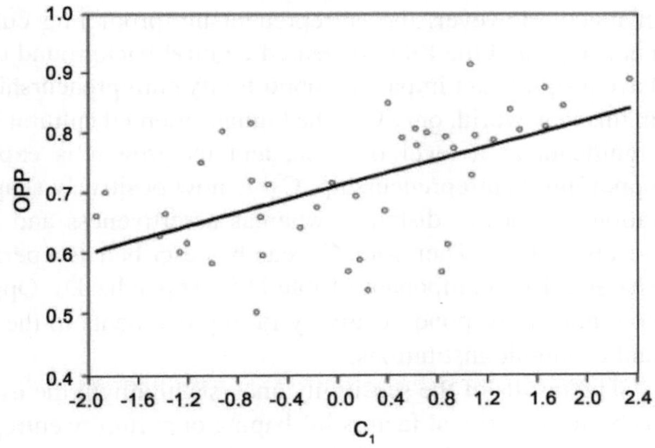

Fig. 14.2 Correlation between Opportunity Entrepreneurship (OPP) and the Promoting Entrepreneurship component (C_1). *Note*: OPP is measured in percentage points. C_1 is a principal component and its values are over and below zero

that increasing the cultural background components that promote entrepreneurship, and improving transactions and institutions would have a positive effect on opportunity entrepreneurship. In contrast, increasing the levels of the cultural background components that increase efficiency (C_3) would inhibit the opportunity entrepreneurship levels. However, it is also clear that the components of C_3 that have this effect are all human-oriented. This therefore changes its character away from efficiency, and toward human orientation.

Because of concerns that opportunity entrepreneurship may be endogenously determined by either TI or C_1, we used the Davidson and MacKinnon test (1989, 1993), to determine the relationship between OPP and TI, and between OPP and C_1. The second and the third columns of Table D.5 (Appendix D) show the exogeneity test and the regression results. We were concerned that opportunity entrepreneurship was endogenously determined by either TI or C_1 because of the strong positive correlations in Figs. 14.1 and 14.2, so we used the Davidson and MacKinnon test (1989, 1993), to determine the relationship between OPP and TI, and OPP and C_1.

To test the hypothesis, we used an instrumental variable correlated with the suspect variable (TI or C_1) but not with the error term of the opportunity entrepreneurship equation. The choice of the appropriate instrument is a crucial step. The values of the exogeneity tests, 0.85 and 0.92, suggest that the results in Regression 1 were not influenced by any endogeneity between opportunity entrepreneurship and TI or C_1. The estimations for the basic model, presented in Regression 1, are consistent and unbiased.

Next, we caused a shock to the economies by increasing the values of performance orientation, future orientation, assertiveness and institutional collectivism by 30 % and by decreasing the values of uncertainty avoidance by 30 % for the countries scoring below the average in each variable. In other words, we created a more opportunity entrepreneurship-oriented world.

The results of this are set out in Table D.4 (Regression 4). The more opportunity entrepreneurship-oriented world produced two statistically significant structural differences (Table D.4, Regression 4). The variables that make up TI were not changed. However, the entrepreneurship-promoting cultural background component (C_1') and the future-oriented cultural background component (C_3') no longer have a significant impact on opportunity entrepreneurship. Unlike the basic model, in this new world, only C_2', the human-oriented cultural background, is statistically significant at a level of 1 %, and its growth is expected to adversely affect opportunity entrepreneurship. C_2' is now positively shaped by performance orientation and power distance, whereas assertiveness and human orientation have a negative effect. Therefore, C_2' can be described as a performance-oriented cultural characteristic component (Table D.5, Appendix D). Opportunity entrepreneurship continues to respond positively to improvements in the transaction characteristics and economic institutions.

The results of the sensitivity analysis highlight the usefulness of these variables as basic and critical factors in shaping opportunity entrepreneurship. If there was a timeless way to shape a background culture promoting opportunity entrepreneurship, then there would be no reason to worry about cultural background anymore and changes would have no further effect on opportunity entrepreneurship. Thus, cultural background is seen to be crucial only in the earlier stages of opportunity entrepreneurship development.

However, our findings indicate that institution improvement always remains relevant in improving opportunity entrepreneurship, irrespective of the cultural background. This conclusion is quite interesting since it separates the effects of policy on cultural background, such as education, political stability, knowledge improvement, from the effects of policies applied to the institutional framework.

In conclusion, Table 14.3 sets out the results in relation to the hypotheses. The table is divided into two parts; one for the basic model and one for the sensitivity analysis.

Hypothesis 1, that all elements of cultural background affect levels of opportunity entrepreneurship, is partially satisfied in both the basic model and the sensitivity analysis. In the basic model, through the promoting entrepreneurship PC (C_1) all variables seem to affect opportunity entrepreneurship, except for the levels of

Table 14.3 The conclusions in relation to the hypotheses

	Not satisfied	Partially satisfied	Satisfied
Basic model			
Hypothesis 1		X	
Hypothesis 2			X
Hypothesis 3			X
Sensitivity analysis			
Hypothesis 1		X	
Hypothesis 2			X
Hypothesis 3			X

assertiveness and uncertainty avoidance of the societies. However, of the factors affecting efficiency (C3), only gender egalitarianism and human orientation satisfy hypothesis 1. After the sensitivity analysis, all variables except for performance orientation affect levels of opportunity entrepreneurship. There is obviously a significant relationship between the cultural background of the societies and opportunity entrepreneurship levels. Hypotheses 2 and 3 are fully satisfied in both the basic model and the sensitivity analysis. Opportunity entrepreneurship levels therefore have a significant relationship with transaction costs in the economic relationships and economic institutions in the societies.

14.7 Overall Relationships Derived and Policy Implications

The cultural background of societies significantly shapes opportunity entrepreneurship levels. The individual cultural dimensions may positively or negatively affect opportunity entrepreneurship: a cultural background promoting entrepreneurship seems to influence it positively, while a cultural background favoring the achieving of efficiency reveals the negative side of the same cultural dimensions, in terms of their impact on opportunity entrepreneurship. At the same time, the relationship between transaction characteristics and the nature of economic institutions, and the levels of opportunity entrepreneurship fully confirms that low levels of overall risk and corruption, less time needed to start up new businesses, low corruption, and high levels of literacy, property rights protection and respect for the rule of law, are all conditions conducive to opportunity entrepreneurship, thus creating new business opportunities.

By creating a more opportunity entrepreneurship-oriented world, we observe that cultural characteristics can inhibit businesses. The effect of this change in the societies examined was extensive. The culture of societies seems to be geared more toward humans and not toward performance. Power inequalities and the assertiveness of society members decreases the number of possible business opportunities. Under these circumstances, the promotion of entrepreneurship is no longer dependent on cultural background, but only on the transaction and economic institutions characteristics. We believe this state can be characterized as "entrepreneurial maturity".

This chapter's findings have particularly important implications for economic policy. First of all, it is clear that some influences on the state of the economy, such as the levels of opportunity entrepreneurship, have a medium to long-term effect on economic activity. In addition, it is also clear that cultural background, transaction characteristics and the nature of economic institutions have effects on opportunity entrepreneurship. It therefore seems likely that investments and interventions in these two areas could have medium to long-term significant impact on opportunity entrepreneurship. This is particularly interesting because previous findings have suggested that opportunity entrepreneurship is extremely difficult to influence, but this work demonstrates that a wider social and political environment might affect it. For example, the level of risk and uncertainty in the economy could be considered as a factor in shaping the economic conditions that affect opportunity entrepreneurship.

There are therefore two levels of policy implication: (a) investment in education to improve cultural background in relation to entrepreneurship and (b) lessening transaction costs and carrying institutional reorganization to improve economic institutions, and thus encourage opportunity entrepreneurship.

Investment in education is the fundamental way to enhance cultural background to favor entrepreneurship. Because it drives increases in productivity, education brings about social and economic attributes that enhance opportunity entrepreneurship levels. Such investments could be interventions in years of schooling, levels of attainment and areas of study. Through investing in education, societies can improve their stock of opportunity entrepreneurs who have acquired the necessary skills to develop new technologies themselves or to adopt and use foreign technology (Fossen and Buttner 2012).

Economic policies to lessen transaction costs could also improve opportunity entrepreneurship levels. For example, reducing bureaucracy, perhaps by simplifying regulations and application procedures, would make it quicker to set up a new business and start earning money. Achieving stability at political, economic and financial levels would be related to lower levels of composite risk. Achieving economic and social progress, democratic values and a strong civil society could lower corruption. Investments in education would lead to higher literacy levels and thus lower costs in economic transactions. Lastly, institutional reorganization to provide better legal protection on property rights, clear laws that are fully enforced by the state, better formation and implementation of law, improved dispute settlement and easier access and operation of state legal systems would enhance opportunity entrepreneurship.

References

Audretsch DB (2007) The entrepreneurial society. Oxford University Press, New York, NY

Baum JR, Oian JD, Erez M, Schnell ER, Smith KG, Sims HP et al (1993) Nationality and work role interactions: a cultural contrast of Israeli and US entrepreneurs' versus managers' needs. J Bus Ventur 8(6):499–512

Davidson R, MacKinnon JG (1989) Testing for consistency using artificial regressions. Econom Theory 5:363–384

Davidson R, MacKinnon JG (1993) Estimation and inference in econometrics. Oxford University Press, New York, NY

Easterly W, Ritzen J, Woolcock M (2006) Social cohesion, institutions, and growth. Econ Polit 18 (2):103–120

Fossen FM, Buttner TJM (2012) The returns to education for opportunity entrepreneurs, necessity entrepreneurs, and paid employees. Discussion Paper, Freie University of Berlin, School of Business and Economics

Fukuyama F (2001) Culture and economic development: cultural concerns. In: Smelser NJ, Baltes PB (eds) International encyclopedia of the social and behavioral sciences. Elsevier Internet publication, Amsterdam, pp 3130–3134

Hausman JA (1978) Specification tests in econometrics. Econometrica 46:1251–1271

Knight FH (1971) Risk, uncertainly, and profit. The University of Chicago Press, Chicago, IL, Originally published in 1921 by Houghton Mifflin Company

Leiblein MJ, Macher JT (2009) The problem solving perspective: a strategic approach to understanding environment and organization. In: Silverman BS, Nickerson JA (eds) The economic institutions of strategy – advances in strategic management, vol 26. Emerald Group, Bingley, pp 97–120

Petrakis PE (2011) Entrepreneurship, university research, and growth: European north vs. south, entrepreneurship/book 2. In Tech, ISBN 979-953-307-861

Petrakis PE, Kostis PC (2013) The effects of culture, transactions and institutions on opportunity entrepreneurship, working paper, April.

Schumpeter J (1934) The theory of economic development. Harvard University Press, Cambridge, MA

Shane S, Venkataraman S (2000) The promise of entrepreneurship as a field of research. Acad Manag Rev 25(1):217–226

Spulber DF (2003) The intermediation theory of the firm: integrating economic and management approaches to strategy. Manag Decis Econ 24:253–266

Stiglitz N, Foss NJ (2009) Opportunities and new business models: transaction cost and property rights perspectives on entrepreneurship, vol 26. Emerald Group, Bingley, pp 67–96, doi:10.1108/S0742-3322(2009)0000026005 DOI:10.1108/S0742-3322%282009%290000026005#Permanent URL: 10.1108/S0742-3322(2009)0000026005

Thomas AS, Meller SL (2000) A case for comparative entrepreneurship: assessing the relevance of culture. J Int Bus Stud 31:287–301

Wennekers ARM (2006) Entrepreneurship at country level: economic and non-economic determinants. ERIM, Rotterdam

Wennekers ARM, Uhlaner L, Thurik AR (2002) Entrepreneurship and its conditions: a macro perspective. Int J Enterp Educ 1(1):25–64

Wennekers S, Thurik AR, Van Stel AJ, Noorderhaven N (2008) Uncertainty avoidance and the rate of business ownership across 21 OECD countries, 1976–2004. J Evol Econ 17(2):133–160

The Effects of Cultural Background and Knowledge Creation on Self-Employment and Entry Density Rates

15

The purpose of this chapter is to identify and quantify the effects of knowledge and culture on the entrepreneurship of societies. The concept of entrepreneurship is approached through two different variables: (a) self-employment rates and (b) entry of new firms to the economy. Romer (1986) and Lucas (1993) formalized the explicit introduction of knowledge into macroeconomic growth models. This introduction shifted the focus of policy to knowledge, which became particularly potent in terms of its impact on growth when compared with the traditional factors of physical capital and labor, where no knowledge spillovers or free access by third-party firms was possible (Audretsch 2007).

The order of the chapter is as follows. Section 15.1 sets out the theoretical background and more specifically the concepts of entrepreneurship identification and knowledge, as well as the effects of knowledge on economic behavior, and its place in the Institutional/Post-Keynesian model. Section 15.2 covers the data used in the empirical analysis. Section 15.3 describes the methodology employed, that is, the empirical model and measurements, while Sect. 15.4 includes the empirical work and discusses the results. Finally, Sect. 15.5 sets out the relationships identified as a result of the work.

15.1 Entrepreneurship Identification, Knowledge and Cultural Background

The identification and the exploitation of entrepreneurial opportunities are an important part of the entrepreneurial process. The theory of entrepreneurship identification has resulted in three basic schools of thought on the identification of investment opportunities (Companys and McMullen 2007).

This chapter is a summary of a scientific paper by Petrakis P.E. and Kostis P.C. (2013) on the Review of Economics and Finance, Vol 3, No 2.

P.E. Petrakis, *Culture, Growth and Economic Policy*,
DOI 10.1007/978-3-642-41440-4_15, © Springer-Verlag Berlin Heidelberg 2014

The Economic School defines an entrepreneurial opportunity as an objective phenomenon that exists in time and space, which may be unknown to some people (Shane 2003; Shane and Venkataraman 2000). Better access to information and knowledge improves the ability of a person to identify entrepreneurial opportunities (Shane 2003; Shane and Venkataraman 2000). Kirzner (1973) argues that opportunities exist, but someone has to identify them. According to Mitchell et al. (2007), entrepreneurial cognition is the knowledge structures that people use to make assessments, judgments or decisions involving opportunity evaluation, venture creation and growth. This school therefore attributes entrepreneurial opportunities to the distribution of information regarding the material opportunities that exist in society (David and Foray 2003).

The School of Culture suggests that entrepreneurial opportunities are subjective and not objective constructions or phenomena (Sarasvathy et al. 2003). According to Weick (1979), entrepreneurial opportunities exist only to the extent that individuals comprehend their existence, and not in an objective way waiting for someone to discover them. The existence of a specific cultural background forms the basis of a sustainable competitive advantage (Rindova et al. 2003). Business opportunities are defined through social interactions, and differences in the distribution of knowledge are the primary source of business opportunities. However, differences in the cognitive level that influence the capability to perceive entrepreneurial opportunities are based on culture and not on the amount of factual information available or past experiences (Shane 2003). Additionally, entrepreneurial opportunities can be actively created by entrepreneurs themselves (Sarasvathy et al. 2003).

Finally, the Sociopolitical School suggests the important role that administrative mechanisms play in the definition of entrepreneurial opportunities (Granovetter 1985). It emphasizes the objective properties of entrepreneurial opportunities, and the political procedures that are exercised to bring pressure to bear on potential entrepreneurs to seize suitable opportunities (Fligstein 1996). This school considers that entrepreneurial opportunities exist and evolve into complex networks of social relationships, which shape economic activity. The placement of actors in a concrete network determines the mass of critical resources and information that the actor may dispose to exploit such opportunities (Burt 1992). The mechanisms of management are, in fact, the rules of the game that affect both the behavior of individuals (DiMaggio and Powell 1983) and the conditions imposed by the external environment.

Regardless of the methodology with which recognition of entrepreneurial opportunities is approached, two key factors seem to play a role first in the identification of entrepreneurial opportunities and then in their activation as entrepreneurship events: knowledge and the cultural background of societies.

Knowledge is considered to be a valuable commodity and concepts such as knowledge sharing and lifelong learning have become increasingly prevalent in business practices. Martins (2011) states that knowledge is more than information, since it involves understanding obtained through learning and experience. De Witte and van den Brink (2013) suggest that even without major increases in (public) funding, improvements in educational outcomes and thus knowledge improve economic performance.

According to Karlsson et al. (2004), knowledge can be defined as scientific knowledge, technological knowledge and entrepreneurial knowledge. The first two definitions of knowledge are more associated with incumbents. Entrepreneurial knowledge, on the other hand, comprises specific knowledge tied to the market and the functioning of an economy and is connected to what is required to introduce an innovation (Schumpeter 1911). Moreover, the ability to recognize and capitalize on entrepreneurial opportunities can be considered as part of the cognitive background of a person.

The expected economic value of knowledge or of a new idea varies significantly among economic actors. Different levels of education, background and experience create different conditions associated with knowledge, the degree of uncertainty, information asymmetries and the cost of transactions and so lead to different decisions (Audretsch 2007). In line with the Cultural School, these differences may lead to discrepancies in identification, evaluation and decision-making concerned with the realization of entrepreneurial opportunities among economic actors, because of different perceptions of the expected value of a new project.

Between knowledge with a potential commercial value and knowledge that is actually commercialized there is a knowledge filter (Audretsch et al. 2006). The knowledge filter activates knowledge and transforms it into business activity. The concept of knowledge management has been extensively researched, as it is considered one of the roots of business development (Nonaka 1994; Randeree 2006). If businesses use knowledge properly, they gain a competitive advantage by becoming more sustainable and innovative. Businesses have an integrated wealth of knowledge, established through their working practices, management systems and human resources (Petrakis and Kostis 2012).

Organizational knowledge is not easily imitated by a firm's competition, which results in a sustainable competitive advantage and a strategic asset for businesses (Bollinger and Smith 2001). The challenge for businesses is to be able to capture that knowledge and to leverage it through their operations. The investments in new knowledge by firms and organizations not only create an opportunity for a comparative advantage to these firms, but also form the conditions for knowledge to spill over to other firms as well (Griliches 1992). As far as the theoretical relationship between culture and entrepreneurship is concerned, see Chap. 14.

15.2 The Data

The data for self-employment and entry density are defined in Table 15.1, and consist of the mean performance of each country for the time period 2008–2009. For the variables expressing cultural background, the reference period is 1995–1997. A more detailed explanation of these variables is set out in Table 12.1 in Chap. 12. The data for knowledge creation and knowledge impact are from 2009.

Table 15.1 Definition of variables and data sources

Variables		Definition	Reference period	Data source
Self-employment		Self-employed workers are those who, by working on their own account or with one or a few partners or in cooperative, hold the type of jobs defined as a "self-employment jobs"	2008–2009	International Labor Organization
Entry density		The number of newly registered limited liability companies per 1,000 working age (15–64) people	2008–2009	The World Bank Entrepreneurship Snapshots 2010 "Measuring the Impact of the Financial Crisis on New Business Registration"
CREATION	Knowledge creation	It includes four indicators that are the result of inventive and innovation activities: patent applications filed by residents both at the national patent office and at an international level through the Patent Cooperation Treaty; utility model applications filed by residents at the national office; and scientific and technical published articles in peer-reviewed journals	2009	Global Innovation Index 2011, INSEAD
IMPACT	Knowledge impact	It includes three statistics representing the impact of innovation activities at the micro and macroeconomic level: increases in labor productivity, the entry of new firms, and spending on software		

Notes: The 45 countries in the sample represent 78.86 % of the global GDP, 2009 (IMF Database). The countries are Argentina, Australia, Austria, Bolivia, Brazil, Canada, Colombia, Costa Rica, Denmark, Ecuador, Egypt, El Salvador, Finland, France, Georgia, Germany, Greece, Hong Kong, Hungary, Indonesia, Ireland, Italy, Japan, Kazakhstan, Malaysia, Mexico, Morocco, the Netherlands, New Zealand, Philippines, Poland, Portugal, Russian Federation, Singapore, Slovenia, South Africa, Korean Rep., Spain, Sweden, Switzerland, Thailand, Turkey, United Kingdom, United States and Venezuela

The small sample size on self-employment and entry density mean that the analysis could not be deepened.

Our limited degrees of freedom (due to the small sample available to us because of our limited number of observations on Self-employment and Entry Density rates) do not permit us to deepen our analysis in this respect. These variables are precisely defined in Table 15.1.

15.3 The Methodology Employed

We examined the following two hypotheses.

$$\text{Self-Employment}_i = \beta_0 + \beta_1 * \text{CULT}_i + \beta_2 * \text{CREATION}_i + \beta_3 * \text{IMPACT}_i + \varepsilon_i \quad (15.1)$$

$$\text{Entry Density}_i = \gamma_0 + \gamma_1 * \text{CULT}_i + \gamma_2 * \text{CREATION}_i + \gamma_3 * \text{IMPACT}_i + \varepsilon_i \quad (15.2)$$

In other words, both self-employment and entry density levels depend on cultural background, knowledge creation and knowledge impact. CULT is the principal component (PC) that arises from the variables expressing cultural background, after a Principal Component Analysis (PCA) (see Chap. 12); CREATION refers to knowledge creation and IMPACT refers to knowledge impact. We also carried out a check for endogeneity among the variables, using a version of the Hausman test (Hausman 1978) proposed by Davidson and MacKinnon (1989, 1993).

We included a sensitivity analysis to evaluate the effect of culture and knowledge on self-employment and entry density rates under changing circumstances. For each hypothesis, we created eight different possible combinations of cultural background and knowledge, through increasing or decreasing the values of the variables. Each variable was increased or reduced by 30 % for the countries scoring below or above the average. Power distance and uncertainty avoidance, which are adversely scored, were reduced by 30 % for countries scoring over the average score of the sample (and vice versa). Figure 15.1 sets out the sensitivity analysis. After the sensitivity analysis, we ran a new PCA with the new PCs for cultural background. In each case, we evaluated the effect of the new PCs in combination with the new variables for knowledge, first on self-employment and then on entry density rates.

We also performed a structural change check relating the alternative circumstances to the basic scenario (see Chap. 12 for a more complete explanation of this technique). This led to conclusions about the new configuration and conditions of self-employment and entry density rates.

15.4 Empirical Work and Discussion of the Results

Four PCs were identified for cultural background (CULT_1, CULT_2, CULT_3 and CULT_4 in Table E.1—Appendix E) that explain 32.88 %, 25.02 %, 13.30 % and 10.77 % of the total variance and have initial eigenvalues of 2.96, 2.25, 1.19 and 0.97 respectively. CULT_1 is determined by the positive effects of performance orientation, future orientation, institutional collectivism, in-group collectivism and uncertainty avoidance, and the negative effects of humane orientation. CULT_2 is positively shaped by performance orientation, gender egalitarianism, institutional

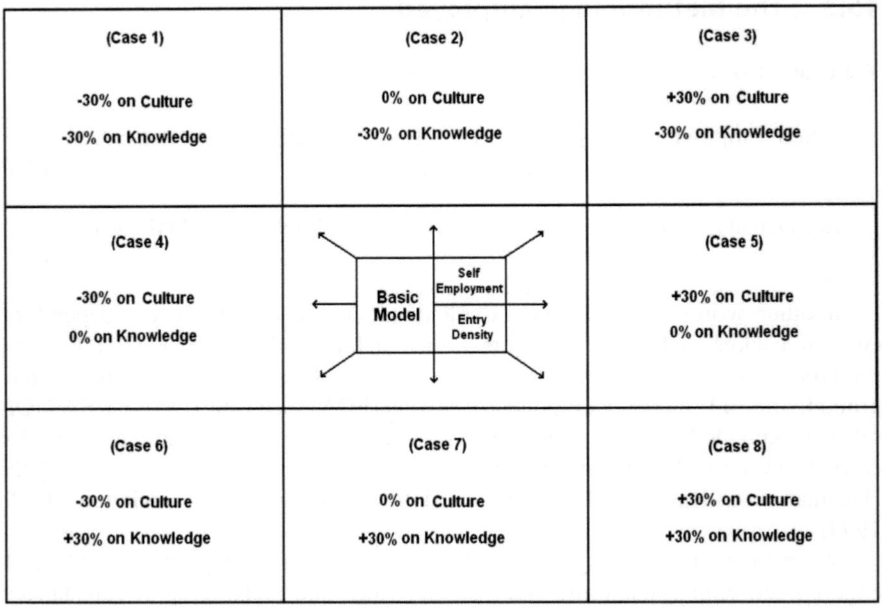

Fig. 15.1 The sensitivity analysis

collectivism and humane orientation, whereas assertiveness, power distance and uncertainty avoidance have a negative effect. The positive effects of performance orientation, gender egalitarianism, assertiveness, in-group collectivism and power distance and the negative effects of humane orientation determine $CULT_3$. $CULT_4$ is determined by the positive effects of assertiveness and human orientation.

Table E.1 (Appendix E) sets out which variables affect each principal component. Table E.2 and E.3 set out the relationships and correlations between the variables. Table E.2 (Appendix E) sets out the empirical results of the estimated regressions. It shows that an increase in $CULT_1$ would result in increased self-employment. However, an increase of $CULT_2$ or knowledge impact would decrease self-employment rates. An increase of $CULT_1$, $CULT_2$ or knowledge impact would increase the Self-Employment rates.

Knowledge creation does not seem to affect either the self-employment or entry density rates. It therefore seems likely that knowledge creation has a longer-term effect on entrepreneurship, perhaps over 10 years or more. We were concerned that self-employment might be endogenously determined by $CULT_1$, knowledge creation or knowledge impact, or entry density by $CULT_3$ or knowledge impact. We therefore carried out a version of the Davidson and MacKinnon (1989, 1993) test. The results suggest that there is no endogeneity, and the outcomes from the original analysis are sound.

Next, we caused a shock in the economies by increasing or decreasing by 30 % or maintaining constant the values of the variables expressing cultural background and knowledge, and run a new PCA, creating new variables. Table E.4 shows the PCA results after the decrease or the increase of the variables that represent cultural background.

The shock in the economies produced some statistically significant structural differences, which are shown in Table E.5 (Appendix E) and Table E.6 (Appendix E).

There was a statistically significant structural change for levels of self-employment in all cases where we reduced the cultural background by 30 %, whether or not the level of knowledge was changed (Cases 1, 4 and 6). After the sensitivity analysis, the impact of $CULT'_1$ was transformed from positive to negative in Case 1, and disappeared in Cases 4 and 6. $CULT'_2$ also ceased to have an impact in all three cases. Simultaneously, new PCs appeared as statistically important: $CULT'_3$ has a positive impact in Cases 4 and 6 and $CULT'_4$ has a negative effect in Case 1. Increased knowledge creation reduced self-employment in all three cases. Knowledge impact continued to have a negative effect except in Case 6.

A statistically significant structural change was observed in three different groups of cases for entry density. In cases where knowledge was reduced by 30 %, regardless of the change to cultural background (Cases 1, 2 and 3), the effect of $CULT'_1$ disappeared. In Case 1 the effect of $CULT'_3$ was also lost, whereas in Cases 2 and 3 its positive impact was reinforced. In all three cases increased knowledge impact caused greater entry density.

In cases where knowledge was increased by 30 %, regardless of changes to the cultural background (Cases 6, 7 and 8), $CULT'_1$ ceased to have an effect when cultural background was constant or increased, but had an increased effect when cultural background was increased. $CULT'_3$ had a reduced impact when cultural background was increased or maintained, but the effect disappeared when cultural background factors were reduced. When cultural background factors were increased, two new PCs started to have a negative effect on entry density ($CULT'_2$ and $CULT'_4$). In all three cases the positive effect of knowledge impact was decreased.

The final group of cases had a reduction in cultural background of 30 %, with different changes in levels of knowledge (Cases 1, 4 and 6). In the first group of Cases, where the dependent variable is Entry Density, the effect of $CULT'_1$ disappears as far as cultural background is concerned. Likewise, in Case 1 the effect of $CULT'_3$ is also lost, whereas in Cases 2 and 3 its positive impact is reinforced. With regard to the variables of Knowledge, in all three cases the positive impact of Knowledge Impact on Entry Density is strengthened. In the second group, the positive impact of $CULT'_1$ is lost in Cases 6 and 7, while it is intensified in Case 8. On the contrary, the positive impact of $CULT'_3$ is reduced in Cases 6 and 7, while it disappears in Case 8. At the same time, in Case 6 there are two new PCs for cultural background with a negative effect on the Entry Density ($CULT'_2$ and $CULT'_4$). As far as Knowledge is concerned, in all three cases the positive effect of Knowledge Impact is decreased. Finally, with regard to the third group, in all three cases, $CULT'_1$ ceased to have an impact. Cases 1 and 6 have been described above. In Case 4, an increase in $CULT'_2$ reduced entry density, while $CULT'_3$ remained unchanged. Finally, increased knowledge impact had an even greater effect on entry density under these new circumstances.

15.5 The Overall Relationships Derived

Factors that promote and suppress entrepreneurship have been defined with considerable clarity to highlight the importance that improvement in particular conditions of knowledge and culture would have on self-employment and entry density rates. From the work described above, it is clear that an increase in knowledge impact reduces self-employment rates, but increases entry density rates. However, knowledge creation does not seem to affect either self-employment or entry density rates, perhaps because its effect is longer-term and so was not seen within the time frame studied. Cultural background of societies seems to affect both self-employment and entry density rates, although different components have different effects.

If the value of cultural background components is reduced, this affects both self-employment and entry density rates under all circumstances. Under these new circumstances, increased knowledge impact reduces self-employment rates even more, as does increased knowledge creation. However, knowledge creation does not seem to play any role in determining entry density rates, although increasing or decreasing the variables representing knowledge as a whole does affect entry density rates, whether or not cultural background is changed.

References

Audretsch DB (2007) The entrepreneurial society. Oxford University Press, New York, NY

Audretsch DB, Keilbach MC, Lehmann EE (2006) Entrepreneurship and economic growth. Oxford University Press, New York, NY

Bollinger AS, Smith RD (2001) Managing organizational knowledge as a strategic asset. J Knowl Manage 5(1):8–18

Burt RS (1992) Structural holes: the social structure of competition. Harvard University Press, Cambridge, MA

Companys YE, McMullen JS (2007) Strategic entrepreneurs at work the nature, discovery, and exploitation of entrepreneurial opportunities. Small Bus Econ 28:301–322

David PA, Foray D (2003) Economic fundamentals of the knowledge society. Policy Futures Educ 1(1):20–49

Davidson R, MacKinnon JG (1989) Testing for consistency using artificial regressions. Econ Theory 5:363–384

Davidson R, MacKinnon JG (1993) Estimation and inference in econometrics. Oxford University Press, New York, NY

DiMaggio PJ, Powell WW (1983) The iron cage revisited: institutional isomorphism and collective rationality in organizational fields. Am Sociol Rev 48:147–160

Fligstein N (1996) Markets as politics: a political-cultural approach to market institutions. Am Sociol Rev 61:656–673

Granovetter MS (1985) Economic action and social structure: the problem of embeddedness. Am J Sociol 91(3):481–510

Griliches Z (1992) The search for R&D spillovers. Scand J Econ 94(Supplement):29–47
Hausman JA (1978) Specification tests in econometrics. Econometrica 46:1251–1271
Karlsson C, Friis C, Paulsson T (2004) Relating entrepreneurship to economic growth. CESIS Electronic Working Paper Series, No. 13
Kirzner IM (1973) Competition and entrepreneurship. University of Chicago Press, Chicago, IL
Lucas RE (1993) Making a miracle. Econometrica 61:251–272
Martins JM (2011) Knowledge transfer to the subsidiaries: a case study of multinational enterprise operating in overseas. Rev Econ Finance 1:74–84, Article ID: 1923-7529-2011-03-74-11
Mitchell RK, Busenitz L, Bird B, Gaglio CM, McMullen J, Morse E, Smith B (2007) The central question in entrepreneurial cognition research. Entrep Theory Pract 31:1–27
Nonaka I (1994) A dynamic theory of organizational knowledge creation. Organ Sci 5(1):14–37
Petrakis PE, Kostis PC (2012) The role of knowledge and trust in SMEs. J Knowl Econ. doi:10.1007/s13132-012-0115-6
Petrakis PE, Kostis PC (2013) The effects of cultural background and knowledge creation on self-employment and entry density rates. Rev Econ Finance 3:18–32
Randeree E (2006) Knowledge management: securing the future. J Knowl Manage 10(4):145–156
Rindova VP, Pollock TG, Hayward M (2003) Celebrity firms: the social construction of market popularity. Academy of Management Conference, Seattle, WA
Romer P (1986) Increasing returns and long-run growth. J Polit Econ 94(October):500–521, 1002–37
Sarasvathy SD, Dew N, Velamuri SR, Venkatamaran S (2003) Three views of entrepreneurial Opportunity'. In: Acs ZJ, Audretsch DB (eds) Handbook of entrepreneurship research. Kluwer, Boston, pp 141–160
Schumpeter JA (1911) Die theorie wirtschaftlicher entwicklung, Berlin: duncker & humblot, english edition: the theory of economic development (1934). Cambridge University Press, Cambridge
Shane S (2003) A general theory of entrepreneurship – the individual-opportunity nexus. Edward Elgar, Cheltenham
Shane S, Venkataraman S (2000) The promise of entrepreneurship as a field of research. Acad Manage Rev 25(1):218–228
Weick K (1979) The social psychology of organizing, 2nd edn. Addison-Wesley, Reading, MA
Witte D, den Brink V (2013) The efficiency of education in generating literacy: a stochastic frontier approach. Rev Econ Finance 2:25–37, Article ID: 1923-7529-2012-01-25-13

16 Cultural Background, Growth and Economic Policy

The stages of economic growth cover the transition from being a low-income country to becoming a middle-income one and, finally, a high-income one (advanced economy). This transition is not easy and, in most cases, comes up against obstacles and lack of appropriate resources. There are many examples of countries that have experienced high growth rates and significantly increased their standards of living, without, however, managing to evolve into advanced economies. High growth rates were followed by periods of stagnation, or even recession, and then by growth again, meaning that such countries have been unable to exit from this vicious cycle and reach a permanent level of higher income.

We describe this phenomenon as the "Cultural Growth Trap", and by doing so, we attempt to explain the failure of middle-income countries to present and sustain economic development and avoid years of stagnation or economic recession. We consider that, except where low productivity is the main factor behind the middle-income trap, cultural background can explain the deeper sources of low income growth rates in middle-income countries.

Later on, we discuss whether there is an ideal cultural background to increasing growth. This chapter closes with reference to issues of economic policy and, more particularly, austerity policy and the neo-Keynesian approach to stabilization policies, using South Europe as a case study.

The chapter is structured as follows. Section 16.1 explains the middle-income trap, and Sect. 16.2 sets out the reasons why the majority of countries fall into this trap. The phenomenon of the "Cultural Growth Trap", as an explanatory factor, is set out in Sect. 16.3. Section 16.4 concerns the ideal cultural background for growth. Section 16.5 makes reference to austerity policy and cultural requirements. Section 16.6 discusses the neo-Keynesian approach to production and employment and its cultural requirements and, finally, Sect. 16.7 discusses South Europe as a case study, where cultural background influences the way stabilization works.

P.E. Petrakis, *Culture, Growth and Economic Policy*,
DOI 10.1007/978-3-642-41440-4_16,

16.1 The Middle-Income Trap

Development economics tries to explain the basic factors that promote or suppress the economic evolution of particular countries. It is a crucial matter that has attracted the interest of many scholars. The rapid economic growth of emerging markets has lifted millions of people out of poverty. However, the question that is raised is whether growth will continue, to lead low-income countries toward a convergence with high-income countries.

The World Bank classifies countries in accordance with a basic criterion, which is the gross national income (GNI) per capita. On this basis, each economy is classified as low-income (GNI per capita of $1,025 or less), middle-income ($1,026–$12,475) and high-income ($12,476 or more). In the course of economic growth, developing countries face the threshold of the poverty trap, at first, and then, provided that they overcome this, the middle-income trap.

By using the term "poverty trap" (Gill and Kharas 2008), development economics literature attempts to interpret the reasons why certain poor countries develop at slower rates than the developed world. This is contrary to what one would expect, given their comparative advantage regarding high capital returns, the use of redundant workforce and the import of cheap technology from developed countries.

The "middle-income trap" (Gill et al. 2007) refers to the situation in which poor countries have overcome the poverty trap and have reached the ranks of middle-income countries, without, however, being able to climb to a higher income level. The economy reaches a certain level of income per capita, by making use of its advantages, but gets stuck at that level and fails to grow to advanced-country levels (Kharas and Kohli 2011).

The constant increase of income per capita over time to higher levels is the pattern expected from every steadily-growing economy. However, in some cases, middle-income countries do not follow this pattern, and periods of rapid growth instead give way to periods of stagnation or decline.

16.2 Why Do Countries Fall into the Middle-Income Trap? An Economic Explanation

The basic explanation for why middle-income countries fail to evolve into advanced economies focuses on sharp slowdowns in productivity (Agénor et al. 2012). Eighty-five percent of cases where the rate of output growth has slowed can be explained by slowing of total factor productivity growth and not by a decline of the capital accumulation growth (Eichengreen et al. 2012).

To understand the reasons why the majority of developing countries fail to evolve into rich countries, we should consider the basic factors of every stage, from low-income to high-income level (Fig. 16.1).

At the first stage, low-income countries are characterized by low levels of productivity. The large margins for improvement therefore give them the opportunity to boost their production levels in an easy way. The rapid growth of

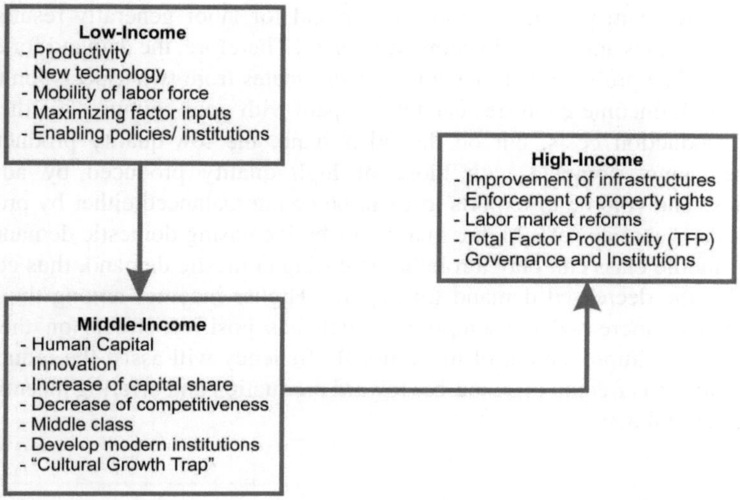

Fig. 16.1 The basic characteristics of a country's income level evolution

low-income countries is mainly caused by the mobility of the labor force from low productivity activities (e.g., agriculture) to higher productivity activities (e.g., industrial production). The economy is mainly based on agriculture, with the labor force being characterized by low levels of specialization. The shift of a redundant labor force toward industrial production constitutes a distinctive example of the way low-income countries tend to grow. This procedure leads to urbanization growth.

Low wages, because there is plenty of labor, make low-income countries competitive, so their exports thrive. Their goods and services become attractive to developed countries, since they can be bought more cheaply than if they were produced in those countries.

Through the inflow of currency from other countries, poor countries acquire the necessary resources to develop their infrastructure, introduce new technologies and improve their productivity. Apart from the accumulation of capital, incoming resources are also channeled toward the improvement of living standards (works of public benefit) and human capital (education).

By making use of the bigger margins available for improvement at this first stage, poor countries follow a strategy of organizing the supply side economy, thus maximizing the effectiveness of the basic growth factors. Furthermore, they tend to establish policies promoting the smooth operation of the institutional background.

After an economy manages to evolve to the middle-income stage, it faces new challenges. The original strategy no longer applies and the economy also faces new challenges, in both its internal and external environments. Growth tends to be more capital- and skill-intensive in manufacturing, whereas an increase in the service sector is considered necessary to serve the new interconnections created to support the production side.

The increase in production and the demand for labor generally results in an increase in wages and a drop in competitiveness. Therefore, the demand for exports is reduced. The problem that then emerges originates from two aspects: on the one hand, middle-income countries cannot compete with poor countries, as they have higher production costs, but on the other hand, the low-quality products they produce cannot compete with those of high quality produced by advanced countries. The volume of exports lost can be counterbalanced either by providing products and services of a higher quality, or by increasing domestic demand.

The middle class can play a role in increasing domestic demand, thus compensating for the decreased demand for exports. Higher incomes among the middle class lead to increased consumption, which has positive effects on the entire economy. The improvement of institutional efficiency will assist the reduction in uncertainty, thus freeing up resources toward production and offering incentives for entrepreneurial activity.

16.3 The Cultural Growth Trap

The Cultural Growth Trap is the concept to describe the situation where a society has increased its standards of living, but the dominant cultural background does not allow it to experience further economic growth and evolve into a developed economy.

According to a World Bank report from 2012, out of the 101 middle-income economies in 1960, only 13 had become high-income ones by 2008 (Fig. 16.2). Those countries were Equatorial Guinea, Greece, Hong Kong SAR (China), Ireland, Israel, Japan, Mauritius, Portugal, Puerto Rico, the Republic of Korea, Singapore, Spain and Taiwan.

Table 16.1 presents the cultural background of middle-income and high-income countries, according to data from Hofstede et al. (2010). The differences among the existing cultural models between the two groups of countries are quite obvious. The scores for each cultural dimension were weighted averages by population.

Middle-income countries appear to accept, to a greater extent, social and economic inequalities and the accumulation of power in a small proportion of the population. In societies where power and wealth accumulate among just a few people, social tensions are created. There are signs of a lack of social cohesion, holding back economic growth. However, such a situation may be constructive, as it may encourage lower social classes to take the initiative, for example, by engaging in rent-seeking activities.

The degree of individualism or collectivism in society plays an important role in the determination of human behavior. The prevalence of collectivism and team spirit prevents individual initiative, thus restraining individual action within a defined context. At the same time, the cohesive bonds created within the group prevent communication and cooperation with third parties. In contrast, societies rewarding individual initiative and independent action tend to achieve better economic results. Individuals act to maximize their personal benefit and, consequently,

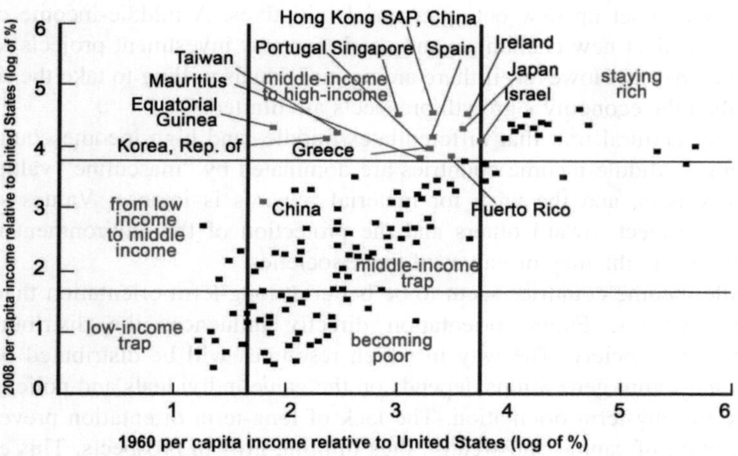

Fig. 16.2 Per capita incomes relative to the United States, 1960 and 2008. *Source*: World Bank (2012)

Table 16.1 The cultural model of middle-income and high-income countries, according to Hofstede

	Power distance	Individualism	Uncertainty avoidance	Masculinity	Long-term orientation	Indulgence
Middle-income countries	44.67	46.56	62.06	45.75	47.24	49.22
High-income countries	30.36	44.72	43.41	31.73	34.70	37.06
High-income countries	30.36	44.72	43.41	31.73	34.70	37.06

Source: Hofstede et al. (2010) and the author's calculations. Weighted averages according to population

Notes: Middle-income countries: Argentina, Brazil, Bulgaria, Chile, China, Colombia, El Salvador, India, Indonesia, Iran, Latvia, Lithuania, Malaysia, Mexico, Morocco, Pakistan, Peru, the Philippines, Romania, Russia, Serbia, Thailand, Turkey, Venezuela and Vietnam

High-income countries: Australia, Austria, Belgium, Canada, Croatia, Czech Rep., Denmark, Estonia, Finland, France, Germany, Greece, Hong Kong, Hungary, Ireland, Italy, Japan, South Korea, Luxembourg, Malta, The Netherlands, New Zealand, Norway, Poland, Portugal, Singapore, Slovak Rep., Slovenia, Spain, Sweden, Switzerland, Trinidad and Tobago, United States and Uruguay

the prospects for society are also better. Nevertheless, the levels of individualism are approximately the same levels in both groups of countries.

Middle-income countries generally feel uncomfortable with uncertainty and ambiguity. However, high-income countries accept the existence of risk and uncertainty. The degree of society's risk aversion directly influences the functioning of the economic system. The members of societies with low sensitivity to risk tend to be reluctant to set up new entrepreneurial initiatives. A middle-income country comes up against new challenges and needs for new investment projects to drive economic growth. However, if there are no individuals willing to take the risk and invest, then the economy's growth prospects are limited.

Another cultural trait that differentiates middle- and high-income countries is masculinity. Middle-income countries are dominated by "masculine" values such as assertiveness, and the wish for material rewards is intense. Values such as solidarity, respect toward others and the protection of the environment occupy low positions in the map of values of these societies.

Middle-income countries seem to be better at long-term orientation than high-income countries. Future orientation directly influences the distribution of resources in a society. The way in which resources will be distributed between present and future generations depends on the value individuals and policymakers attribute to long-term orientation. The lack of long-term orientation prevents the accumulation of capital and wealth, thus limiting growth prospects. This element may constitute the driving force behind the evolution of middle-income countries to high-income ones.

Finally, middle-income countries allow relatively free rein to enjoying life and having fun ("indulgence"). By contrast, individuals in high-income countries tend to be more restrained, and behavior is more determined by strict social norms.

This model of cultural values, therefore, identifies some important differences between these two groups, which may explain the divergences in economic outcome. High-income countries accept the existence of inequalities to a lesser extent than middle-income countries and have lower risk aversion. Middle-income countries tend to have higher future orientation, dominance of "masculine" values and a preference for indulgence.

Hence, the question posed is why most countries face difficulties in sustaining growth to higher income levels, such that only 13 have managed to evolve into advanced economies since the 1960s. Finding the deeper causes is a difficult undertaking, but could shed light on this question.

The transition of a country from one level to another is linked to the fulfillment of basic requirements, which are different for each level (see Fig. 16.3). Initially, transition from lower to middle level is linked to the satisfaction of basic needs and improvement of living standards. The situation becomes different as an economy shifts from middle- to high-income level, given that the incentives of economic activity differ. At this point cultural change comes to the fore.

The satisfaction of human needs acts as the driving force for growth. The transition from agriculture to new forms of economic activity, in conjunction with the industrialization of production, increases productivity, thus offering new jobs and the safeguarding of basic survival needs. During this phase, members of society aim to increase prosperity, by combining the available production factors with greater efficiency. The dominant cultural background does not affect the way decisions are taken.

However, the picture changes as societies progress. The comparative advantages they had as poor countries have now been eliminated and they are standing on the

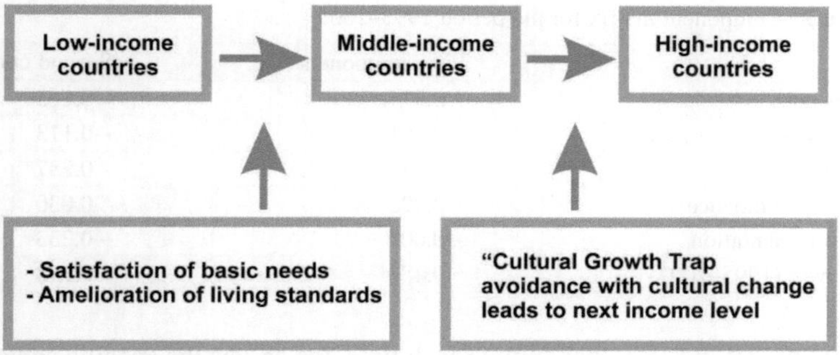

Fig. 16.3 The basic requirements

verge of either progress or stagnation. Living standards have improved, and the number of individuals living below the poverty line has dropped. Further increases in income per capita need additional effort. Cultural values and stereotypes affect both individual and collective decisions, by influencing goals and priorities. The dominant cultural background may not favor the increase of national wealth and may also prevent the undertaking of entrepreneurial activity.

Therefore, to understand why many countries fail to break free from specific growth thresholds, it is necessary to look at cultural values.

16.4 Ideal Cultural Background and Growth

Is there an ideal cultural background favoring economic growth? A positive answer to this question has been implied in the previous sections. It appears that societies with pro-growth characteristics can break free from the middle-income growth trap, but that those without a similar cultural portfolio may struggle. However, before we search for the appropriate cultural background, there is still one more issue to examine: the means to achieve economic growth, or the economic system.

Until now, we have considered cultural background and the economic system to be inter-associated in a complicated manner, while accepting that this is consistent with the characteristics of the capitalist system. Nevertheless, the productive capitalist system undergoes different stages of development and transformation of its own. Its characteristics in the various stages of development are different, depending on its historical evolution and origin. Therefore, financial capitalism has its own particular characteristics, as do the systems of capitalism created in the aftermath of the collapse of the former communist states in Eastern Europe, state capitalism in oil-producing states and the form of capitalism developed in the Chinese economy.

Different cultures coexist with capitalist institutions in a different manner. The different elements building cultural background may also have a determinative effect on the efficiency of economic institutions. Hence, the original question must be rephrased as follows: Is there an ideal cultural background, consistent with the

Table 16.2 Component matrix for the period 1995–2007

	First component	Second component
Power distance	0.874	0.165
Individualism	−0.881	−0.113
Masculinity	0.145	0.287
Uncertainty avoidance	0.092	0.830
Long-term orientation	−0.009	−0.233
GDP growth (1995–2007)	0.487	−0.748

capitalist model in force, that applies each time and serves the specific social goals set by societies? Rephrasing the question provides a better description of the different social dimensions of the search for the ideal cultural background and the relationships between answers to this question.

For this purpose, in our attempt to approach the basic characteristics of cultural background that correspond to a dynamic growth profile, we developed a particularly loose quantitative method of examination. Basing this on the data of Hofstede et al. (2010), we attempted to depict observed changes in the cultural background of 62 countries[1] over the period 1995–2007.

The methodology we adopted was as follows. To represent the complexity of the cultural background's variables, we employed the Principal Component Analysis (PCA) method. Table 16.2 presents the component matrix for the entire period (1995–2007). The cultural dimensions of Hofstede et al. (2010) and the growth rate in GDP (1995–2007) were also integrated. Two principal components emerged: the first component captures 30.08 % of the total variance, and the second component captures 24.11 % of the total variance. The variables that affect the PC configuration take values of partial correlation greater than 0.3.

The first component is determined by the positive effect of power distance and the negative effect of individualism positively connected with GDP growth. Power distance and collectivism tend to shape a cultural background that favors growth. The second component is determined by the positive effect of uncertainty avoidance with the negative effect of GDP growth. Risk aversion can be determined as a hold-back factor in undertaking economic activity and, consequently, its effect on GDP is negative. The interactions among power distance, individualism and risk aversion tend to favor GDP growth.

The acceptance of inequalities in society contributes to economic development, by encouraging individuals to take entrepreneurial initiatives, and express rent-

[1] The 61 countries in the sample constitute 88.52 % of the global GDP in 2007 (IMF Database). The countries are: Argentina, Australia, Austria, Bangladesh, Belgium, Brazil, Bulgaria, Canada, Chile, China, Colombia, Croatia, Czech Rep., Denmark, El Salvador, Estonia, Finland, France, Germany, Greece, Hong Kong, Hungary, India, Indonesia, Iran, Ireland, Israel, Italy, Japan, South Korea, Latvia, Lithuania, Luxembourg, Malaysia, Malta, Mexico, Morocco, the Netherlands, New Zealand, Norway, Pakistan, Peru, the Philippines, Poland, Portugal, Romania, Russia, Serbia, Singapore, Slovak Rep., Slovenia, Spain, Sweden, Switzerland, Thailand, Trinidad and Tobago, Turkey, United States, Uruguay, Venezuela and Vietnam.

seeking behaviors. When reaching high levels, the perception of risk and uncertainty acts as a factor holding back growth.

What emerges from this simple exercise is that positive growth rates are indeed linked to certain basic cultural dimensions, at a global level and on average and for the specific period of time under examination. These are increased power distance and decreased individualism. Increases in levels of masculinity and uncertainty avoidance reduce levels of growth.

Much more research and study is needed to draw full conclusions about the elements building an ideal cultural background. However, the approach here has provided an insight into some of the basic elements.

16.5 Austerity Policy and Cultural Requirements

In brief, the austerity program for competitive and fiscal consolidation established across many economies in the recent recession requires the simultaneous creation of a positive external flows balance and a positive fiscal surplus. It is known, though, that these two targets, internal and external balancing, conflict with each other, when applied to economies that do not have control over foreign exchange rate. Creating external balance through internal depreciation leads to aggravation of the level of economic activity and decrease of GDP. This makes any reduction in the debt-to-GDP ratio very difficult.

Those in favor of the implementation of austerity and supply side programs consider that problematic economies should be in a position to increase their net international investment position in a creditworthy manner. However, the extent and the speed at which this change will take place must be suitable to accelerate the Adjustment Goal (internal and external balancing) of the austerity program. Achieving this goal depends on (a) the figure for private and public debt levels (stocks) and (b) the net balance of the current account (flows) (Roubini 2011) and more particularly on the net balance of the current account in relation to international tradable goods. Therefore, this latter figure (stocks) should become positive, in order to consequently decrease stock as well. If there were flexible exchange rates, a depreciation in the exchange rate would suffice at first, with the other conditions being stable. Since there is no ability to change the exchange rate, those in favor of the implementation of austerity and supply side programs claim that such depreciation must take place mainly through a decrease in the cost of labor. Such thinking does not apply with a floating exchange rates system, nor when we convert a system of stable exchange rates to one with floating exchange rates. The procedures there can be uncontrollable.

When everything else is steady, the Adjustment Goal (i.e., extent and speed) economically depends on five basic parameters: (a) the share of tradable goods and services in production, (b) the share of non-tradable goods in consumption, (c) the flexibility of demand for tradable against non-tradable goods and services, (d) the share of domestic production in the tradable goods and services and (e) the flexibility of demand for domestically-produced tradable goods against those produced abroad. In effect, during the interim period for the achievement of the adjustment goal, the consequent restructuring produces signals (i.e., change in relative values and destruction of certain sectors and fields), which once again trigger entrepreneurship, which will shape the new model.

The bigger the Adjustment Goal, the bigger the sacrifices required and the longer the time required for its achievement. If an attempt is made to shorten the time (i.e., adjustment speed), then the annual extent of the sacrifices that will be required will also grow. Structural adjustment can occur through changes in demand for internationally-tradable goods (merchandise) and internationally non-tradable goods (homes, land). The bigger the production of tradable goods in a periphery country, the easier it is for that country to realize the adjustment in the current account balance and regain its lost competitiveness. For this reason, for instance, it can be argued that the countries of the European core should accept an appreciation in their real exchange rate, and at the same time the periphery countries should accept a depreciation. Therefore, in the periphery countries, a decrease in demand for tradable goods is required to reduce the volume of imported products. At the same time, the countries in the rest of the world should increase their demand for tradable goods, which they will import from the periphery countries. In order for this to occur, the prices of non-tradable goods in the periphery need to fall, and the prices of the same products in the rest of the world need to rise. In this way, the periphery countries will have low prices for non-tradable goods, whereas the rest of the world will have high prices for consumption goods, and will therefore substitute them with "cheap" ones, imported from the periphery. In this manner, the countries of the periphery would undergo a depreciation of their true exchange rate, which would improve their exporting capacity.

In essence, austerity and supply side policy suggests that structural reforms should be undertaken largely across three dimensions: (a) increase in the share of tradable goods in production, (b) improvement in the flexibility of the price between non-tradable goods and tradable goods and (c) reforms in the labor market.

These structural changes require and lead to shifts in resources between tradable and non-tradable sectors. This not only takes some time to achieve, but results in increasing unemployment and under-employment of capital force.

The following are therefore seen in economies: (a) wage cuts, (b) change in relative prices, (c) unemployment and under-employment of capital force. These characteristics lead to a decrease in demand and to recession. It is therefore clear that decreasing demand is a pursued and expected outcome that accompanies the restructuring of economies.

In light of this analysis of austerity and supply side programs, it becomes clear that achieving a specified change in the relationship or ratio between net international investment position and GDP, that is, the reason for pursuing the decrease in demand, is not at all certain. The only certainty is that it changes slowly. This occurs because the denominator, GDP, also decreases, meaning that it is very difficult for the ratio to reach a steady rate. However, where the goals concern the public debt to GDP ratio, and given that public debt is only part of the net

Fig. 16.4 Economic adjustment, time, speed and social flexibility

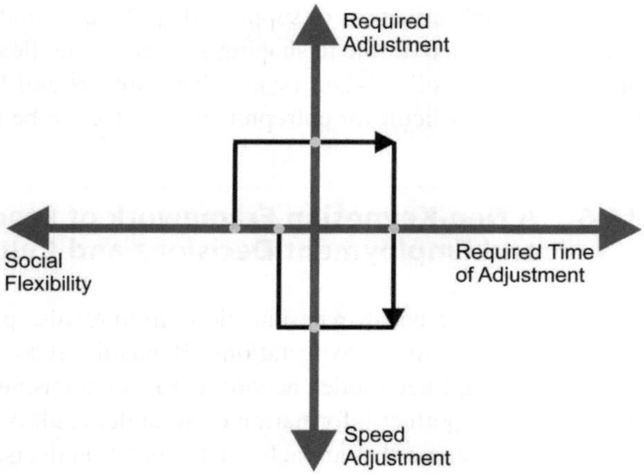

international investment position, things become even more complicated and obscure.

Of course, it should be noted that any society that implements an adjustment program has only certain social capacity to adapt to the new conditions. The circumstances shaping a society's adjustment flexibility and speed are linked to cultural background, history and social composition. Thus, social flexibility makes the adjustment problem even more complicated. In reality, it could make its solution very difficult or even impossible, given that social flexibility must ideally be combined with required time of adjustment, required adjustment and speed of adjustment.

The strategic dilemmas of countries implementing similar policies can be described through a decisions figure, which links the required adjustment, the required time of adjustment, the speed of adjustment and social flexibility (see Fig. 16.4). If the required adjustment is given, it is not at all certain that social flexibility can be appropriately combined with the required time of adjustment and the speed of adjustment.

Social flexibility is a general variable, through which cultural background enters the picture. It is very difficult for a society with a dominant tendency toward uncertainty aversion to keep up with the requirements created by new signals in economy, which lead to the reorganization of entrepreneurship in tradable sectors. In terms of the economy's orientation, the renunciation of introversion and the growth of extroversion are essential for the success of a supply side policy. Introversion, though, is built on in-group collectivism, and extroversion requires members with "masculinity" and love of risk. Furthermore, if the society does not have a long-term orientation, it is difficult for it to accept the needs to decrease debt with respect to GDP, and to 'purify' the economy's net international position, as a way to stabilize the economy. Given that supply side policies lead to an increase in income inequalities, which may encourage economic activation in the future, then it is clear that power distance has a dominant role in social behavior, with a mixed effect on the effectiveness of supply side policies. Finally, the level of collectivism plays a determinative role in shaping an ideal social flexibility. If the society insists on defending a collectivism (state) that controls and holds back private activity, then it is very difficult for entrepreneurial forces to be unleashed.

16.6 A Neo-Keynesian Framework of Production and Employment Decisions and Cultural Requirements

According to the neo-Keynesian view, individuals' production and employment decisions are based on expectations. Benhabib et al. (2013) cast the Keynesian insight in a simplified model, according to which businesses produce goods without having a priori perfect information on total demand. At the same time, the level of demand and income that are achieved depend on decisions made by businesses, in terms of the products produced and levels of employment. They characterize rational expectation as the equilibrium of their model. They conclude that despite the lack of any non-convexities in technologies and preferences, many points of rational expectations equilibria might emerge. They add that sentiment-driven equilibria are likely to be the result of the signal extraction problem faced by firms when production decisions must be made prior to the realization of demand.

Sentiment-driven fluctuations can be significantly influenced by levels of pessimism or optimism in society, or—in Keynes' terminology—by "animal spirits". Nevertheless, in the model of Benhabib et al. (2013) and contrary to Keynes' allegation, sentiments give rise precisely to self-fulfilling rational expectations equilibria, despite the fact that they constitute the outcome of the "weighted average of quantitative benefits multiplied by quantitative probabilities" that turn out to be correct.

Hence, households can estimate the amount of the real wage, by relying on their sentiments regarding total demand and their aggregate preference shock. By contrast, businesses try to obtain information on consumer sentiments and total demand by relying on market and consumer behavior research. The signals they receive are imperfect (i.e., the signal extraction problem), although they still attempt to use them to get a total view of the level of demand. Therefore, businesses hire household employees, by offering nominal wages, which have an expectation of the realization of output and, therefore, of prices and the real wage.

When businesses have reached a level of balance (and equilibrium is the rational expectation), then the estimations made by households based on sentiments will be self-fulfilling, meaning that the goods markets and the labor market will clear at realized prices, household expectations of prices and real wages will be correct and firms' forecasts of consumption demand will be confirmed. In this context, the actual equilibrium distribution of output will be consistent with the distribution of consumer sentiments in a stochastic self-fulfilling equilibrium.

Because of the zero lower bound, there are multiple equilibria consistent with rational expectations (Benhabib et al. 2001a, b, 2002). The lower bound depicts a non-monotonic relationship between consumption increase and expected inflation, which decreases the total demand when levels of inflation are sufficiently high, and increases demand when monetary policy hits the lower bound. This situation creates difficulties in the functioning of total demand, which results in the existence of sunspot equilibria, in which waves of pessimistic expectations can bring the economy into a temporary liquidity trap. A loss in confidence is deflationary, sends real interest rates soaring and causes large drops in output and welfare (Mertens and Ravn 2010). Economic activity then decreases to a much greater extent than in economies where higher rational expectations are observed. Here, the expectation of a future recovery fuels intertemporal substitution and makes firms reluctant to cut prices. Hence, according to this analysis, when an economy has deeper uncertainty aversion or is subject to increasing uncertainty, then it refuses to shape expectations, which can drive it toward realization of investments or employment increase.

The whole issue becomes even more complicated when society displays the permanent characteristic of increased levels of risk and uncertainty. In such conditions, what is needed is a special adjustment program, which will create positive future expectations. Under these circumstances, a program of economic and social intervention aiming to increase expectations of success could be much cheaper in economic and social terms than any stabilization package.

16.7 Stabilization Policy and Cultural Background in South Europe

As we have ascertained in Chap. 8, common cultural traits can be seen in the countries of southern Europe. The primary forces that shaped the social model in these countries, including geography, development, and history, may have had very different origins, but seem to have resulted in some common characteristics.

In Chap. 8, we noted that the cultural background of the south comprises a mixture of characteristics. A high score for the acceptance of inequalities is distinctively shown in the GINI coefficient, which is quite high. The score for uncertainty aversion is also high, as is the level of risk experienced by the social model. All risk indices (i.e., total, political and economic) are higher in relation to other countries of Europe and particularly those in northern Europe. The low future orientation and the short-term view is a distinctive feature of southern Europe, as well as a lack of results orientation. The acceptance of entrepreneurship by the public seems to be at much lower levels in southern Europe. A "masculine" organization of society is observed in these countries, which takes it a long way from social solidarity and care for the weak. A world full of uncertainty and with low level of collective trust leads to the accumulation of individual wealth, as the ultimate safety net. A much higher level of individual wealth is seen in the south than in the north. Perhaps people in northern European countries rely on being able to use services to improve their quality of life that do not depend on levels of individual wealth accumulation. In southern Europe, there is denial of the value of assertiveness and little encouragement of competition in social relationships.

Finally, gas emissions in the Mediterranean countries are very high, showing that environmental conditions are not highly regarded.

As the value of individual achievements is downgraded, together with a simultaneous increase in promotion of the principle of competition and a lack of faith in collective activity, a strong tendency for self-employment is created. At the same time, creative entrepreneurship is not promoted. The strong support of southern European society toward masculine values is expressed through personal independence and, hence, self-employment. Consequently, a satisfactory interpretative ideological platform is created regarding the very high levels of self-employment in the south, which is also backed by the lack of orientation and trust toward the future.

The swelling of a shadow economy, however, is the result of the concurrence of a series of values. The most important role is played by denial of institutional collectivism and reduced trust toward institutions, in conjunction with the dominance of in-group collectivism, particularly of the family group. At the same time, an important role is also played by low future orientation, including pessimism, that leads people away from long-term reservation of resources. The lack of future orientation is, thus, linked to the more general tendency for political and social belief. A dominant example of these tendencies is the swollen fiscal deficits and the public debt in the countries of the south, which are clearly higher than those of the north. Under these circumstances, it is difficult to plan any intervention of a stabilizing nature, that is, which would improve the net international position of the country, as well as investment expectations, because it could easily result in the opposite effect.

It is obvious that any program should have a central core, with certain elements: (a) the shaping of a future perspective to reduce uncertainty, (b) the promotion of collectivism, founded on respect for individualism, (c) the renunciation of introversion in favor of extroversion, (d) the acceptance of inequalities, as an interim stage of understanding a more equal society and (e) a well-built balance between the present and the future.

References

Agénor P-R, Otaviano C, Jelenic M (2012) Avoiding middle-income growth traps. VoxEU.org, 21 December

Benhabib J, Schmitt-Grohe S, Uribe M (2001a) The perils of Taylor rules. J Econ Theory 96:40–96

Benhabib J, Schmitt-Grohe S, Uribe M (2001b) Monetary policy and multiple equilibria. Am Econ Rev 91:167–186

Benhabib J, Schmitt-Grohe S, Uribe M (2002) Avoiding liquidity traps. J Polit Econ 110(3):535–563

Benhabib J, Wang P, Wen Y (2013) Uncertainty and sentiment-driven equilibria. NBER working paper no. 18878, March 2013

Eichengreen B, Park D, Shin K (2012) When fast growing economies slow down: international evidence and implications for China. Asian EconPap 11:42–87

Gill I, Kharas H (2008) An east Asia renaissance: ideas for economic growth. World Bank, Washington, DC

Gill I, Kharas H, Bhattasali D et al (2007) An east Asian renaissance: ideas for economic growth. World Bank, Washington, DC

Hofstede G, Hofstede JG, Minkov M (2010) Cultures and organizations-intercultural cooperation and its importance for survival, 3rd edn. Mc Graw Hill, New York, NY

Kharas H, Kohli H (2011) What is the middle income trap, why do countries fall into it, and how it can be avoided? Global J Emerg Mark Econ 3:281. doi:10.1177/097491011100300302

Mertens K, Ravn MO (2010) Fiscal policy in an expectations driven liquidity trap. C.E.P.R. Discussion Papers, No. 7931

Roubini N (2011) Four options to address the eurozone's stock and flow imbalances: the rising risk of a disorderly break-up, 1 Nov., Roubini.com

World Bank (2012) China 2030: building a modern, harmonious, and creative high-income society. World Bank, Washington, DC

Appendix

Appendix A

Table A.1 Probit analysis—contribution and time preference

Variables	Coef. (SE)							
ldist	0.001* (0.001)	0.001 (0.001)						
sdist			0.003 (0.010)	0.004 (0.022)				
presr					0.053*** (0.019)	0.054 (0.039)		
presw							0.041** (0.019)	0.03 (0.038)
period	−0.055*** (0.012)	−0.054** (0.022)	−0.054*** (0.012)	−0.054*** (0.019)	−0.053*** (0.015)	−0.052 (0.034)	−0.053*** (0.015)	−0.62** (0.031)
ld*per		−0.001 (0.001)						
sd*per				−0.001 (0.003)				
presr*per						−0.001 (0.006)		
presw*per								0.002 (006)
Obs	1,380	1,380	1,380	1,380	900	900	900	900
LRChi^2	215***	215***	215***	215***	113***	114***	111***	111***

Notes: * statistical significance at the 10 % level, ** statistical significance at the 5 % level, *** statistical significance at the 1 % level

P.E. Petrakis, *Culture, Growth and Economic Policy*,
DOI 10.1007/978-3-642-41440-4, © Springer-Verlag Berlin Heidelberg 2014

Table A.2 Probit analysis—contribution and trust

Variables	Coef. (SE)			
trusR	0.040***		0.053***	
	(0.011)		(0.014)	
trusW		0.017**		0.046**
		(0.012)		(0.023)
period	−0.034***	−0.007**		
	(0.011)	(0.008)		
trusR* period			−0.007***	
			(0.002)	
trusW * period				−0.006*
				(0.003)
Obs	900	900	900	900
LR Chi^2	12.67***	2.02**	13.59***	4.11**

Notes: * statistical significance at the 10 % level, ** statistical significance at the 5 % level, *** statistical significance at the 1 % level

Table A.3 Probit analysis—contribution and uncertainty/risk (behavioral approach)

Variables	Coef. (SE)					
risk_37	0.220***			0.276***		
	(0.069)			(0.078)		
risk_38		0.114**			0.156***	
		(0.046)			(0.052)	
risk_39			0.142			0.365*
			(0.102)			(0.203)
Period	−0.036***	−0.028**	−0.005			
	(0.012)	(0.012)	(0.007)			
risk_37 * period				−0.040***		
				(0.012)		
risk_38 * period					−0.023***	
					(0.008)	
risk_39 * period						−0.045
						(0.032)
Obs	900	900	900	900	900	900
LR Chi^2	9.96***	6.07**	2.01	12.33***	8.90**	3.37

Notes: * statistical significance at the 10 % level, ** statistical significance at the 5 % level, *** statistical significance at the 1 % level

Table A.4 Probit analysis—contribution and uncertainty/risk (descriptive approach)

Variables	Coef. (SE)			
UNCER	0.037***		0.061***	
	(0.012)		(0.016)	
UNCEW		0.036***		0.063***
		(0.013)		(0.020)
period	−0.027**	−0.020**		
	(0.011)	(0.009)		
UNCER * period			−0.008***	
			(0.002)	
UNCEW * period				−0.008***
				(0.003)
Obs	900	900	900	900
LR Chi^2	8.76**	8.06**	13.36***	10.15***

Notes: * statistical significance at the 10 % level, ** statistical significance at the 5 % level, *** statistical significance at the 1 % level

Table A.5 Probit analysis—contribution and social capital

Variables	Coef. (SE)							
Sc_1	0.065**				0.063***			
	(0.014)				(0.015)			
Sc_2		0.065***				0.059***		
		(0.013)				(0.014)		
Sc_3			0.121**				0.197***	
			(0.057)				(0.068)	
Sc_4				0.181***				0.188***
				(0.045)				(0.050)
period	−0.053***	−0.057	−0.023*	−0.047***				
	(0.013)	(0.013)	(0.012)	(0.013)				
Sc_1*period					−0.008***			
					(0.002)			
Sc_2*period						−0.008***		
						(0.002)		
Sc_3*period							−0.030***	
							(0.010)	
Sc_4*period								−0.026***
								(0.008)
Obs	900	900	900	900	900	900	900	900
LR Chi^2	21.65***	22.53***	4.48*	15.62***	16.21***	16.35***	8.60**	14.07***

Notes: * statistical significance at the 10 % level, ** statistical significance at the 5 % level, *** statistical significance at the 1 % level

Appendix B

Table B.1 Descriptive statistics

Variables/statistics	N	Median	Mean	St. Dev.	Min	Max
GDP annual growth rate	41	3.416	3.641	1.83	0.92	10.25
Performance orientation	41	4.110	4.107	0.41	3.20	4.90
Future orientation	41	3.860	3.861	0.52	2.85	5.07
Assertiveness	41	4.130	4.109	0.35	3.38	4.79
Power distance	41	5.180	5.154	0.39	3.89	5.64
Uncertainty avoidance	41	4.150	4.192	0.62	2.88	5.32
Gender egalitarianism	41	3.465	3.435	0.34	2.50	4.08
Institutional collectivism	41	4.290	4.292	0.46	3.25	5.22
In-group collectivism	41	5.270	5.042	0.75	3.53	6.36
Humane orientation	41	3.940	4.046	0.46	3.32	5.12
Investment rates	41	22.396	22.363	4.07	15.82	37.35
Average years of schooling	41	8.732	8.835	2.29	3.58	13.00
Working population (age 25+) growth	41	0.136	0.135	0.05	0.06	0.23

Table B.2 Descriptive statistics for cultural background variables after a 30 % increase in value

	Variables/statistics	N	Median	Mean	St. Dev.	Min	Max
+30 % on efficiency orientation	Performance orientation	41	4.550	4.659	0.37	4.11	5.33
	Future orientation	41	4.390	4.389	0.34	3.71	5.07
	Assertiveness	41	4.620	4.668	0.37	4.13	5.32
	Power distance	41	3.927	4.279	0.57	3.62	5.15
	Uncertainty avoidance	41	3.612	3.565	0.36	2.88	4.18
+30 % on social orientation	Gender egalitarianism	41	3.930	3.897	0.31	3.25	4.42
	Institutional collectivism	41	4.900	4.896	0.37	4.23	5.58
	In-group collectivism	41	5.525	5.536	0.43	4.59	6.42
	Humane orientation	41	4.758	4.700	0.34	4.10	5.19

Table B.3 Descriptive statistics for cultural background variables after a 30 % reduction in value

	Variables/statistics	N	Median	Mean	St. Dev.	Min	Max
−30 % on efficiency orientation	Performance orientation	41	3.320	3.426	0.40	2.88	4.10
	Future orientation	41	3.150	3.231	0.33	2.71	3.86
	Assertiveness	41	3.353	3.435	0.42	2.89	4.09
	Power distance	41	5.600	5.825	0.52	5.06	6.70
	Uncertainty avoidance	41	4.780	4.822	0.41	3.74	5.43
−30 % on social orientation	Gender egalitarianism	41	2.849	2.866	0.34	2.43	3.40
	Institutional collectivism	41	3.640	3.608	0.40	3.01	4.29
	In-group collectivism	41	3.948	4.024	0.36	3.53	4.94
	Humane orientation	41	3.490	3.486	0.36	2.87	3.99

P.E. Petrakis, *Culture, Growth and Economic Policy*,
DOI 10.1007/978-3-642-41440-4, © Springer-Verlag Berlin Heidelberg 2014

Table B.4 Principal component matrix

		PEOC	PSOC1	PSOC2	MESOC
Efficiency orientation	Performance orientation	0.78			0.35
	Future orientation	0.82			
	Assertiveness	−0.38	−0.78		
	Power distance	−0.69		−0.53	
	Uncertainty avoidance	0.85			
Social orientation	Gender egalitarianism	0.78	0.41	0.70	−0.38
	Institutional collectivism	0.46	0.36	0.50	0.71
	In-group collectivism		0.41	−0.53	
	Humane orientation		0.46		

Note: We only present the values of partial correlations that are greater than 0.3 in terms of absolute values

Table B.5 Basic model

	Dependent variable: GDP
CAP	0.17*** (3.58)
L	8.11* (1.68)
HC	−0.14 (−1.59)
PEOC	−0.04 (−0.18)
PSOC1	0.42* (1.82)
PSOC2	−0.26 (−0.98)
MESOC	0.11 (0.48)
Adjusted R^2	0.86
F-statistic	39.43***

Notes: Values in parentheses include t-test statistics for the coefficients of the regressions

Significance at the 1 % and 10 % levels is denoted by *** and *, respectively

Table B.6 Correlation matrix

Variable	GDP	CAP	L	HC
CAP	0.438***			
L	0.444***	0.156		
HC	−0.384***	−0.059	−0.545***	
PEOC	0.005	0.126	0.023	0.140
PSOC1	0.199	−0.047	−0.067	−0.006
PSOC2	−0.382**	−0.180	−0.483***	0.343**
MESOC	0.182	0.191	0.192	−0.019

Notes: Significance at the 1 % and 5 % levels is denoted by *** and **, respectively

The correlations between the PCs expressing cultural background are not reported, as there is zero correlation between them

Table B.7 Sensitivity analyses and structural change

	Case (1)		Case (2)		Case (3)		Case (4)		Case (5)		Case (6)		Case (7)		Case (8)	
	S.A.	S.C.	S.A.	S.C.	S.A.	S.C.	S.A.	S.C.	S.A.	S.C.	S.A.	S.C.	S.A.	S.C.	S.A.	S.C.
CAP	0.18*** (3.68)		0.16*** (3.47)		0.18*** (3.69)		0.20*** (4.08)		0.19*** (4.09)		0.17*** (3.53)		0.17*** (3.47)		0.18*** (3.80)	
L	11.23** (2.53)		10.41** (2.26)		12.71*** (2.84)		10.78** (2.40)		12.74*** (2.84)		11.75** (2.42)		9.45* (1.89)		13.30*** (2.77)	
HC	−0.21*** (−2.42)		−0.16* (−1.96)		−0.24** (−2.63)		−0.25*** (−2.74)		−0.26*** (−2.91)		−0.21** (−2.30)		−0.16* (−1.75)		−0.26*** (−2.81)	
PEOC′	0.18 (0.82)		−0.12 (−0.53)		0.29 (1.29)		0.24 (1.09)		0.32 (1.46)		−0.22 (−0.93)		−0.19 (−0.79)		−0.16 (−0.71)	
PSOC1′	−0.40* (−1.77)		−0.24 (−1.02)		−0.46** (−2.08)		0.33 (1.32)		0.44* (1.72)		0.24 (1.03)		−0.08 (−0.33)		0.17 (0.73)	
PSOC2′	−0.10 (−0.44)		−0.05 (−0.22)		−0.26 (−1.03)		0.13 (0.81)		−0.22 (−0.99)		−0.27 (−1.07)		−0.34 (−1.41)		−0.68* (−2.60)	
MESOC′	−0.48** (−2.06)		−0.45* (−1.97)		−0.42* (−1.82)		−0.47* (−1.93)		−0.46* (−1.96)		−0.38 (−1.55)		0.03 (0.14)		0.23 (0.97)	
dum × PEOC″		0.22 (0.69)		−0.08 (−0.24)		0.33 (1.02)		0.29 (0.89)		0.35 (1.09)		−0.18 (−0.54)		−0.15 (−0.44)		−0.12 (−0.37)
dum × PSOC1″		−0.83** (−2.54)		−0.66** (−2.01)		−0.89*** (−2.76)		−0.09 (−0.26)		−0.06 (−0.18)		−0.18 (−0.55)		−0.51 (−1.46)		−0.25 (−0.77)
dum × PSOC2″		0.15 (0.43)		0.21 (0.58)		−0.004 (−0.01)		0.45 (1.27)		0.008 (0.02)		−0.01 (−0.03)		−0.07 (−0.21)		−0.42 (−1.11)
dum × MESOC″		−0.59* (−1.79)		−0.57* (−1.72)		−0.53 (−1.62)		−0.58* (−1.72)		−0.33 (−1.27)		−0.50 (−1.45)		−0.07 (−0.22)		0.11 (0.34)
Adjusted R^2	0.87	0.87	0.86	0.87	0.88	0.87	0.87	0.87	0.88	0.87	0.89	0.87	0.86	0.86	0.88	0.87
F-statistic	43.58***	41.41***	40.21***	39.82***	45.13***	42.11***	42.15***	40.75***	44.52***	40.94***	40.59***	40.00***	37.39***	38.39***	44.43***	41.80***

Notes: Values in parentheses include t-test statistics for the coefficients of the regressions

In the structural changes, the variables PEOC″, PSOC1″, PSOC2″, and MESOC″ and the groups for the basic growth factors are included, but their estimates are not displayed because they are the same as in the basic model. In addition, we include the products of the groups of the basic growth factors with the dummy variable, but they are not displayed

Significance at the 1 %, 5 % and 10 % levels is denoted by ***, ** and *, respectively

Appendix C

Table C.1 Principal component matrix of transaction costs

		Transaction costs and economic institutions (TI)
Transaction characteristics	Starting a business	−0.75
	Corruption	0.97
	Composite risk	0.88
Economic institutions	Property rights	0.95
	Rule of law	0.97

Table C.2 Principal component matrix of culture

	Pro-growth orientation (C_1)	Pro-social orientation (C_2)
Performance orientation	0.73	
Future orientation	0.80	
Assertiveness	−0.37	0.44
Power distance	−0.78	−0.45
Uncertainty avoidance	0.88	
Gender egalitarianism		0.47
Institutional collectivism	0.75	−0.33
In-group collectivism	−0.60	−0.59
Human orientation	0.37	−0.72

Table C.3 Correlation matrix

Variable	Transaction costs and economic institutions (TI)	Pro-growth orientation (C_1)
Pro-growth orientation (C_1)	0.651***	
Pro-social orientation (C_2)	−0.488***	4.47E-16

Note: Significance at the 1 % level is denoted with ***

Table C.4 Regression results

	Basic model
Dependent variable	Transaction costs and economic institutions (TI)
Pro-growth orientation (C_1)	0.63*** (6.52)
Pro-social orientation (C_2)	−0.49*** (−5.13)
Adjusted R^2	64.5 %
F-statistic	34.49***

Notes: Values in parentheses include the t-statistics for the coefficients of regressions. Significance at the 1 % level is denoted with ***

P.E. Petrakis, *Culture, Growth and Economic Policy*,
DOI 10.1007/978-3-642-41440-4, © Springer-Verlag Berlin Heidelberg 2014

Appendix D

Table D.1 Descriptive statistics

Variables/statistics	N	Median	Mean	St. Dev.	Min	Max
Opportunity entrepreneurship	42	4.185	4.121	0.41	3.20	4.90
Performance orientation	42	3.915	3.873	0.52	2.85	5.07
Future orientation	42	3.433	3.423	0.35	2.50	4.08
Gender egalitarianism	42	4.110	4.111	0.35	3.38	4.79
Assertiveness	42	4.295	4.294	0.46	3.25	5.22
Institutional collectivism	42	5.295	5.035	0.76	3.53	6.36
In-group collectivism	42	5.180	5.158	0.39	3.89	5.64
Power distance	42	3.950	4.038	0.47	3.29	5.12
Human orientation	42	4.160	4.215	0.63	2.88	5.32
Uncertainty avoidance	42	79.226	76.730	8.70	58.18	89.29
Composite risk	42	32.000	43.583	39.30	2.00	159.50
Starting a business	42	4.107	4.104	2.48	0.34	7.91
Corruption perceptions index	41	98.900	95.717	5.82	66.00	99.70
Literacy rate	42	63.636	62.996	20.77	10.00	90.00
Property rights	42	0.615	0.638	0.22	0.27	0.95
Rule of law	41	1.360	2.086	1.54	1.00	7.00
Birth rate	42	10.875	13.489	5.05	7.42	26.01
Patents	42	4.185	4.121	0.41	3.20	4.90

Table D.2 Principal component matrix

	Promoting entrepreneurship PC	Human orientation PC	Efficiency PC	Transaction characteristics and economic institutions
	C_1	C_2	C_3	TI
Performance orientation	0.69	0.34	0.43	
Future orientation	0.74		0.31	
Gender egalitarianism		−0.62	−0.52	
Assertiveness	−0.32	−0.31	0.73	
Institutional collectivism	0.75	0.32		
In-group collectivism	−0.58	0.64		
Power distance	−0.74	0.31		
Human orientation	0.30	0.76	−0.30	
Uncertainty avoidance	0.86			
Composite risk				0.93
Starting a Business				−0.65
Corruption perceptions index				−0.94
Literacy rate				0.59
Property rights				0.34
Rule of law				0.95

P.E. Petrakis, *Culture, Growth and Economic Policy*,
DOI 10.1007/978-3-642-41440-4, © Springer-Verlag Berlin Heidelberg 2014

Table D.3 Correlation matrix

Variable	OPP	TI	C_1	C_2	C_3	BIRTH
TI	0.622*					
C_1	0.606*	0.608*				
C_2	−0.213	−0.477*	0.034			
C_3	−0.220	−0.003	−0.179	−0.116		
BIRTH	−0.374*	−0.666*	−0.107	0.537*	−0.081	
PAT	0.243	0.533*	0.487*	−0.030	0.091	−0.502*

Note: Significance at the 1 % level is denoted with *

Table D.4 Results of regressions

	Regression 1	Regression 2	Regression 3	Regression 4	Regression 5
	Basic model	IV weakness	IV weakness	Sensitivity analysis	Structural change
Dependent variable	OPP	TI	C_1	OPP	OPP″
C_1	0.033*** (1.95)				
C_2	−0.012 (−0.72)				
C_3	−0.021*** (−1.70)				
TI	0.044*** (1.93)			0.050* (2.60)	
BIRTH		−0.098* (−7.84)			
PAT			0.365* (4.21)		
C_1'				−0.014 (−0.80)	
C_2'				−0.035* (−2.73)	
C_3'				0.018 (1.25)	
dum × C_1''					−0.048** (−1.96)
dum × C_2''					−0.022 (−1.04)
dum × C_3''					0.039** (2.06)
dum × TI					0.007 (0.242)
Constant	0.699* (53.57)	1.576* (7.12)	−0.680* (−3.38)	0.702* (54.26)	
Adjusted R^2	0.43			0.45	0.44
Exogeneity test		0.85	0.92		

(continued)

Table D.4 (continued)

	Regression 1	Regression 2	Regression 3	Regression 4	Regression 5
	Basic model	IV weakness	IV weakness	Sensitivity analysis	Structural change
Partial instrumental variables R^2		0.54	0.26		
Partial F-statistic		61.54	17.77		

Notes: The parentheses include the t-test statistics for the coefficients of the regressions
In Regression 5, we also used the variables C_1'', C_2'', C_3'', TI'' and the constant but do not display their estimates because they are the same as in Regression 1 (the basic model)
Significance at the 1 %, 5 % and 10 % levels, is denoted with *, ** and ***, respectively

Table D.5 Principal component matrix after the sensitivity analysis

	Human orientation PC	Performance orientation PC	Future orientation PC
	C_1'	C_2'	C_3'
Performance orientation		0.71	
Future orientation			0.82
Gender egalitarianism	−0.56		
Assertiveness	0.51	−0.59	
Institutional collectivism			0.56
In-group collectivism	0.81		
Power distance	0.66	0.53	
Human orientation	0.46	−0.65	
Uncertainty avoidance			0.50

Appendix E

Table E.1 Principal component matrix

	$CULT_1$	$CULT_2$	$CULT_3$	$CULT_4$
Performance orientation	0.57	0.53	0.39	
Future orientation	0.85			
Gender egalitarianism		0.78	0.40	
Assertiveness		−0.48	0.42	0.67
Institutional collectivism	0.72	0.41		
In-group collectivism	0.71		0.46	
Power distance		−0.79	0.34	
Humane orientation	−0.38	0.40	−0.43	0.61
Uncertainty avoidance	0.81	−0.32		

Note: Only the values of partial correlations that are greater than 0.3 in absolute value are included

Table E.2 Relationships between the dependent variables and each of the other variables

Variables	Self-employment	Entry density
c	43.88*** (5.98)	−6.97*** (−4.65)
$CULT_1$	5.70** (2.28)	0.98* (1.85)
$CULT_2$	−3.46* (−1.93)	−0.48 (−1.32)
$CULT_3$	−1.32 (−0.68)	0.84** (2.19)
$CULT_4$	0.96 (0.54)	−0.30 (−0.83)
Knowledge creation	−0.13 (−1.50)	0.01 (0.64)
Knowledge impact	−0.33* (−1.69)	0.32*** (8.00)
Adjusted R^2	0.442	0.710
F-statistic	6.81***	17.76***

Notes: The parentheses include the t-test statistics for the coefficients of the regressions
Significance at the 1 %, 5 % and 10 % level, is denoted with ***, ** and *, respectively

P.E. Petrakis, *Culture, Growth and Economic Policy*,
DOI 10.1007/978-3-642-41440-4, © Springer-Verlag Berlin Heidelberg 2014

Table E.3 Correlation matrix

Variable	Self-employment	Entry density
$CULT_1$	0.60**	−0.23
$CULT_2$	−0.23	−0.17
$CULT_3$	−0.19	0.43**
$CULT_4$	0.06	−0.16
Knowledge Creation	−0.52**	0.13
Knowledge Impact	−0.48**	0.81**

Notes: Significance at the 5 % level is denoted with **
The correlations among PCs expressing cultural background are not reported because of the fact that there are none

Table E.4 PCA after the sensitivity analysis

	−30 % on cultural background				+30 % on cultural background			
	$CULT_1'$	$CULT_2'$	$CULT_3'$	$CULT_4'$	$CULT_1'$	$CULT_2'$	$CULT_3'$	$CULT_4'$
Performance orientation	0.312	0.621	0.371	–	–	0.793	–	–
Future orientation	0.371	–	−0.558	0.567	0.847	–	–	–
Gender egalitarianism	0.513	–	0.572	–	−0.558	0.680	–	–
Assertiveness	0.596	−0.480	–	–	–	–	–	0.931
Institutional collectivism	−0.639	–	–	−0.362	−0.589	–	0.352	–
In-group collectivism	–	0.716	–		0.412	0.621	0.384	–
Power distance	−0.583	–	–	0.586	–	−0.662	0.405	–
Humane orientation	–	−0.503	0.501	0.399	−0.444	–	−0.695	–
Uncertainty avoidance	0.520	–	−0.494	−0.368	0.866	–	–	–

Notes: Only the values of partial correlations that are greater than 0.3 are included
The case of −30 % on cultural background is applied to Cases 1, 4 and 6, while that of +30 % on cultural background is applied to Cases 3, 5 and 8. In Cases 2 and 7, where only knowledge is modified, the powers that shape the cultural background PCs are those in Table 14.2

Table E.5 Results of sensitivity analysis and structural change for dependent variable self-employment

	Case 1		Case 2		Case 3		Case 4		Case 5		Case 6		Case 7		Case 8	
	S.A.	S.C.	S.A.	S.C.	S.A.	S.C.	S.A.	S.C.	S.A.	S.C.	S.A.	S.C.	S.A.	S.C.	S.A.	S.C.
c	61.98***		49.33***		58.91***		52.01***		48.88***		46.36***		40.25***		43.68***	
	(6.38)		(4.82)		(5.68)		(7.52)		(6.44)		(8.20)		(6.79)		(7.08)	
$CULT_1'$	−0.07**		5.52**		3.97		0.25		4.31		0.12		6.11**		4.90*	
	(−0.04)		(2.23)		(1.60)		(0.13)		(1.66)		(0.06)		(2.46)		(1.88)	
$CULT_2'$	2.88		−3.47*		−2.58		2.33		−2.30		1.86		−3.45*		−2.07	
	(0.18)		(−1.93)		(−1.41)		(1.12)		(−1.25)		(0.89)		(−1.92)		(−1.12)	
$CULT_3'$	3.09		−1.97		−1.62		3.55*		−0.83		3.90*		−3.45		−0.72	
	(0.19)		(−1.09)		(−0.93)		(1.77)		(−0.45)		(1.92)		(−1.92)		(−0.38)	
$CULT_4'$	−3.54**		0.78		3.12		−3.09		2.72		−3.17		1.05		2.45	
	(−0.22)		(0.44)		(1.58)		(−1.59)		(1.32)		(−1.59)		(0.59)		(1.17)	
Knowl Creation′	−0.41***		−0.25*		−0.42***		−0.22**		−0.23**		−0.15**		−0.08		−0.15**	
	(−0.44)		(−1.87)		(−2.89)		(−2.50)		(−2.38)		(−2.18)		(−1.27)		(−2.09)	
Knowl Impact′	−0.88***		−0.54		−0.76**		−0.49**		−0.38*		−0.30**		−0.20		−0.22*	
	(−0.34)		(−1.59)		(−2.24)		(−2.66)		(−1.95)		(−2.45)		(−1.61)		(−1.69)	
dum × $CULT_1''$		−5.15*		0.73		0.76		−4.94		−0.30		−5.37*		−0.42		−0.84
		(−1.65)		(0.26)		(0.27)		(−1.59)		(−0.11)		(−1.74)		(−0.15)		(−0.30)
dum × $CULT_2''$		5.18*		0.01		1.46		5.29*		1.32		5.18*		0.03		1.37
		(1.95)		(0.00)		(0.58)		(1.98)		(0.52)		(1.93)		(0.01)		(0.54)
dum × $CULT_3''$		4.51		−0.99		−0.92		4.78*		0.08		5.16*		0.49		0.61
		(1.61)		(−0.39)		(−0.36)		(1.72)		(0.03)		(1.86)		(0.19)		(0.24)
dum × $CULT_4''$		−5.03*		−0.09		1.57		−4.41*		1.56		−4.24		0.06		1.49
		(−1.96)		(−0.03)		(0.60)		(−1.71)		(0.58)		(−1.62)		(0.02)		(0.55)
dum × Knowl Creation″		−0.16		−0.08		−0.18		−0.04		−0.07		−0.002		0.03		−0.02
		(−1.15)		(−0.59)		(−1.24)		(−0.40)		(−0.62)		(−0.02)		(0.29)		(−0.25)
dum × Knowl Impact″		−0.04		−0.06		−0.005		0.03		0.06		0.08		0.04		0.10
		(−0.25)		(−0.39)		(−0.03)		(0.23)		(0.48)		(0.73)		(0.41)		(0.89)
Adjusted R^2	0.456	0.434	0.449	0.445	0.475	0.450	0.438	0.436	0.448	0.444	0.415	0.429	0.434	0.438	0.427	0.436
F-statistic	7.14***	6.69	6.97***	6.95***	7.64***	7.06***	6.70***	6.73***	6.94***	6.92***	6.19***	6.57***	6.61***	6.77***	6.47***	6.73***

Notes: In each case, there are two independent parts to be tested: Sensitivity Analysis, denoted as S.A., and Structural Change, denoted as S.C.
The parentheses include the t-test statistics for the coefficients of the regressions
Significance at the 1 %, 5 % and 10 % level, is denoted by ***, ** and *, respectively
In the structural changes, the variables $CULT_1''$, $CULT_2''$, $CULT_3''$, $CULT_4''$, Knowl Creation″ and Knowl Impact″ are also included but do not display their estimates because they are the same as in the case of the sensitivity analysis

Table E.6 Results of sensitivity analysis and structural change for dependent variable entry density

	Case 1		Case 2		Case 3		Case 4		Case 5		Case 6		Case 7		Case 8	
	S.A.	S.C.	S.A.	S.C.	S.A.	S.C.	S.A.	S.C.	S.A.	S.C.	S.A.	S.C.	S.A.	S.C.	S.A.	S.C.
c	−11.62***		−10.35***		−11.96***		−8.49***		−8.05***		−5.45***		−4.18***		−4.91***	
	(−4.11)		(−4.02)		(−4.25)		(−5.52)		(−4.91)		(−4.37)		(−3.37)		(−3.63)	
$CULT_1'$	0.13		0.70		0.78		−0.24		1.23**		−0.21		0.78		1.09*	
	(0.24)		(1.13)		(1.22)		(−0.57)		(2.24)		(−0.48)		(1.46)		(1.92)	
CULT2′	−0.87		−0.31		0.25		−1.01**		0.13		−0.83*		−0.59		−0.07	
	(−1.41)		(−0.70)		(0.51)		(−2.12)		(0.33)		(−1.73)		(−1.57)		(−0.17)	
CULT3′	0.72		1.50***		1.39***		0.84*		0.78**		0.81*		0.72*		0.64	
	(1.27)		(3.43)		(3.16)		(1.90)		(2.05)		(1.80)		(1.77)		(1.59)	
CULT4′	−0.09		−0.14		0.73		−0.69		−0.45		−0.76*		−0.39		−0.26	
	(−0.18)		(−0.32)		(−1.38)		(−1.65)		(−1.01)		(−1.76)		(−1.08)		(−0.57)	
Knowl Creation′	0.04		0.03		0.06		0.02		0.02		0.01		0.004		0.01	
	(1.22)		(0.89)		(1.56)		(1.15)		(1.18)		(0.81)		(0.31)		(0.67)	
Knowl Impact′	0.55***		0.51***		0.55***		0.36***		0.34***		0.23***		0.20***		0.22***	
	(5.71)		(5.85)		(5.94)		(8.69)		(8.03)		(8.43)		(7.56)		(7.51)	
dum × CULT1″		−1.01		−0.85		−1.01		−1.31**		0.02		−1.04		0.46		0.60
		(−1.30)		(−1.31)		(−1.50)		(−1.99)		(0.03)		(−1.58)		(0.78)		(1.00)
dum × CULT2″		−0.06		0.13		0.49		−0.42		0.57		−0.44		−0.11		0.48
		(−0.09)		(0.22)		(0.83)		(−0.73)		(1.07)		(−0.76)		(−0.21)		(0.88)
dum × CULT3″		−0.12		0.82		0.71		0.01		0.01		−0.06		−0.42		−0.37
		(−0.18)		(1.45)		(1.20)		(0.02)		(0.03)		(−0.11)		(−0.80)		(−0.70)
dum × CULT4″		0.34		0.08		−0.21		−0.33		−0.11		−0.53		−0.06		−0.03
		(0.54)		(0.14)		(−0.35)		(−0.61)		(−0.20)		(−0.96)		(−0.11)		(−0.06)
dum × knowl creation″		0.007		−0.002		0.01		0.002		0.007		0.01		0.008		0.01
		(0.19)		(−0.06)		(0.41)		(0.09)		(0.30)		(0.43)		(0.41)		(0.56)
dum × Knowl Impact″		0.08**		0.09**		0.08**		0.001		−0.005		−0.06***		−0.06**		−0.06**
		(2.28)		(2.57)		(2.16)		(0.04)		(−0.18)		(−2.45)		(−2.46)		(−2.50)
Adjusted R^2	0.458	0.571	0.586	0.642	0.559	0.622	0.669	0.688	0.689	0.699	0.655	0.681	0.688	0.691	0.661	0.682
F-statistic	6.76***	10.21***	10.65***	13.39***	9.67***	12.37***	14.81***	16.26***	16.10***	17.06***	13.97***	15.74***	16.09***	16.48***	14.35***	15.83***

Notes: In each case, there are two independent parts to be tested: Sensitivity Analysis, denoted as S.A., and Structural Change, denoted as S.C.
The parentheses include the t-test statistics for the coefficients of the regressions
Significance at the 1 %, 5 % and 10 % level is denoted by ***, ** and *, respectively
In the structural changes, the variables $CULT_1''$, $CULT_2''$, $CULT_3''$, $CULT_4''$, Knowl Creation″ and Knowl Impact″ are also included but do not display their estimates because they are the same as in the case of the sensitivity analysis